WaterLover

Lorraine Eljuga

Essential Earth

Lorraine Eljuga's website can be visited at
http://www.lorraineeljuga.com

First published 2021 Essential Earth Pty Ltd
Copyright © Lorraine Eljuga, 2021

Cover design: Natasha Snow Designs
(https://natashasnow.com/)
Publisher: Essential Earth Pty Ltd
Printed & bound: Ingramspark Australia
ISBN 978-064899-60-7 (Paperback)
ISBN 978-064899-67-6 (eBook)

In too Deep ... and the lies begin

ONE

THERE's a reason I'm afraid of my own shadow. I am a vile, cruel monster who has no rights to love and yet, here I stand, heart in hand, asking her to love me.

Every morning I wake, I ask myself why would she give me the time of day? How she can even look at me and call me her own and yet every day, I have no answers. Every day, I fail her.

Fail myself.

So far, I've worked out, that a hundred and forty-seven definitions describe who I am.

I've counted them.

Many times.

And still, there must be more.

They all fit, all justify, making me possibly the most cunning predator that ever lived.

I don't mean in the killing sense.

I'm certainly no murderer, not of the flesh kind anyway. Of the heart, well, I'm guilty as charged, your honour. People often say that when their heart is broken, they want to die ... so maybe I am a killer ... to some degree. As it is, I've got zero chance of getting out of this world wearing a halo or at best, out on parole for good behaviour, regardless of how much good I do from now on.

It won't matter though.

None of it will.

I can't possibly make up for all that I've done. To start with, I can't erase the last seven years of my life.

Seven deceptive, lust-filled, unscrupulous years.

You see, my problem is ... in the last four months, I might have developed a conscience - something I didn't think I was capable of having. And something I hadn't foreseen, altering me in such a way, I hardly recognise the person I used to be. All because I met the girl I've been dreaming about since my lungs felt their first breath. I say that long ago because I can't remember a time when she wasn't waiting for me whenever I closed my eyes. When darkness fell, and my life became a speck of dust, loneliness killing me slowly ... she was always there.

When I actually came face to face with her, when I saw her in the flesh and discovered she was real, something broke inside me. Or was it that something healed inside me? I can't tell. That moment happened in a blink – too short a time to ponder on. All I know, is it changed me.

Forever.

Never able to change back.

My one regret ... I wish I hadn't lied to her. I wish I hadn't done half the things I've done to get to know her. I wish she hadn't fallen in love with me ... because it isn't *me* she truly loves.

She doesn't know the real me.

The person she sees in the flesh every day is an illusion, a hunter, an insect without remorse, without guilt, a criminal, a villain … living within my skin, seducing, manipulating, devouring everything it wants.

That one regret now watches, gleeful, allowing karma to ladle me into a large bowl, ready to make a meal out of me …

The room has no air and my chest is barely inflating. Her face is a hundred thousand hearts breaking all at once.

And it's all my fault.

Her posture is slowly wilting under the weight of my words.

And I can't do anything to fix it.

Her eyes are searching, searching my face for reasons, searching my hands that are wound in a tight ball of why I would be saying this, my legs that won't stop shaking.

And I deserve every last drop.

In this bedroom of my house, Ember adopted as her own, my life is about to disintegrate around me … about to die … about to be kicked into the dirt, trodden in, and ground to a fine powder as though it never even existed. The life I fooled myself into believing I could have, is no more. My dreams, replaced with nightmares.

No more laughter.

No more chances to tuck that familiar lock of hair behind her ear that she plays with when she's nervous. No more tender moments, where time stops because I am caught up in her smile. No more occasions when her fingers accidentally brush against my skin, breaking me, gripping me with the most intense, mind-blowing pleasure that it would take a million words and a million years to unravel.

No more …

And yet it is nothing less than I deserve.

She sits wedged up against the pillows, no longer cradled in my embrace, her knees drawn up, arms hugging protectively around them … trying to keep me out, trying to deflect my words. She stares at me, not blinking, hardly breathing, trying to coax some kind of explanation from my mouth, her jaw staunch, lips tight. They tremble a little before she gathers herself again. It is torture of the worst kind.

I cannot bear to watch, and yet I haven't earnt the right to look away. Time freezes between breaths. Scaring me. A week could pass and I wouldn't notice nights becoming days or dawn finding a place amongst the stars.

Finally, she releases me from the torment and buries her face into her hands.

I could cry out if I was capable of such a thing. I want to, except I don't know how to make it happen. I don't think I possess the ability to cry, having no memory of ever doing so.

Dark, diseased patches grow over my heart that no amount of forgiveness will ever heal. I slink back into the murky depths, where my true soul lies, where I deserve to be, knowing I haven't inflicted the worst on her yet.

Every muscle inside me is bunched, cramped, tight, twisted in knots, waiting … oxygen hating me, air refusing to enter my body as though it knows I don't deserve it. Waiting … waiting … waiting.

Her lack of response is a blunt knife, carving the final remnants of my heart into an impossible nothing. My entire existence has come down to one easy sentence.

One single sentence defining who I truly am …

I'm a liar and a thief, and I prey on girls like her for the satisfaction of my own needs.

This conversation is long overdue, but that's not who I am, not to *her* anyway. She's nothing like the *other* girls.

My heart falls out of rhythm.

Trying to stop, knowing it has to beat to keep me alive. Trying to stop again, to punish me, to scare me, to hammer hard and then diminish by its own will, indecisive and yet in total distress, preparing for the worst. And yet cracked wide open and vulnerable and so wanting to be loved. But only by her.

The world around me is numb as though no pain exists outside of me. And now, my biggest fear, is that it will be all too much for her and she will give up on me and leave before I have the chance to explain how I managed to fuck up the one perfect thing in my life.

I need to tell her now, but I'm not sure I remember how to talk, or want to risk it, my throat burning from every swallow, strangling with each breath. Guilt chokes up from all the nasty, selfish areas of my body, leaving a sour taste in my mouth.

I have found hell on earth.

I am hell. Definition number twenty-seven … pure evil.

No good lives here.

She wriggles her toes and refolds her arms.

She is very much alive. And very much opposite to everything I am.

She is the life-raft in the midst of my hurricanes – winds that blow in from nowhere, memories of being kicked hard in the gut until my vision distorts, and I vomit over my schoolbag all because my family has money, making me a target for bullies at the tender age of nine. The wannabe dependable figure in my life, my father, when he inadvertently forgets to text me to say he's away on the French Riviera for the next three months and I didn't even get the memo he was back from his last trip. She's always been there.

The truth is … I love her.

I love her in numbers I can't count because they don't exist – no more than you can count raindrops on a stormy night or the tiny grains of sand held tightly by an only child who would love a dog to play with, love for him to curl up on the end of his bed to comfort him, but never has, because dogs spread disease. I love her when nothing makes sense, when my heart wants to close, and steal itself away, if only to hide from the pain of never being able to hold her, kiss her.

Those words will mean nothing to her now if I say them, so I don't. I lock them away in the safe behind the Monet print in my father's study.

But … there is a fine line between *loving* someone and *deserving* them and I don't deserve her. My search for her has been all about me, not her, never about her or what she wants or what is good for her. It's me, and what I want. Definition number sixteen … selfish.

'Liar? *Thief*? What are you saying, River? I don't understand.'

The desperation in her voice shatters all of the carefully structured and hardened places in my heart until nothing but blank canvas's and empty closets reside there.

Definition number one and two and three … I'm a cold-blooded. Calculated. Heartbreaker.

Undeserving and unable to look at the way her bottom lip quivers any longer, I drop my gaze to the floor. Her breathing shifts from non-existent to fast, shallow sips.

I-I can't bear it.

I reach out my hand to her, to offer something … anything …

She refuses me.

And rightly so.

I square my shoulders, feeling the steady, unravelling thread of rejection. My chest lifts slovenly with the last hopeful breath I might take next to her, and I then let it out slowly. I raise my head.

'I am not proud to say, the first time I had sex, I was thirteen years old. It was with a girl much older than I was, and you might think I was naïve or even mature for my age or she should have known better, but the truth is …'

I pause.

Mouth dry.

Stomach in knots and dreading my next words.

Words that will destroy *her* and take me apart, seam by seam, stitch by carefully constructed stitch.

'I *instigated* it all, Em. *I* made it happen.' Definition number fifty-five … manipulator.

Ember blinks and blinks, each time harder and longer than the one before, as though she is expecting something new to happen.

'What does it have to do with us?' Her cheeks have lost that pinky glow. That beautiful pink that tells me when she's embarrassed or excited. The room start to blur around me as my world tumbles in.

I don't know where to start … how do I explain that I've lived with this vile curse since puberty. Since I first heard the beast. Since I felt his evil presence inside me … running the show … dictating my intentions. How can I possibly make her understand that I only pretended to be a boy of seventeen so I could meet her – who then lied to get a fake birth certificate so I could see her with my own eyes - who lied over and over and did terrible things, hurt people, crushed an innocent girls heart in the process, a good … decent girl, just so I could reach out and touch her skin to convince myself she was real and I wasn't going mad.

My fingers run through my hair as I search the entire world for the right thing to say, but I am still left with nothing.

Nothing.

Words keep piling up in my mouth … begging to be released. I want to say, it has nothing to do with us, and yet it has everything to do with us. My fingers find their way up to massage my temples. I can't look at her as I drop them back into my lap. I try again.

'I'm not seventeen, Em. I'm twenty.' I stop to let my words marinate. I want to see her eyes, read how she's feeling, because her emotional state screams in my head.

Breaks every bone in my body.

I hate that I can read emotions better than I can read a book. It's also part of this fucking curse I know I'll never be rid of.

'I am not who you think I am.'

I glance up long enough to see a frown clouding her beautiful coppery eyes.

'And what *exactly* does that mean?' she asks. There is a dry, cutting edge to her tone and my heart rips open wider.

My fists grip tighter, and release, and then even tighter until pain echoes inside me to stop. I've never actually said the words out loud and now it's come to it, I'm not sure I can. I deliberate, trying different words on for size, trying to soften the blow.

And that's precisely the problem.

There are no words in the English language to sugarcoat having sex with over three *thousand* women. For that is what it must be – even if I was to say I screwed two women a day for the last three years is undercutting my calculations …

By a mile.

Sometimes it was four girls a day.

Hundreds of blurred faces of the female persuasion, zip across my vision as a haunting reminder, a carousel of easy lays and empty love.

Ember adjusts her position. Slowly. Painfully slowly. As though she doesn't want me to see her move, give away how she is feeling. But I do see it. I see every little thing she does, every crease in her face, every measured blink, even how many breaths she might take at once. I see everything.

The words I can't hold back any longer scratch against my tongue, trying to claw their way out. 'I need to have sex … and lots of it.'

Thumping is all I can hear. My heart. Her heart. Both. I can't be sure.

Ember inches further away from me.

The thumping stops.

Pain chases pain around my body, two high speed vehicles recklessly looking for the ultimate end.

Definition number twenty-one, twenty two, twenty three … Womaniser. Fraud. Imposter.

I am crippled by her expression. Find myself examining every square inch of her face.

For all the sorrow and hurt chiseled deeply into her jaw, her lips, her brow, her eyes, she is still the most beautiful person I have ever met and if she leaves, and I never see her again, I will cling to those memories until the last ounce of life leaves my body.

'And me? Why haven't you had sex with me? What's wrong with me?' She looks over herself and shakes her head. Self-repulsion fills her eyes. 'Oh, I get it. It's because I'm not good enough for your list, right?' She bites down hard on her lip, her eyes closing with the pain. Tears spill out.

I am undone.

I have hurt this gorgeous girl so deeply. There is no coming back from this. How can I start to explain myself? The truth is, I can't. But I try anyway.

'No. No. That's just it. You're too good for me. I didn't want to ruin things between us.'

'How is sharing love, ruining things, River? I thought we had something special.'

'We do and it will ruin things, love. Believe me.'

Because I know who I am, I want to say.

Because I know what I'm capable of, I want to scream.

'Because I'm not in control ... and I'm not who I want to be. I want it to be *me* who ...' I'm struggling to make myself clear because she doesn't know the half of what I've had to endure.

'In case you haven't figured it out by now. I'm in love with you, River,' she says between sobs. 'I have been, ever since I saw you with your stupid hands in your pockets, standing at the school gate. Do you have any idea how you make me feel ... made me feel.' Another tear runs down the crease of her nose and lands on the duvet cover. She watches the circle growing, spreading, until the dark spot reaches it's full diameter, her fists knotted in the sheets.

She looks up at me, face tear-stained and tired. 'And just so you know, I'm already ruined, beyond what you could *ever* do. What difference would having sex with me

12

make, if you're nothing more than a common thief.' Her lips have tightened. I feel the burn of acid in her tone, burning through every layer inside me, melting right through to my bones.

Gutted.

Dead from the heart up, numb from the hips down.

'You're right, I am no good and yet, it would make all the difference in the world ... to me.' I look up, incapable of breathing.

'You use women ... for sex.'

'Not anymore ...'

Ember sighs.

It's a soft, slow murmur of air that doesn't say she's angry anymore or impatient. It's a sigh of confusion. There's pain there too.

'Start from the beginning, River. Tell me everything ... I want to know everything.'

I don't have to start from the beginning.

This past year is all I'll need.

Twelve months before

I zip up my jeans.

Some cheap blonde gazes up at me, make-up smeared, hair in a nest, naked from the waist up, a black vinyl skirt barely covering the places I've just been. Her eyes are glassy, mouth hanging open.

I scowl at her.

I've seen this unfocused look before. She is love-drunk from my presence. Just like the rest of them.

Me? I feel nothing. Just like always.

Empty from the chest up. Drained from the waist down.

No lust.

No empathy.

No respect.

In fact, everything about her repulses me now. The quicker I'm out of here, the better. Definition number ten – repulsive.

Her confused plea, thinking we have something *special,* begging me to take her home with the promise of more sex won't change my mind. I got what I came for and so did she. I'm a callous bastard, you see, no big news

14

there, and I cast her aside as another score to my ever growing list.

I swing my legs over the side of the bed.

'But, I don't even know your name,' she coos.

'And that's the way I roll.'

Like I said, callous.

Already heading back into the hallway, I slip my t-shirt over my head, not giving her another thought. Half an hour ago, I couldn't get her in this room quick enough, my body convinced she was the sexiest chick that ever walked this side of the River Mersey. Long legs that flex like a yoga instructor, tits way bigger than a handful, and a mouth that will say and do anything I want. Less than ten seconds after it's over, she is little more than the taste of garbage on my tongue.

Look, it is what it is.

I've stumbled down that dark alleyway of guilt a long time ago and it holds nothing but pain and sleepless nights. So, I tell myself, it is what it is, tomorrow will be just the same as today, so get on with it. I've lived with it long enough now to know, no amount of changing will make a difference and I won't ever be free of it, so grow a pair and deal with it.

The soft moans coming from the next two bedrooms leave nothing to the imagination. Naked bodies sprawled across double beds, arses in the air, no shame, no inhibitions. The third is a little more discreet. Dark, huddled figures, fully clothed, gyrate on chairs or in corners. This is definitely my kind of gig.

The room making the most noise is the kitchen.

Looks like shots are up!

Skimpy clad girls throw back loaded cocktails and laugh, drowning out some poor drunk trying to out-sing the artist on a karaoke machine. I swipe the nearest glass and down the liquid in one gulp.

It burns.

The taste of aniseed floods my mouth. My first guess is Absinthe. It dulls my senses, switching off my memory for a few short seconds.

I am at peace.

And then I'm not.

I hear my name being chanted as I knock back another.

And that's my limit tonight.

I can't afford to fall prey to its hallucinogenic properties again that had me up for thirty hours straight a while back. Any more alcohol than that, intensifies my *carnal needs* rather than sending the big guy downstairs to sleep. Unless of course I want to forget who I am and what I've done, and then I wind up at the bottom of a tequila bottle until I pass out.

Again, not a smart idea either – threatened with a criminal record for drunk and disorderly took a lot of phone calls and a pay-off to a not-so-honest copper. Wally tells me all too often, alcohol and I don't mix well.

'Hey, River, we're going to borrow Simmo's car. You wanna come for a spin?'

A distraction ... just what I need. I've had my standard quota of girls tonight – three in total, enough to tie me over until tomorrow.

It *should* see me through.

Sometimes it doesn't.

Sometimes, I find myself in real trouble.

'Yeah, why not.' I follow Leo to the front door.

Three pairs of tits in short skirts block my exit. I haven't *had* any of these girls tonight, but they're the kind I usually go for. Gagging for a good time and no self-respect.

It's true.

I don't have any standards, but I do have rules.

No Nannas.

Over sixteen.

No married women; the irate husbands are too much to handle.

And none of the girls I go for have red hair.

'River, don't go,' they whine. I have no idea how they know my name. A hand with glossy purple nail varnish slides up my arm to my shoulder. Another hand creeps up my back to my other shoulder, then a hand on my back and one on my chest.

'Hey, Thor,' shouts Leo. 'Are you coming or not?' His words have double meaning for me.

I want to do both.

I can be done with these girls in twenty minutes, if only he'd wait, but Leo hates waiting. When he wants to do something, you either do it, or you get left behind.

The decision to leave should be easy enough and yet I find myself holding back, not breathing, jaw locked tight, that familiar ache in my groin, rearing it's ugly head.

The temptation is back. Quicker than normal.

It's more pain now than pleasure.

Tightness pulls in my chest. Builds in my muscles. That strong addiction, begging me to give in. It's so hard to resist when the pressure intensifies. I reach deep inside, concentrating with everything that I have, until I feel something shift. Sometimes it works, sometimes it doesn't. Today it has.

I take in a shallow breath and rake my fingers through my hair. This round I win.

The car horn blasts twice.

Daniel McBride, Leo's sidekick, and the only other person I call friend, is sitting in the front seat. 'C'mon dude, ditch the bitches.' His arm dangles out of the car window of some guys'ancient beige cortina, his fingers busily picking at the rusted paintwork. He *also* doesn't like to wait.

The first step away is always the hardest.

Their fingers glide down my skin like steam over ice, chest burning, my body fighting me every inch of the way, still trying to convince me, I've made a mistake. The only way I can leave, is to tell myself I can be back here in an hour if things don't work out. I'm confident they'll still be here, and probably spoiled, but beggars can't be choosers as my father would say, and in my world, sloppy seconds are better than none at all. Then I can satisfy the devil living inside my skin. Definition number five – conceited.

'Wait up,' I yell back.

I break contact with them.

Air freezes around me and any heat I once felt flushes away with the carnal urge. I jog towards the car, my body hating me every step of the way.

Daniel's goofy grin widens as I draw closer. 'I don't know how you do it, bro. You can get any girl you want, including my girlfriend, if she was here, and yet you go for those dogs all the time.' He gesters his chin at the three slags behind me. 'I don't understand it.'

'Me either,' I lie. Lying is easy … like I was born to do it.

I've never told him that I spent an entire weekend with his girlfriend when they broke up the first time. She certainly wasn't anything to write in your diary about, even if I was into that write-your-pathetic-feelings-down kind of guy, besides I don't know what Daniel is worrying about. He's never short of a girlfriend. Quaffed hair, a streamline body and a Justin Bieber smile, is apparently all it takes to snag a chick these days. Poor, Leo, however, is not. He's your typical joker, everyone's best mate, prematurely going bald at twenty one, reminds me of Jack Black, and his crooked nose was the result of cricket bat and an irate younger brother.

'It's the eyes,' says Leo.

Oh fuck, not this again. The depth, brightness, colour, vibrancy, alluring and hypnotic capabilities of my eyes have been discussed at length, not only by friends, but strangers too. Eyes have a lot to answer for.

They are my weapon.

Most predators have something that attracts their prey, and I've come to understand, for me, it's my eyes. The rest of me isn't bad, according to what girls have said, but

I can't, won't, don't, believe them. I can't believe them because what they see in me isn't real.

Girls can't keep away from me.

And not just one or two chicks– it's all females, from fifteen to fifty five.

I am a magnet for them.

I don't have to say or do anything.

They come and seek me out.

They're all under the same spell.

And I have no idea how to break it.

It's a curse I've lived with, that I haven't told anyone about, not even Wally.

It keeps me dark and hidden and in pain.

And I don't feel many emotions either. Not like everyone else does. Mostly, they are non existent – except for anger, lust and love, and all have their limitations.

Anger is my constant companion and generally my first reaction to any given situation. It's always been there, as long as I can remember, but I'm learning a lot about it through Wally.

Lust moved in and changed me in a single blink when I was twelve. It has dominated and controlled every action, been behind every decision and takes up all available space in my head. It requires endless feeding.

Love is subjective - I don't feel it when people express it to me and I don't sense it when regarding anyone. The closet form of love that I cling to, or what I desperately hope is love, is to one solitary human – but I'm not a hundred per cent sure she's even real.

That's another part of the curse.

And pain … I feel pain in every form.

I take a breath and climb in the back of the car.'Where are we off to?'

'Going to see a man about a dog,' says Leo over his shoulder. That's code for going to the Rasta's lair to score. Leo isn't big into it, mostly because living at home with his gran, and working part-time as a lifeguard, means he doesn't have the money for it. Occassionally though, when he'd won at the tracks, he liked to get high.

Leo floors it and the first thing I do is zip up my jacket. Daniel does the same.

'It's the middle of winter, Leo, for fuck sake, man. Why the fuck do we have to have the windows down when its minus four outside? In case you hadn't noticed, we don't exactly live in the Bahamas, you know?' Daniel rolls his eyes at me when Leo doesn't answer. He probably can't hear anything above his "doof doof" music which is breaching the Neighbourhood Watch's loud noise curfew. Daniel shakes his head and mouths the word 'dickhead' to me as we speed along Chase Parade.

The street we turn into, on the other side of town, is dark for a reason. Glass lays scattered at the base of a lamppost, a large stone amongst the debris. Most areas in England, especially in Sheffield, have a dodgy end. The Rasta's Lair is in the better part of the dodgy end.

The off-white terraces are a bit more up market than your standard council house terraces, but not by much and at least here, the end houses aren't stewn with graffiti. Concrete steps lead up to a highly-polished black front door, complete with a brass knob, and if this was our destination, I'd be thrilled. Instead, I look to the mossy staircase leading down to the basement level. A black, wrought-iron fence, something you might have found Emily Pankurst chained to, partially surrounds it.

Leo swings around in his seat. 'You guys wanna wait here? I'll be five secs.'

'No way,' says Daniel, already reaching for the door handle, 'I've always wanted to see in there.'

I get out of the car, and decide it's probably not a good time to draw attention to the huge boot-print on the front door near the letterbox. The red paint-job is invitation enough that hell, or something similar, lurks within. I get the feeling, this isn't going to end well.

'Can't be too bad, if they're playing reggae music down there.' That is the dumbest thing I've ever heard Daniel say.

The poor lad has led a sheltered life from what I can gather. His parents are devout Christians, and Daniel and his twin sister, Juliette, had spent a lifetime wrapped up in Saturday *and* Sunday School, no mobile phones or Facebook and seven o'clock curfews until the day before their eighteenth birthday. One of the first things I remember him telling me was that he was surprised he'd even graduated puberty the way his mother had stunted his life. He's more than made up for lost time, and hanging out with me has only accelerated his new found love of trouble.

Leo is first down the steps, me bringing up the rear. He knocks on the door twice before a giant of a man opens it. He's bald, at least six six, and wearing an impressive two inch black spear through his bottom lip. His voice though, is surprisingly soft.

'And you're here to see …?'

'Mandrell,' says Leo confidently, 'we're here to see Mandrell.' The giant opens the door wider and ushers us into a bright yellow hallway glowing like the inside of a lemon. The place stinks of ganja and week old chicken masala.

'This way.'

The giant leads us to the end of the corridor and pushes us through a hanging, beaded doorway. 'Wait here.'

People of all classes are packed into a dingy room that doesn't smell any better than the one we've just came out of. A distinguished looking gentleman, wearing a suit and tie, stands in one corner chatting to a dirty cheap brunette with holes in her stockings. A middle-aged woman, wearing an apron and slippers is sitting in an antique armchair to my left, bouncing her knees up and down as she knits one, pearls one, and four young lads, still in high school by the look of their acne, huddle closely, one

21

biting his nails. They don't take much notice of us as we push past them.

A seedy looking fish-tank, glass green with algae, omits the only light in the room, casting an eerie, zombie like glow across these dropouts that don't interest me in the slightest. That is until my attention snaps into gear – my brain yells out, *check out the redhead*. She is standing beside a cute Asian girl in Doc Martens. She shakes her head, her hair a blaze of fire down her back.

The colour is a perfect match.

The length is spot on.

My body follows suit, the same way it always does in these situations; it locks into position, my muscles cease to work, blood refuses to flow. I hold my breath, not sure whether moving will stimulate her to notice me. Normally, that's all it takes. I've waited a long time for this moment, and as much as I want to indulge in it, I hold back.

As though she is suddenly aware of my presence, she spins around to face me. Adrenaline pools in my feet bringing my heart to a skidding, deathly halt.

Another letdown.

'Fuck,' I mumble.

It isn't her.

It isn't the girl I've been dreaming about – the one girl responsible for stealing my heart, convincing me I am capable of some form of love, even though I've never met her.

Daniel frowns, his eyes searching every inch of my face. 'What's up, bro?'

'Nothing,' I say, although it sounds more like a growl. I don't want to be here anymore. I want to head back to the party so I can release my frustration on the three willing victims I'd left on the doorstep. A menage et trois plus one sounds cool. 'How long is this going to take, Leo?'

'Half an hour, at the most. Why? You got some place you need to be?'

Daniel raises his eyebrows at me.

'I guess not.' The girl with the red hair, is now staring at me. I try to tune her out, half-hating myself for the attention I'm creating, half-unintentionally driving the desire forward. In less than ten minutes, the females in the room won't be able to stop themselves from coming over and slipping their phone numbers into the back pocket of my jeans, most compelled to have a cheap feel while they're at it. If I'm lucky, that's all that will happen.

I'm now counting seconds.

I need to leave.

The giant is back and beckons to Leo. 'Just you.' Leo nods to us and follows the giant through a second beaded doorway.

A few seconds later, an irate voice extends from the same entrance. 'I said, get your fucking hands off me.' A lad, my age, or perhaps a year younger, is escorted out by the giant and his manhandling twin. Apart from the spear in his lip, the two are identical. 'I know the way out, you fucking retards. You don't have to drag me out by the neck.' There's a twang to his accent. He's definitely not from around here.

The two heavys' let go of the boy's shirt and drop him two inches to the floor. The boy re-adjusts himself and flips back his blond hair. A stupid, childish grin spreads across his face. First impressions … I think he's a tosser and deserves everything he gets.

The redhead takes to him straight away, and he threads his arm around her waist and pulls her into him. 'Where have you been hiding, gorgeous?'

She giggles.

I hate her even more.

'Are you wearing contact lenses?' she asks him. I don't know why it interests me to hear what he has to say, maybe because it's a question I get asked a lot. I find myself waiting for his response.

'No, babe. They're the real thing. Just like me.'

Yeah, tosser … like I thought.

Wearing her like a scarf, he walks towards me. I have to admit it, his eyes are kind of freaky in this low light, like brand new five pence pieces, straight off the press.

He stops directly in front of me. 'You alright there, mate?' He looks me up and down, with that stupid smirk still on his face.

I'm about to tell him *exactly* what I think of him, when a scuffle and the sound of a door slamming down the hallway, instantly puts me on edge. I turn in the direction of the noise, hearing footsteps stampeding towards us. A man sporting a pink bandana, sweat dripping from his head and carrying a package under his arm bursts through the doorway, sending beads everywhere.

'You guys better split. Cops are gonna be here any minute.'

Daniel and I make a dash for the way we came in. 'Don't go that way, dude,' says the man with the package. 'They're right behind me, and I pity whoever's car's parked outside. It's been impounded.'

'Fuck,' says Daniel, 'we're trapped.'

TWO

ᴀᴛ that moment, Leo shows up, stuffing a small plastic bag into the pocket of his jeans.

'What's going on?' he asks, confused.

'It's a raid,' says Daniel. There's something euphoric in the way he speaks. His face has that naïve excitement only a seven year old can produce. 'Simmo's car's been seized.'

'Christ,' mumbles Leo, rolling his eyes.

I take a quick inventory of the room. Most have already taken off, and I spy a familiar pair of slippers disappearing around a maroon coloured curtain, a set of knitting needles under her arm. Daniel sees it too.

'Cool. A back door,' he says excitedly. 'It's just like in the movies.' I want to shake him by the shoulders and tell him this is serious. But, there just isn't time.

A door opens and the biting winds of an English winter come at us with everything it's got. The temperature is way past the shivering stage, no clouds, no moon and a strong chance of snow before the night's out,

I'd wager. I pull the lapels of my jacket together and brace myself against the cold.

'Move, will you.' The sound of raised voices behind me, force me to dig my fingers harder into Daniel's back as the familiar stench of the law closes in. I end up giving him a hearty shove, ignoring his persistent monologuing that this is the coolest thing he's ever done.

Once outside, Daniel and Leo are soon swallowed up by a mob of people fleeing from upstairs windows and other secret doorways. The colourful language of shits and fucks as desperate dopeheads pick their way through a maze of marijuana plants competes with the neighbourhood dogs that have taken up a chorus.

I hear a police siren.

'This way,' Leo shouts. But I can't see him, to see which way *that* is. I blindly navigate my way through the darkness, snapping woody bushes and plants underfoot, and steer around what looks to be a patch of staked-out tomato plants. Relief hits me when I feel concrete beneath my feet.

A small light flicks on from the house next door, giving me just enough light to see the back gate is open and only a few steps away. I have no idea where Daniel or Leo are. I can only suppose they've made it out ok.

I slip through the dark opening just as several flashlights shine around the garden.

I sprint down the alleyway, my feet hitting puddles and god knows what else, expecting to find Leo and Daniel at the end. I am not expecting to find the tosser, with his back flat against the wall, breathing heavily.

'What's …'

'Sshh.' I haven't been shushed since I was eight years old. I didn't think people *did* that anymore. The boy removes his finger from his lips and listens. Now that everything is quiet, I hear voices too. They seem to be getting further away.

'My bike's over there,' he says in a hushed voice. 'You need a lift somewhere?'

I could say no. I could say that I think he is an egotistical prick, and I have no desire to spend another second with him, but phoning Wally from jail again isn't something I'm keen on either. I haven't exactly had a smooth run with the law over the last few months.

'Sure,' I whisper.

We hang in the shadows for a few minutes before dodging around a handful of parked cars. We sprint up the street and across a partially fenced-in playground. The boy is fast, and I'm having a little difficulty keeping up, which I hate, considering how much time I devote to the pool. The cocktails from the party aren't helping either, and my head is still spinning from the Rasta's lair.

Finally, he slows to a jog and then to a walk. His customary smirk is back. 'Do you always live your life by excuses?'

His question is right out of the blue. '*What*?' But it's like he's just plucked the answer straight out of my head.

The boy laughs. 'Never mind.'

A motorbike is parked at the kerb in front of a church and although my knowledge of bikes is minimal, it looks pretty flashy.

He reefs the keys out of his pocket and swings his leg over the seat. 'No helmet?' I ask.

'What are ya … a sheila or something?'

'*Sheila*?'

'You know, a chick, a girl,' he explains, rolling his eyes. 'Well, do you wanna lift or not, or do you have to ask for Mummy's permission first?'

The thought of sharing a cell with a couple of drunks, faces polished red and purple from brawling, and spoiling for another fight, plus a transvestite shoplifter winking at me from across the room, doesn't excite me one bit. Been there, done that.

The voices from before have been replaced by wailing sirens which begin to echo around the entire block. I don't answer, instead, I throw my leg over the bike and hold onto the rack at the back. The boy guns it, flying so fast,

27

my adrenaline keeps any chance of hyperthermia at bay. It's exhilerating, borderline suicidal.

Fifteen minutes later, and several yelled directions of where to go, we finally pull into my driveway. I glance up at the outside light which has been left on for me.

'Sweet digs, bro. Mummy waiting up for you?'

'Yeah, something like that. Anyway ...' I glance up the driveway for a second time, 'thanks for the lift ...'

'Skye. Skye Buchannan,' says the boy, producing his fist for me to pound.

'I'm River Fulton,' I say, dismounting. I bump this fellow escapee's knuckles, who, now that I'm staring at him, seems strangely familiar to me. 'Have we met before?'

Skye laughs. 'Is that the line you're going with, loverboy. No wonder you were looking to get high.' He doesn't even let me answer. 'No, we haven't. I'd remember. Maybe our mums were at the same hippy camp or something, *River*.' I want to rub the smirk off his face with my elbow.

The more time I spend with him, the more I dislike him. 'Do you deliberately go out of your way to piss people off?'

'Why, am I getting to ya?' He is, just a little, but there's no way I'm going to give this jumped-up little shit the privelege of knowing that.

He laughs heartily and claps me on the back.

I wince. 'Like I said, thanks for the lift.'

'No problemo,' says Skye, still smiling. He revs the bike and floors it before I even take a step. Tosser.

I check my watch. Shit ... it's way after four. I'm likely to get a right bollocking for this.

The front door opens just as I line up my key in the lock and a man steps into the light, dressed in a chequered dressing gown and slippers. His face is drawn and eyes sleepy. His hair, though, is immaculate.

'How many times have I told you not to go ...'

'Ease up, Wally. I'm tired. Can we do this in the morning?' I slide past the man who came to my rescue two years ago. It was just after my parents died in a boating accident. They'd gone to Tenerife for a week without me, as usual, and while on board a yacht, blue skies and calm seas, they'd fallen overboard and drowned. They were excellent swimmers and experienced divers and yet their bodies were never recovered. No rip, no tide, no man-eating shark and no evidence they had ever existed. Wally, had been the second option as far as my primary carer was concerned.

My dad's cousin, Terry, and his wife, Anabeth, had been posted as legal guardians, but being childless, they knew nothing about bringing up a seventeen year old with "severe emotional difficulties" – according to what was written on my court record when custody was finally handed over to Wally, my dad's ex-business partner and long term family friend, five months later. Wally had been married, but his wife, Janine, died suddenly a few years back from a brain tumour, leaving the poor man devastated. He's seen the best and the worst of me, and I of him, and yet he still treats me with the utmost respect.

I take the stairs, two at a time, ignoring the elegance of a house, much too large for the both of us. This house and I are strangers, the same way my parents and I were. When they were alive, most days consisted of very little conversation, unless I was in trouble, baked beans on toast for one at mealtimes, and weekends of why the hell was I born? Even now, everytime I dip my hands into their bank account it feels like grave robbing.

I throw myself onto my bed and pass out in seconds.

Sparrows tweet outside my window the next morning, trying to tease me out of a dream.

The dream I'd willingly put my life on hold for.

If I could stay asleep forever, just so I can see her face, I would, in a heartbeat because this half-life shit is no life at all.

29

I refuse to open my eyes. I'm not yet ready to say goodbye to her for another day.

The long hours in between are my worst nightmares. Is it selfish to simply want to hold the delicate image of her face a few seconds longer, just to witness the colour of her eyes change like they've done countless times before? Her eyes are not trouble, they are perfection, and the ripples of bronze that flow down her back in glorious, enticing waves as she shakes her hair catches me up in a frenzy of knots every time. I can almost taste the subtlty of her perfume on my lips – a perfume I have yet to decipher.

She is my dream girl.

My body aches for her in a way that is so unique from the used-up tramps I'm used to. To start with, its not sex that propels me towards her, although I'd be a down and out liar to say I haven't thought about it.

It's *something* else.

Something stronger.

Something I can't fully explain.

I want to say its love, but having never experienced what love feels like, I'm not sure it's that. I want it to be love. I hope it's love.

I have to believe I am capable of it.

I have to believe there is something inside me that is good and wholesome and deserves to be happy, instead of the callousness I inflict.

I roll onto my back and think about opening my eyes.

Pain of the worst kind dives into my body and begins its daily slaughter. The dreaded compulsion is back, evident by the relentless agony growing in my groin and legs.

Please don't fucking start this early.

I haven't the energy to go and find a willing participant this time of the morning, and they always are, *willing*. And sure, taking care of this *myself* would seem an easy solution, but I've learnt the hard way. Three times I've experimented, to know it presents more

30

complications than it's worth and I'll never go there again. Masturbation amplifies my need to fifty, a hundred, a thousand, a million women instead of the three or four I've assigned myself to get through the day – becoming *not* the release or the remedy to the problem, but an addition that only more sex can anaethetise.

And turning a blind eye and abstaining from both doesn't help either. I am punished with the worst kind of torture this world can bring upon anyone. It's a pain that works its way into every inch of me, turning headaches into migraines, body aches into bone-crunching agony and light fevers into bed soaking sweats. It's an unforgiveable and crippling infliction. *It* doesn't care whether I toss and turn with guilt for the thousands of girls that have fallen prey to me. *It* doesn't care that I'd rather be dead than go through this every day. *It* doesn't care what I want.

It doesn't care.

This curse takes what it wants, from who it wants, when it wants. I am merely the pawn.

Gingerly, I stretch my arms above my head, ignoring my need to piss. I want to lie here a little longer and bask in the fading vision, but I know I can't. I don't want to get up. I don't want to move. I don't want to face another empty day without her. But laying here is not an option either.

It's impatient.

It's controlling.

This desire wants its fill.

Stomach cramps quickly turn to nausea. I need to get in the shower before the burning, tearing, ripping begins and pins me to the bed for the whole day. *There is no way in hell I can go through that again.*

One whole day and night of the most excruiciating pain I've ever had, until I accidently spilt a whole glass of water over myself giving me immediate relief. It's a lesson I don't need to re-learn.

I inch my eyes open and squint at the clock.

It's already nine.

I end up sitting in the bottom of the shower bay for an hour before I can muster the strength to get up. The cramps have dissipated for now but they will return if I don't find my first release. They always do.

I squirt something green and smelling like flowers into a flannel, and wash my hair and body with it. I towel off, and pull on last nights jeans. I peer into the mirror and rake a hand over my chin. I can get by another day without a shave.

Wally is immaculately dressed, as usual when I come down to breakfast. He lowers his paper. 'Rough night?'

I've had worse. 'You know, the same old story. Rave music, too many shots and loads of vomit.'

Wally's face says he's after more information. 'And if you were a complete stranger, I would believe you, River. I mean, you can't dance, you don't drink …' I raise my eyebrows. 'Much,' he accentuates, 'ruling out the vomit aspect. So, tell me. What was her name?'

I open my mouth to deny the allegation.

'Were you safe?' Wally is staring intently at me.

'Wha …' I'm lost for words. I'm always *safe*. I now regret being so open with him in the beginning regarding my sex life, and look for a quick way out of the conversation.

'Did Leo or Daniel phone?'

Wally shakes his head. 'You expecting a call from them?'

I'm not, I just thought they might have. 'No, not really.' Wally goes back to his paper.

The breakfast bowls and cereal are still sitting on the kitchen bench and I help myself to cornflakes, aimlessly gazing out of the window.

I lose myself for a few seconds in a dreamy, kind of floaty way until something amazing happens. *Her* face begins to emerge through the thick veil of my unconsciousness.

32

This is a welcome first!

Normally, conjuring a crystal clear picture of my dreamgirl with my eyes wide open is the hardest thing to do. I've tried so many times, I've lost count.

It's too hard.

And hurts too much.

I figure, there must be something wrong with my brain because even though I've seen her a thousand times in my dreams, I can't seem to bring together a clear memory of her beauty whilst I'm awake. I have to rely on old, faded images of her in times of need. Times when pain finds me hunched over in the dark, staring into my palms, looking for answers, looking for a way out of this hell. But right now, in this moment, with my eyes open, I see her. As if I'm staring straight at her.

My heart discovers a rhythm it's never felt before, bringing with it an intense rush of ... dare I say ... *emotions*. I can't tell if I'm happy, horny or want to cry though, which in my world, is freaking weird.

And awesome.

Emotions, for me, are generally measured by the teaspoon. The black concrete driveway blurs around her as she smiles at me for the first time.

I am a new kind of broken.

This warm, and happy place, where a low buzz has taken hold of my body, is a place I've never been to before and feels strangely serene and light. It's where hunger vanishes and wishes seem real and within reach, but like all good things in my life, it ends before it has chance to begin.

A large black bird hops onto the window sill and scares the shit out of me, popping my little bubble of serenity.

'Fuck,' I mumble, spilling the cereal all over the bench. I look up to bang on the window to scare off the bird, but it's already gone. Irritated, I blow out a disappointed breath, scoop up the spillage, add them to my bowl and crunch my way to the table. Wally looks up at me and frowns.

'What?' I feel milk dribble from the corner of my mouth.

'Boys,' says Wally, shaking his head. He says it in a way that makes me feel about fifteen but he means nothing by it. I hold back a smile. Wally is as easy going as a lazy morning in bed. 'No work today?' This time he doesn't bother to lift his gaze.

I work part-time at the pool with Leo. He got me the job four months ago, not that I need one. My parents are frigging loaded ... were loaded, I mean, I'm loaded ... whatever, at the time I said yes, I was bored, and wanted something more in my life than combing the streets looking for an easy lay. Now, I actually look forward to it.

'Yeah, but not for a few hours.' I have the afternoon shift. 'I'm heading off early so I can swim before I start.' Wally nods his head.

It isn't for fitness, although swimming certainly has its benefits. My body doesn't have an inch of undefined muscle on it, anywhere. Definition number twenty-nine – egotistical.

I've been swimming since before I could walk. When I was younger, my mother used to tell her posh, stuck-up friends, the ones that drank too much wine and bathed in god awful perfume that burnt your nose if you got too close, that I was part fish, not that she would've known. She never hung around long enough to see me in the water. I'd hear her telling them she'd had a water birth with me, and that I was born completely enclosed in the amniotic sac or whatever it's called, giving way to some kind of pyschic abilities. And then she'd laugh, and they'd all laugh with her, in this fake, tittering kind of laugh that doesn't even sound like true laughter. And then they'd all smile and re-adjust their lipstick or cake another layer of powder on their noses. I'm now convinced the five lessons a week were for her benefit, not mine.

All I know is, water has an effect over me, untouched by anything else. It's a guilt free way of controlling the urges and keeping the pain at bay. Swimming is the only thing that makes me feel *normal*.

I yawn loudly.

Wally glances up from his paper, his head tilted, eyes full of questions. 'I hope I'm not going to get a visit from any irate parents today about some poor girl you seduced, because to tell you the truth, River, I'm over it. When are you going to grow up and stop acting like you have something to prove?'

Shit. I'm back on his radar. Note to self – no more yawning near Wally when his standard speech about sex and girls, and what ungodly hour to come home at, has not quite hit the boil yet.

I huff out my irritation. 'I don't have anything to prove. Can I help it, if I don't fit in anywhere?'

Wally looks up at the ceiling and then back at me. 'I know, I know.' He lets out an exagerrated sigh. 'You're *different* than everyone else.'

'I am,' I protest.

I never really mixed well at school, despite attending a private school for boys and one that accepted a select few, especially if their families donated ludicrous amounts of money to the school's board and welfare fund like mine had. But it isn't just that. I've always felt different, no better or worse than them, it's just my brain works on an entirely different level to theirs.

'Can I *perhaps* suggest dating then? It's an old fashioned approach, way back when these useless things weren't around …' Wally reaches over and taps the screen of my phone, 'and it's also a way of getting to know a girl by taking her out to dinner and actually talking to her rather than …' He breaks off.

Every muscle in my body clenches. 'You know I don't like to date.'

'Then can I recommend you keep your pecker in your pants. You might live longer. *I* might live longer.'

I scowl.

'Georgia, *wasn't* it?' His fingers glide over his chin, reminding me of the blow he'd received from her father, that *I* should've got.

'You said we weren't going to bring that up again, and anyway, I'm only interested in one girl, you know that.'

Silence surrounds me.

Suffocates me.

Overwhelms me as her face comes back into focus for the second time in as many minutes. I lose all concentration and stare through Wally's head.

'I suppose you had *another* dream about her.' I exhale softly and rub my forehead. He doesn't understand. How could he? No one does. 'You have conjured this phantom girl from nothing, son, and it's tied you up in all kinds of knots.' Wally knows about the girl with the fiery red hair, and how she visits me every night in my dreams. I now regret opening my mouth and telling him about it, because I'm sure he thinks I'm drowning in grief or something. Truth is, I can't get her out of my mind, even if I want to, and for the record, I *don't* want to and besides, the weirdest part of all of this is, like I explained to him many times, is that I don't have any control over what I dream about, anymore than he does.

'But she ...'

Wally interrupts. 'You know there's a name for this kind of thing.'

I frown. '*Thing*?'

'It's called Schizophrenia.'

I stare him straight in the eye, my jaw tense. 'I'm not nuts, Wally. Okay?'

Wally sniffs. 'I'm worried, River. I'm really worried. This has been going on ever since your parents passed away and it's time you dropped it.' I sneak a shallow breath in, half grimacing at the fact I'd failed to mention to him it's been happening long before then. 'My advice is, date a real girl. Dream about a real girl, and you'll snap out of it. Stop wasting your time on someone that doesn't exist.'

'How do *you* know she doesn't exist,' I fire back at him.

'Have you ever tried to look for her?'

I shrug.'Well, no.'

'Exactly. If you've never met her and won't look for her, I can only deduce you are indulging in some fantasy rather than looking for someone more ... ' Wally lowers his eyes.

'More what?'

He rustles his paper. 'Never mind. I shouldn't have said anything.'

We never get in this deep and I'm curious to see what he thinks is going on in my life.

'You brought it up, Wal. Let's hear it.'

Wally huffs. His head angles to one side as he looks at me. '*I think*, you'd rather fall for a girl who isn't real because that way you'll never be hurt again. Don't forget, lad, I've watched you grow up. I've seen the spaces in your life that haven't been filled before *and* after your parents death.'

I have to admit, he's half right. The hurt part I can deal with, and do deal with ...everyday, not particularly well, I might add, but I get by the best way I can. Falling for a girl that visits me in my dreams every night was never part of the plan, but it's so much more complicated than that. I just don't think I'm ready to confide in him about my sexual addiction, especially not since his *Schizo* reference. White coats. Padded rooms. Straightjacket. One pyscho coming right up.

'It might look that way to you, but I can't help the way I feel about her. It's like I've known her my entire life.' I can't tell him that I feel like she calls out for help even though she's never said a single word to me. That would really seal the lid on my capacity to function as a *responsible* adult.

37

Wally has that look on his face again like he's heard this a million times before. 'The way you do this to yourself, is only torturing you more. Let her go, River.'

He rises, dumps the paper onto the table and walks towards me. His hand falls to my shoulder. 'Let it go, son, or it'll destroy you.'

I know he means well, but how can I let go. The more I think about it, the more I realise it's *her* who visits me… visits me with eyes that blaze like molten lava, not the other way around.

I close my eyes and draw on all my strength, mentally trying to push her aside. My heart becomes stone, becomes glass, slows right down until it wants to stop.

I can't. It feels wrong to do it.

She won't let me.

She lives inside me, in a place so deep that's she's as much a part of me as I am.

I know she's real.

She has to be.

THREE

'DRIVE carefully,' calls out Wally.

I lift the keys from the hook and close the door behind me. In the time it takes me to make my way across the driveway, the garage doors are already up.

And there it is … staring right at me, as bold as brass, just like the man himself - my father's red BMW 3 series.

It isn't a car I would've chosen for myself, a Porche Spyder is more my style, although Wally had strongly advised me to reconsider when I'd shown him the price tag. Affording it and deserving it were the words Wally used in his argument and having the money there, doing nothing, doesn't mean it can be spent. In all honesty, any car that doesn't come with a ghost is ok by me. The Audi S8, which hardly sees the light of day now, shares the space next to the BMW. It was my fathers work car and something I drive as a last resort.

I sit in the driver's seat of the BMW, meditating through the usual waves of nausea. You see, I can still smell him. I can still smell the strong, almost musty, metallic odour of my fathers's aftershave, and it's as strong now as it was two years ago. As much as I try to forget him, and the invisible man he was to me, he is more a part of my life *dead* than when he was *alive*. Even the stupid things he used to say still go around in my head. His constant reminders sneer at me from everywhere - his house, his cars, his possessions, his time, his effort, his bath, furniture, pens, fridge. Anything he owned had "his" in front of it. Not family cars or family home or family holiday. Everything was his. Everything except me. I was somebody else's.

I take a deep breath in and blow it out, remembering the mantra I'd taught myself eight years ago about blocking out the pain – if you hide your heart from him, he can't hurt you, if you hide your heart from him, he can't hurt you.

I can't help wonder how much of him is in me. I have the same selfish tendencies when I want something. I own almost no emotions. And I lie to everyone.

Including myself.

But one solemn vow I have made is that I will do everything in my power to never become a second-rate version of him to my own children, if I have them.

I start the engine.

The numbing effects from the shower are wearing off and I have a hard-on from hell, which feels great for all of about five minutes until the pain kicks in. Impatient voices inside my head start their low, mumuring whispers - *you want this -you need this -this is who you are ... give in*. The beast rears its ugly head and begins it's usual chants for the day

It's easy enough to ignore for now, but I grip the steering wheel tightly anyway and rev the engine to drown them out. The pool is less than fifteen minutes away. I should be able to make it.

I pull into the car park and spot the S girls' - Sophie, Serena and Siobhan outside the main doors of the pool, smoking and chatting. Serena works in the kiosk, Sophie on the front desk and Siobhan is the shift manager. They are all blonde, not too bad on the eye, although Serena outranks the other two by at least three bra sizes.

I park in my usual space and reach over for my bag. I pause before facing them. I know each girl, intimately, Serena more so than the others, and they never let me down when I'm at a loose end. Although recently, I sense something has changed between Serena and I. I see it in her eyes every time she looks at me. I hope for her sake, and mine, she hasn't fallen for me. It happens a lot.

The moment I'm out of the car, their backs straighten, their shoulders are thrown backwards, and the words Gattling Aquatic Centre, written in light blue stretches to capacity across the front of their white t-shirts, especially Serena's. She's just what I need at the moment to take the edge off and is always up for a quickie in the car or the public toilets. A pensive gaze. A touch of her hair. That's all it takes, and she's as easy as that.

Darkness falls over me.

And so it begins for another day.

I want her now.

I want her more than I've ever wanted anything in my life.

The beaSt is rising.

Fast.

The lies are forming.

Some tiny honourable part of me, and I emphasise the word tiny, is dying to be recognised. I feel it stronger than ever, and yet it still shatters and splinters and falls into nothingness everytime I think about my greedy self and what I want. I feel my conscience striving so hard to grow and be strong and break me out of these chains and yet I'm compelled to follow this insidious pattern that has shaped my existence over the last seven years.

It's useless to resist. The addiction is too strong and it certainly doesn't help me as the selfishness of my father slides further into my desires, making me hate him more, and yet spurring on the temptation to drag Serena into the alleyway behind the pool and tick my first one off for the day. Definition number seventeen – seducer.

I'm beginning to hate myself for who I might become.

I grit my teeth and push the thought away before it has chance to take hold.

Serena calls out before I even reach them. 'Hi ya, River.'

I wave.

No smile.

A smile can be dangerous right now, a wink … catastrophic.

'Do you have plans later? I've got the latest episode of Walking Dead, if you're interested.' In short, it means her parents are out for the night and she wants me over for the same reason I want her right now.

My body trembles at the thought. The ramblings in my head amplify. My car keys dig into my palm as I tighten my fist around them. I'm about to concede. I'm about to give into the beast, give in to the lust that is escalating, driving me closer to the edge, closer to guilt, when out of nowhere, a cool breeze touches my face, freeing the demons, freeing my mind, giving me just enough time to take that crucial step away from them.

For three full seconds, reason returns and sanity finds a way in. The good angel on my shoulder says -*you are so close to a guilt-free release -you don't have to hurt anyone's feelings, -this happy little foursome could be fun but the pool is right there -you can do it*

'Maybe,' I call out over my shoulder as I pass them. Good angel or not, I'm still a piece of shit to know when NOT to burn my bridges.

'Aren't we good enough to talk to,' sings out Sophie. Sophie is still dark at me after we had sex at a party two weeks ago and then ditched her for a brunette with a Swedish accent.

Emotionally, they are easy to read. I detect Sophie's annoyance and Serena's lust. Siobhan is a little harder, but certainly not when her clothes are off. I may not have any emotions myself, but I have a definite knack for reading other peoples. When I'm at my strongest, in times like this, emotions are so much easier to read.

This time, my lips welcome a smile and I turn and raise my arms in defeat. 'Sorry, girls. Water waits for no man.'

I hear a giggle, most likely Siobhan. The sound leaves an irritating mark against my skin that I can't wait to wash off.

I continue towards the main entrance, their stares boring holes into my back, twelve gage style, their bodies craving my touch.

As much as I hate what I stand for, moments like these feel amazing. I have defeated the beast and won. Yes, it's a small victory, probably pathetic to every other eighteen year old in the world, who would do anything to get into their knickers, but I don't care. I am in control of my urges, and for the briefest of seconds, I bask in the glory of that power, the same way a smoker refused that longed-for cigarette three months after giving up. Look, it doesn't happen very often. Normally, I'm the one in the ashtray searching for leftover butts.

The most seductive perfume I've ever known greets me at the swimming pool door. I allow the warm, sharp bite of chlorine to seduce my senses for just a second. Any longer, and I could be in trouble. It's sets off a chain reaction in my body. My feet start to tingle, my legs and thighs become light, like I'm wading through feathers. My hips and waist burn with the most urgent of needs. My chest and heart are full to the brim like I am heaven and earth and everything in between, and I am waiting at the gates of hell with a pass that says I'm only here for a short while so make it worth it. My body feels that familiar ache. A heavy pulse throbs painfully in my neck.

I need my water-fix.

43

With no-one manning the front desk yet, not that I ever pay, I throw my legs across the turnstyle and detour through the kiosk, lifting a chocolate bar from the shelf on my way to the changing rooms.

Five minutes later, I stand at the deep end of the pool, looking into the water below, my toes gripping the edge. Tiny splashes tease them as I bask in the thrill of it – that glorious moment before the water hits my skin and makes all the horrors in my life melt away. That miraculous glassy liquid that whispers for me to join it, to smother the evil inside me, returning my body back to me, untainted.

Without another thought, I dive in.

My body surrenders immediately, lifting me to heights that sex has never taken me to. The water permeates my skin making me want to scream out with utter bliss as it soaks deeper and deeper into my bones. My muscles have become frenzied instruments of joy, urging me to go faster, knowing the stronger the stroke, the more intense the gratification. No other feeling on earth surpasses this, except being submersed in a lake or river – fresh water adds a whole new depth to the pleasure, too hard to explain, too complex to put into words. Exhilaration does it no justice. Joy is way too redundant. Eurphoria is close but no closer than the moon is to the stars. I have no true description for how it makes me feel, and for this reason I consider myself different. A word should be able to convey any thought or emotion, although it doesn't seem so in this case. I figure my word has yet to be invented.

Nobody else seems to share this intimate bond that I have with water. I'd figured that out from a very young age, seven maybe eight. The whole world seem to use and abuse it, wasting it and taking it for granted, but for me, every drop is magical. It means something more to me than H2O. It *lives* inside me, as weird as that is to say, and overrides so much of what *should* make me human. I know it sound totally nuts but I can't explain it any other way, other than I must have been at the back of the queue when the lesson on restraining emotional impulses were taught or something like that because I have no knowledge how these work or why we need them. And yet sensing other people's emotions as if they are my own, like with Serena and Sophie, is happening more regularly. And I was perhaps not in the queue at all when the class on controlling sexual urges was implemented. Which brings me to one final conclusion ... I truly believe these two bizarre things have something to do with my affinity to water. So, surely that categorises me as being different, just like I tell Wally all the time.

Bottom line is, when I can't swim, my life is a horror movie in process and my body turns into a walking hard-on. When I'm in control, I am at the top of my game and others' emotions are easier to read.

Different.

I swim the entire length underwater. Thirty metres in total. When I come up at the other end I'm not even out of breath. I can stay down longer but Leo is on duty and he has started to notice my strange affiliation.

With my initial craving slaked and the throb of ecstasy gone, I porpoise back beneath the surface and begin the first of four hundred laps. The more I do, the better I feel and the more control I have. Ten thousand metres should see me through.

I dread the days I can't swim.

Lost in my own watery world requires a considerable whack on the top of the head to get me to stop swimming, according to Leo. He has a sheepish look on his face.

'Dude, you've got five minutes until your shift starts.' I rub my head and look up at him as he retracts the safety pole. I swim to the edge and glance over at the clock.

Torment twists inside me.

Eighteen laps short – I *should* be okay.

'Thanks, mate.' I haul my body out of the water.

Standing behind the glass, separating the pool from the kiosk, the 'S girls giggle and clap their appreciation as I search for the towel I forgot to bring. I dip my head at them but still refuse them the pleasure of my smile. I'm back to being plain old me again, for a little while at least, and as selfish as that sounds, fully aware of my father's hand on the back of my neck, I want me all to myself.

I shower and quickly change, donning the customary white logo shirt and shorts, and make my way back into the pool area.

Leo is walking towards me. 'You get home alright, last night?'

'What does it look like. I'm here, aren't I?' I smirk.

Leo punches me on the arm and then promptly massages his knuckles. 'With muscles like that, nobody would wanna touch you.' I smother a laugh. 'And man, you're eyes are so blue in this room, it's freaky.' He really has a fixation with my eyes and it's getting harder and harder to come up with different excuses. They're always more vibrant once I've been in water.

I could go for the coloured contacts line. I haven't used that in a while. But instead I choose a more comical approach, one that will stop his curiosity instantly. 'Are you hitting on me, bro?'

Leo is the homophobic type. 'Yeah, well … right, anyway, Daniel reckons he saw you getting on the back of some kids' motorbike.'

Two girls in bikinis make their entrance and Leo brazenly gawps at them. My eyes float over to them, but I find them easy enough to ignore.

'Yeah, it was some kid called …' My voice ebbs away. The guy who'd dropped me home last night steps out from behind the bikini twins, wearing a pair of fluro green board shorts. 'Get fucked,' I mumble, blowing the words out with my breath.

Leo's head snaps around. 'I know, stunning, huh? You're a lucky son of a bitch to be on duty with two hotties like that.'

'What? No. I wasn't looking at *them*. Him.' I gesture in Skye's direction.

An enormous laugh explodes out of Leo's mouth, causing Skye Buchannan to look over. 'Don't tell me you've turned to the dark side, Obei Wan?'

'*What*? Fuck no. That's the guy who gave me a lift home last night.' Skye makes a deliberate point of staring at me before his face breaks into a cheeky grin. He raises his hand and offers me a static wave. I acknowledge him with a single nod of my head. *What the hell is he doing here? Come to aggravate me some more?*

Leo's attention returns to the bikini twins. He puffs up his chest and smooths his hand over what little hair he has. 'I'll leave you to it, then. I'll go and make sure those girls are wearing their wristbands.' He struts towards them like an overweight pigeon.

'Right, yeah. Catch ya.'

By the time I reach my perch, Skye is already climbing the ladder to the ten metre diving platform. This platform isn't for the faint-hearted, and on the weekends, it's roped off so the smart-arse twats from the local high school can't shows off to their girlfriends.

I take my seat in the two metre lifeguard chair, watching his every step. I'm not sure who he thinks he's trying to impress, but I lean forward and prepare to enter the water in case his dive goes wrong, and we are in for the biggest belly flop of the century. As much of a tosser as he is, it's still my job to make sure no one gets injured on my shift.

Quite an audience has assembled below him, and I'm surprised to see him confidently turn around and baby step it backwards to the edge of the platform. I can't hold back the gasp as he launches himself backward into the air.

'Holy shit,' I mumble.

For a moment, I feel like my eyes are playing tricks on me. He seems to be hovering, stationary, floating in mid-air, longer than is possible after his initial jump. His knees tuck up and his two triple back somersault is a sight to see. His body performs each rotation as though in slow motion, the pure elation on his face reminds me of how I feel being surrounded by water. For a split second, the tosser is gone, and in his place is a willowy, graceful creature who beckons to my own heart. I see a comrade, a kinship, a brother-in-arms - a like-minded individual seeking the same answers to questions I want. For the first time in my life, I feel a natural connection to someone.

However, it's short-lived.

A round of applause goes up as he surfaces and I find myself clapping too. Skye looks over and nods, his smart arse smirk still managing to needle its' way under my skin.

The next four hours of my shift are spent mesmerised by him as he swan dives, backwards and forwards, into the water, flying through the air with all the elegance of a ballerina. If I didn't know any better, I would say he has the same respect for air as I have for water. The way he moves inside it, with it, not against it and with no fear of falling. His face, every time, portrays peace and unity and I'm disappointed when five o'clock rolls around and it's time to close.

The pool slowly empties of people, with the pair of bikinis' clinging excitedly to each of Skye's arms. I begin my usual wind down routine of dumping all the lost property into the bin and then stop by the kiosk for a takeaway coffee for the trip home. Serena does make the best cappucino. She chats about some concert she's just been to, and how amazing it was, although I'm only half listerning. She knows why I'm here.

'I'll be five minutes,' she says, when I start to fidget. I head into the storeroom to wait for her.

It's dark by the time I cross the dimly lit car park. My car is the only one left and when I look closer, I see someone sitting on the bonnet.

'Thought this sweet ride might belong to you,' says Skye. He is alone and doesn't move as I beep the car open.

'Where's your little entourage?'

Skye's lips twist into a smile, dimples burrowing their way into his cheeks. 'Gone. They're fun and all, but they're not really my type. I've got a thing for redheads ... what can I say.' My body becomes rocks and ice and a thousand shards of glass. My heart, a deserted shell. My brain feels fiddled with, memories shuffled somehow as though he's opened the back door of my skul, had a good look around and found the picture of my dream girl and taken it for himself. 'But you don't find many around these days, do ya – well, no decent ones anyway.'

I try not to let my guard down even though I know he speaks the truth. True redheads aren't seen much in this area. Believe me, I've searched. Orange hair or ginger, carrot top or auburn, and even those artificial girls' who dye the shit out of their hair to look like runway models are a dime a dozen, but to find someone with the same burnt red hair that I long to run my fingers through every night in my dreams, well ... they are as rare as my own laughter these day. 'No, you don't.'

I go for the car door, expecting him to step aside. He doesn't. 'No bike tonight?'

'Umm, no. I needed to walk for once. You know that feeling, when you're sick of a particular form of transport and you just wanna get back to basics?'

'Yeah,' I say, confused and surprised by his response. It says a lot more than ... I just feel like walking. Straight away, I recognise that essence of mystery surrounding him ... that others like to pigeonhole me with. We are uniquely individual yet cut from the same cloth, as my father used to say. I hope to hell I can punch through the irritation to satisfy my curiosity.

'So, what are you up to? What's your poison? Beer, girls, or drugs.'

'None,' I reply. 'Bed.' A quick trip to Sandra Marie's Love Shack and fall asleep to Bladerunner no doubt is what I had in mind, but I don't tell him that. The swim and the ten minute quickie with Selena won't get me through, but Madam Marie always has a few girls lined up for me, just in case – paying for it means no guilt. If I go out, I know I won't be able to stop myself.

'*What*? It's *Saturday* night.'

'Yeah, and I've been working all day.'

As though he's read my mind, he calls me on it. 'You reckon sitting in a chair, perving on girls, *work*? Dude. You're young, healthy, a tad good-looking …' I squint my eyes at him and he laughs. 'Okay, you're drop dead gorgeous.' The sarcasm in his voice pisses me off. I *am* curious about him, but I'm not yet prepared to spend an entire night with him to find out what his deal is. 'Honestly, man. Where's your adventurous side? Lets go and have some fun.'

There's a lot about Skye that could be fun, but I'm really not up for it tonight. 'I'm on a good behaviour bond,' I say, lying through my teeth. Actually, it isn't what I would call a full-on lie. The last few times I've been out, hasn't gone well. Two trips to the police station after fights had broken out, and an all-night stop-out where I'd fallen asleep in some alleyway, smashed out of my head, worrying poor Wally half to death. He'd kindly suggested that I come home at a reasonable hour and keep my nose out of trouble. Wally's reasonable hour is 2am.

'You're over eighteen, you can do what you want.' The dimple is back in his cheek. '*What*? You're parents don't trust you or something?'

My lips tighten. 'My parents are dead.'

Skye lets out a short laugh. I look him over, wondering what he found funny. 'Mine too,' he says with a still smiling. 'Let's get wasted.'

Our eyes lock on. Time slips away quickly before solid words finally enter my brain. 'Ahh, I'm not up for it.'

'Lightweight. I'll flip you for it. Head's we go, tails you can go home to your cosy little bed with your teddy. Deal?'

I haven't even agreed before Skye tosses the coin into the air. It spins fast, over and over, almost intentionally stalling at the top of its ascension only to come down much slower as though gravity doesn't exist. I shake my head, confused, putting it down to being tired. And then, before landing in his palm, the coin performs an extra rotation to rest on heads.

'You ...'

Without thought, I question what I'd seen, but how can I say he'd *coereced* the coin to land on his chosen call, even though that is exactly what happened.

Skye raises his eyebrows at me and leans in closer. 'You ... *what*?' There is a curious tone to his voice as though he desperately wants me to call him on it.

'Nothing. I have to go home and change first.'

Skye bolts around the car and gets in. 'Great. I could do with a little freshen up myself.'

My shoulders sag. It's like looking after an annoying little brother.

FOUR

'WALLY, I'm back.'

Skye lets out a low whistle as I close the door behind him. 'What a cool place, man. Is that real marble?' He trails his fingertips up one of the pillars before heading over to my father's antique grandfather clock. 'The old woman who used to live next door to me in Australia had one of these.' He raps on the woodwork with his knuckle and grins. 'She reckons it was worth a small fortune.' He takes a slow look around. 'How long have you lived here?' He drops his bag to the floor to gaze up at the chandelier.

I ignore him.

Wally appears, immaculate as always, in brown trousers and an Armani shirt. '*Sir*, if I'd had known you were bringing a guest, I would've made extra.'

'What the fuck? You have a *butler*?' I roll my eyes. 'That's the coolest. Do you have maids too?'

'Look …' I begin, tightness growing in my knuckles. The first time Wally pretended to be a butler was at my parents wake. My Aunt and Uncle were concerned for my mental health, so they invited a few of my school friends around, along with dozens of my parents so-called friends. I suppose it was Wally's way to lift my spirits or make me laugh. And it worked. It was funny as hell and totally unscripted, but now I've asked him three times to drop the act whenever someone comes to the house, but he doesn't. I throw him a look that says we're going to discuss this later.

Skye slaps me on the back. 'It's all good. Wally, is it? Well, don't worry, Wally. I've come prepared.' Skye pulls out a silver microwave dish from his backpack. 'That blonde chick from the pool kiosk, Sabrina or Selena or something ...'

'Serena,' I throw in.

'Serena, huh. I was close. Anyway, she thought my backflips were pretty cool, so she gave me ...' Skye pauses to read the label. 'Chilli con carne, whatever that is.'

A smile creeps across Wally's lips and being the respectful man that he is, he wipes it away before Skye looks up. 'It's spicy minced beef, sir.'

'Sounds edible enough. And you can drop the sir shit. The name's Skye.' Skye, launches the frozen meal at Wally. 'Be a pal and heat it up, and I'll be done in a few secs. Which way is the bathroom?'

I point down the hallway to the guest bathroom. 'Second door on the right.'

'Sweet.'

He picks up his bag and takes off, leaving Wally and I staring after him. Skye opens the first door on the right, which is an airing cupboard, even though I'd told him the second, and he looks back and smirks at us. Upon reaching the second door, he disappears inside.

Wally begins to laugh.

'Don't,' I urge. 'He has latched himself onto me like some abandoned puppy. And quit the butler shit, will you?'

Wally is still grinning. 'I like him, River. I think he'll be good for you.' He ignores my last statement.

'What is he … a tonic?' I throw back at him.

Wally's smile grows wider as he shakes his head. 'I suppose I'd better warm this up before his majesty returns. And whilst we on the subject of serving, I should come clean about who I really am.'

I shrug. 'Leave it. Let's keep him guessing a while.'

Wally scowls at me 'It's just another lie, son. In some form or other. Remember that.'

I scowl at Wally for starting this in the first place and bolt up the stairs, if only for a few minutes of peace.

My shower is shorter than I would've liked, and I drag on a clean pair of jeans and shirt. It's cold out, no moon, no clouds, but I imagine the kind of places Skye frequents, don't take into account your everyday geographical wonders. Underground nightclubs that come with an added kick – unlicensed boxing matches, girls for sale or a multitude of highly accessible drugs come to mind. Maybe I'm wrong, but that's my first impression of him.

As I come down the stairs, Wally's laughter wafts through the dining room doorway. The two of them are sitting at the table, eating. Skye has changed outfits too, a grey and black hoodie with some logo on the front, and a pair of black jeans. I look down at my clothes, wondering if I'm too dressy for a dingy nightclub.

'I left yours in the oven,' says Wally, looking up. I head into the kitchen and remove the plate. 'River, did you know the water goes down the plughole the opposite way in Australia?' calls out Wally as I return. He laughs again.

'I do now.' I don't know why I'm suddenly so grumpy. Wally and Skye are really hitting it off, making me feel like an intruder in my own home.

'Where are you fellas off to tonight?' asks Wally. I look up and lean eagerly across my plate. I'm also interested in what Skye has in store for us.

Skye smirks. 'Can you ride a motorbike?'

'Of course I can.' I'd learnt years ago. My father brought me one for my twelfth birthday after a heated arguement on becoming independent. It turned into a one-sided debate by him, with my realisation that becoming independent meant I wasn't wanted around. It was the one and only gift I received outside of christmas.

'Awesome, because tonight isn't for everyone.'

My initial thought is drag racing, but standing in front of the Cage of Death, nearly an hour later, watching two kitted out riders chasing each other inside what looks like a massive steel framed orb, my mouth drops open. The Grease Pit is the last place I thought we'd end up.

'You up for it?' The childish grin on Skye's face returns. No way am I going to back down from this, not even if it kills me, and it's more than likely *going* to. I glance over at the bar area. A little dutch courage is needed.

'I need a drink first.'

'Bikes first, drinks later. You'll want to experience this rush without alcohol dulling your senses.'

I take a quick look around. The whole set up is enclosed inside an old aircraft hangar. Decked out with a huge arena in the middle, the wheel of death sits centre stage, tables and chairs around the edges, a betting booth in one corner, and fully equiped bar in the other. Flashing, multi-coloured lights and thumping bass music transforms it into a nightclub with a twist – just like I'd foreseen. It's only a matter of time before the paid entertainment shows up.

'I'll go and sign us up,' he says, without waiting for my answer. I casually lean against the bar, trying to look like it's the kind of place I come to often.

Skye is back before I have a chance to decide whether to have that drink or not. 'No time for that, loverboy?' His hand falls heavily onto my shoulder. 'We're on in ten minutes. We need to suit up.'

I follow him down to the *shit pit*. I can't make up my mind if it's called that because of the grease everywhere and motorbikes being fuelled or it's from try-hards dumping their nervous bowels.

Skye heads straight over to a guy kneeling down beside a familiar looking bike – the same one he dropped me home on last night. 'Is this yours?'

'I wish,' replies Skye. 'Darcy lets me borrow it occasionally, don't ya Darce?' The man lifts his head. A pair of brown eyes stare at me from behind a mask of grease.

'Yeah, only when you bring it back in one piece,' he grumbles.

Skye's face switches between embarrassment and hurt. 'He's such a joker and besides, it only happened once.'

'Twice,' corrects Darcy. 'Remember …' Skye's face frowns and then suddenly lightens.

'Oh yeah, but that wasn't my fault. That dickhead had it in for me.'

'Whatever,' mutters Darcy, kicking over the engine. He looks me up and down and then turns his attention back to Skye. 'Are you gonna bullshit all night or are you going to get out there and rattle that cage.'

'You betcha,' says Skye.

All I can think of is, what the fuck have I just signed up for.

Ten minutes later, padded out in leather pants and jackets and donning a helmet, we wheel the bikes to the ramp at the bottom of the cage.

Adrenaline out-strips my body of water until I feel almost solid. The crowd has suddenly tripled and the sound of cheers that Skye laps up, echoes around me, leaving me numb. A clock has started its countdown from sixty. Fuck, fuck, fuck.

To be honest, adrenaline and I aren't on the best terms. It sparks way too many emotions, all of which I have very

56

little understanding of, fear, excitement, anxiety, anticipation, hysteria, envy – all channelling through me at break-neck speed, making my head spin. Everything is mixed up and I can barely see the entrance to the cage as I wheel the bike closer. One leg trembles and every muscle in my stomach tightens. What calmness I had before is replaced by spiralling, out-of-control nonsense.

'You alright, bro?' I hear Skye say. 'You gonna puke?'

I feel like it.

'C'mon. It's no big deal if you wanna pike out.'

I grit my teeth and nod for him to move.

Skye pushes his bike through the doorway first, giving me a few seconds to look up, perhaps pray a little, and hopefully clear my head. The noise of the crowd dulls slightly, and perched on the hanging lights above my head sits a large black raven. It peers down at me with a pair of lime green eyes as though I'm the only one in the room. Strangely hypnotising, it stills my erratic senses, streamlining my assorted emotions into one – exhilaration.

I manoevuer the bike into the cage and throw my leg over the seat, listening to the shallow, desperate pattern of my breath. If this is what excitement feels like, I'm all in. Skye is ready too.

A voice booms over a loudspeaker.

'Rider one, ready?' Skye thrusts his hand in the air to a thunderous applause.

'Rider two, ready?' I copy, though not so confidently.

'On the sound of the siren,' bellows the voice. 'Begin your chase.'

Two red lights glow intermittently. I rev up the bike the same time Skye does, all the while, my heart pumping hard in my chest.

The light turns to green. I drop the clutch. The back wheel spins, and I accelerate, sending me forward like a free roaming canonball. The first lap goes past in a blur, the second even faster.

'Equator, equator, equator,' begins the crowd. I look up to see Skye way above me, riding the walls of the centre of the cage with ease. I rise a bit higher, gaining confidence with each lap, still on the opposite side of the cage to him. I suck in a breath and push the bike further so my front tyre is close to his back mudguard. My whole world almost comes to a complete standstill, the more caught up I get in experiencing one simple, solitary feeling at a time. A freedom I haven't felt since I was a small boy floods my mind with, god, dare I say the word, but happiness is what I feel. Not happy to be racing some maniac, but happy that I am capable of being more than a sex addict, more than a liar, more than a fraud.

The crowd begins to chant 'round the world, round the world, round the world.' I'm stunned when I see Skye going completely upside down, circling the cage horizontally. Just when I decide I'm not ready for it, the blast from the siren goes off.

Screams of appreciation and whistles follow. Skye powers down his bike and I do the same until we come to a stop at the bottom.

My body has come alive.

Something has changed, feels different even.

I can't explain it other than it feels like a key has found it's lock and clicked into place. The once organised emotion now hangs in tatters around me, which is what I was expecting, and the rumble of a thousand different feelings are again scattered and loose and not making any sense. But I don't care. It's a start. I glance up to offer my silent thanks to the bird, but it's gone.

Skye removes his gloves and helmet. His eyes are like that first night I'd seen him at the rasta's lair – silver coins, fresh off the mint. We exit and stow the bikes.

'What a rush,' he says breathless.

'Hell, yes.' I have to admit – it was a rush but I couldn't have done it without the help from the bird. I look up again, and Skye copies.

'Whatcha looking at?' he asks, craning his head back. A curious frown is forming.

'Nothing,' I say, like it's a secret.

Skye laughs. 'Let's get a drink.'

'You're not as much of pussy as I thought,' says Skye, holding back a smirk.

I raise my eyebrows. 'And you're not as annoying as you think.'

We both laugh and pull up a couple of stools. The bar reminds me of something from an old western movie. Clad in red wood, cow horns above the bar and red leather seats including salon style booths. All that's missing are the saloon doors and the horses out front.

Skye opens his mouth to order.

'God. You don't drink that Fosters' piss, do you?' I quickly ask.

'I don't drink alcohol. It dulls the senses.' Something in the way he says it makes my eyebrows arc. Dulling my senses is what I do best, but nevertheless, it's a strange reason for sobriety.

'Well, order me a light beer. I'm driving.'

A pretty blonde bartender, wearing what's left of a white t-shirt dress and a brown cowhide waistcoat saunters towards us. 'Didn't think I'd see you back so soon, Skye, especially after what happened last time. You know JT is still looking for you.'

Skye shifts in his seat. 'Yeah, well, that was a rough night.' The lightness from his face disappears.

'You can say that again. I've never seen you so upset. You never did tell me how you got out of that ...'

Skye cuts her off. A fake smile, which I'm sure is soley for my benefit, finds it's way to his lips. 'Can we get a light beer and an iced water thanks, Mel.' The pained look in her eyes, along with my awesome ability to read emotions, tells me she cares about him and that he's in trouble. She shrugs and goes to get our drinks.

I clear my throat. 'What was all that about?'

He checks her out as she bends over to retrieve two glasses. 'Er, nothing. Old stuff.'

I don't let it drop. 'Sounds pretty new to me.'

Skye mumbles something too low for me to hear as Mel brings over the drinks. He looks along the bar to where a buff looking guy winks at her and flexes his muscles at us. 'I see you're still hanging out with that loser. You could do so much better.'

She puts down the drinks and tugs playfully at his chin. 'I couldn't wait for you forever. Besides, you left me with no choice. Gym junkie verses too many secrets, meant Brad and his bulging biceps beat you hands down.'

Skye chuckles. 'He's a lucky guy. Thanks, Mel.' He turns to me. 'You wanna sit at a table?'

'Sure. What's she mean about secrets?'

'Oh, you know, bloke stuff,' he says casually, picking up his drink.

We take a booth furthest away from the bar. My guess is, he doesn't want Mel offering up any more of his life. Anything I want to know, I'm going to have to find out for myself.

'How long have you been in England for?'

Skye shrugs one shoulder. 'Few months. I'm still not sure if I'm gonna stay yet.'

I frown. '*Stay*?'

'Yeah, I came over with my older brother, Dean. It was supposed to be all of us. Dad had a job here but then …' He stops and flicks his hair out of his eyes. 'It's just me and Dean now.'

The muscles in my chest and neck, tighten as the only emotion I have with death, tries to inch its way forward.

Grief.

I'm not a hundred per cent sure it's grief, having nothing to compare it to, so I rolled the dice, stuck a pin in it and attached it to my parents death.

I do, however, recognise the blank stare on Skye's face. I'd bet money he hasn't dealt with theirs either. 'I'm sorry. How did they die?'

'Skydiving.' He sighs heavily. 'I can understand one parachute not working, but two …what are the odds?'

'I'm sorry.' What *are* the odds of both parents dying at the same time. I remember thinking the same when my parents drowned in calm water, both excellent swimmers and divers.

'Thanks.' His eyes glaze over as though he's no longer here. Dreamily, he says, 'well, all I can say is the 22 August is a day I'll never forget.'

Flatline – one second, two seconds, three seconds.

My body is granite, is cold, is marble, is dead. My heart thumps back into some kind of unnatural cadence as blood drains from my face and pools at my feet. It anchors me to the spot. What are the odds of his parents dying on the very same day *mine* did. As much as I want to put this down to some weird coincidence, something inside me says we were meant to meet. We were meant to be friends and with that, our parents were meant to die, in order to bring us to this very moment. A shiver races over my spine and up to the back of my neck.

Something else changes.

The drafty room, with no personality, suddenly charges up with electricity.

I look up.

A redhead is walking straight for us. A familiar ache twists in my groin.

Skye clocks her at the same time. 'Dibs,' he says childishly.

Her face comes into view. 'She's yours,' I mutter.

It isn't *her* – it isn't *my* redhead. The rush is over before it had chance to begin, although it has woken the beast. I twist in anticipation of my next victim.

As though we've beaten the same drum, immediately, the look on his face alters from excitement to boredom. 'On the other hand, I think I'll pass,' he mumbles.

We exchange looks that say so much more than I'm simply not interested. I have no desire to lay my cards on the table and tell this stranger that I've been dreaming about a redhead for years and yet, there is a strange comfort in opening up to him.

I gesture to her with my chin. 'Not good enough for you?' The girl winks at me as she passes, and it takes all of my self control to not drag her into the nearest toilets and find out what she's wearing under that tight black dress. The beast, living inside my skin, wants its fill.

'Something like that,' says Skye with a smirk.

I down my beer. 'I need to go.'

In my haste to leave, the glass I'm holding slips through my fingers. Skye is resting his elbows on the table, eyeing off Mel. He isn't looking in my direction, and yet, his reflexes are out of this world. Inches from the floor, and as though he has some kind of secret pact with gravity, the glass lands safely in his hand. I replay the scene over in my head.

'That was …' No words fit for what I want to say.

'Nothing,' says Skye, 'you saw nothing, because it was nothing.' His face has all the personality of a gravestone. And yet it sounds like a phrase he's used to saying a lot.

I *saw* it.

It sounds totally preposterous that someone can slow down time, but that's what it looked like. The glass hung in mid-air, hovered a fraction of a second so that Skye could get to it in time before it went smashing to the floor. The same way the toss of his coin worked, and his slow-motioned somersaults.

'But you …'

'I said, drop it, River. This isn't the place and certainly not the time.' He smiles and taps his temple. 'Right?'

I have no idea what he means, but he is right. I do have to leave and this can wait. I have to silence the chanting in my head – we *have* to go, we have to *go*, *we* have to go, *we have to go*.

I'm wasting time.

I'm not sure how much longer I can last, especially as more females are flocking into the bar area. This is the main reason I avoid pubs and nightclubs – too many to deal with at once, especially when they have male companions with them. Most of the fights I've got into in the last few months are due to frequenting a pub or nightclub. And I promised Wally, no more fighting, although in my defence, it isn't me swinging the first punch. Guys step up to protect, these poor, deranged women who are drawn to me by some unknown presence, having no idea why – and this is where the manipulator part of me steps up and puffs up his chest. He's an arsehole, you see, doesn't care who he hurts, doesn't care what he has to do to get what he wants. He's a scam-artist and should be locked away from society,

'Let me get your number and we'll catch up for another adrenalien junkie, near death experience soon,' I say.

'What do you mean by that?' asks Skye. A flash of irritation slides across his face.

I'm confused. 'Nothing. Just that if you want to thrash your *mate's* bike again, I'll be up for it.' Skye's face loses its hostility and a smile comes back to his lips. He snatches my phone, types in his number, and then throws it back to me.

'River, if you can't get me on my mobile, Mel will know how to get hold of me.' He winks. 'Don't be a stranger now,' he says and disappears into the crowd.

The tap on my shoulder is right on time. 'Hello, handsome. Wanna buy me a drink?' The first of four girls have singled me out.

'Actually, I'm just leaving …?'

'It's Alexa,' says the blonde. She smooths her lip gloss over with her little finger. 'My name's Alexa.'

'Like I said, I was just leaving.'

Her eyes sadden and her lips pout. 'You need some company?'

I take a quick look around. She wouldn't be my first pick, but she'll do. 'You alone?'

'Mmhmm,' she squeaks.

I smile.

And *that* is how it's *done*. Definition number four - controller.

I don't have to work at it. I don't have to drop a line or coerce them into my arms. It's a natural instinct for them to notice me, and even though they aren't sure why, a more natural instinct for me to be who I am – a fraud.

She links her arm through mine and cuddles in close, purposely rubbing her breast against me as though we've been dating for months. The beast living in my blood, licks it's lips, ramping up my desire to have her.

By the time we reach the carpark, her nails scratch and pinch into my flesh. She's desperate for me, that much is clear, and I know she can't do anything to stop it.

Poor thing.

It's what drives them wild to seek me out in the first place. I've seen girls go half-mad, trying to get into my pants, and even worse, when they can't have me as a permanent boyfriend. It's not pretty, and I don't take any joy in their discomfort. That is why I cut it off early, no names, no phone numbers.

'Nice car,' says Alexa as I give the engine a revving. I'm not here for small talk, and hum my response. The least I know about her, the better. Names equal real people, with hopes, thoughts and feelings.

I drive to the Golden Finch Motel, speeding through two red lights and narrowly missing the gutter as I turn in. This is my usual haunt, and I pull up in front of room eighteen. I hate to admit it, but I rent this room by the week. In the beginning, I'd made the mistake of taking a couple of girls back to my place, hence the *Georgia* scenario Wally got in the way of, and of course, when one particular chick saw the kind of lifestyle I led, she immediately wanted a piece of it. It took me weeks before she finally got the message. We live and we learn. Never again will a chick walk through the front door of my house.

The glove box falls open at the touch of a button and I retrieve the key with it's green plastic tag. Several condoms spill out with it.

Preening in the drop down mirror, Alexa abruptly stops. 'You're not some kind of weirdo, are you?' That is definitely debatable and I ponder on my answer. 'It's just I don't do this kinda thing very often,' she goes on to explain.

I find that difficult to believe. I turn up the charm and wink at her. 'What do you reckon, gorgeous?'

She doesn't look scared, only cautious, and shrugs. 'You look harmless enough to me.'

I offer her my most sincerest smile.'I swear I'm not going to hurt you.' Immediately, I sense her anxiety drop. Her perfume, however, which will remain in the car long after she leaves, and will irritate the shit out of me tomorrow. Chanel No 5 – I would know it anywhere.

I open the car door, knowing she'll follow my lead. She does, too closely, pressing her tits into my back as I stop to open the motel door.

The room isn't anything special – a queensize bed, a tv, not that I've ever switched it on, and a small bathroom.

'Something tells me this isn't your first time here.' Alexa removes her jacket.

'Yeah, I rent this room by the week,' I say sarcastically. She giggles and I grind my teeth.

She shakes back her blonde mane, allowing me to get an eyeful of her huge bust. As quick as that, she reaches down to the hem of her sparkly dress and whips it off in one swift movement. It doesn't surprise me to see she isn't wearing any underwear.

The beast peers over the top of my sanity. She's yours, it hisses.

I am almost conquered.

'One rule,' I say, looking her over.

Her head cocks to one side. 'Which is?'

'No kissing.'

Kissing is personal. My own mother hadn't kissed me very much, *even* as a child, and I'd only ever gone out of my way to kiss two women in my life – one was my nanna when I was seven and she'd brought me my very first pair of flippers and goggles, and the second was Julie Bates at the year eight formal, which was wet and painful due to her braces.

But that isn't the reason.

Kissing is a direct line into their emotions multiplied by ten, into their darkest fears and deepest desires. And for me, that is a dangerous place to be.

'Good, then you won't ruin my lipstick.'

I hold back a smile. Whichever way she wants to look at it, that lipstick is definitely coming off.

Definition number twelve – commanding.

FIVE

LOOKING everywhere and anywhere, I circle the streets, my skin crawling with torment. The fourth girl for the day is always the worst – like the first bite of your favourite dessert - the yearning far more intense and more thrilling than the act itself, and then knowing the glorious satisfaction only happens after the last bite. Except for me, the end is never satisfying, neither are the ones in the middle. Sex is a means to an end.

Alexa is long gone.

So is the waitress from the all night café I stopped at for a takeaway coffee.

But I need one more.

The first, barely scratched the surface, second got me through with minimal discomfort, third stopped the pain, stopped the endless ache. The fourth will ensure I get a good nights sleep and drown out the incessant voice inside my head. The intruder that moved in and didn't ask permission, who never leaves me alone, whispers such evil, that I no longer distinguish who I truly am anymore.

I'm tired.

I want to go home.

Three hours later, I pull into the garage with the full quartet under my belt, completely exhausted. The middle-aged woman loitering on the corner of The Crown and Anchor was just what *she* was looking for, she'd said, regardless that she kept calling out for Dave to go harder. It was quick and barely took the edge off.

Now, it's well after four and I need sleep.

The house is dark and smells like a Chinese takeaway. Wally must've ordered in, and as hungry as I am, I can't bring myself to eat anything. I drag myself up the stairs and fall onto my bed. I'm out in seconds.

I know I'm dreaming when I see her luscious red hair swaying this way and that as she runs ahead of me. The one girl I can't have is the only girl I truly want. And she is only fifty steps away from me. Night after night, I chase her through unfamiliar streets with tall buildings and sharp corners just to get a glimpse of her. Every time I catch up, she slowly, and yet effortlessly, walks away from me - a distance I can never seem to lessen. All I want is to see her face and maybe touch her skin, just to convince myself she is real. In my heart she is, but Wally's words are casting shadows of doubt in my mind.

The gap between us grows.

'Don't go,' I beg.

I drive my legs harder into the ground, drawing on strength I know is there. It's like running on layers of mattresses.

It's no use.

I stop and bend over, gulping down air. It is torment of the worst kind.

Pleeeeease.

Please don't go. I can't bear it when you leave.

I raise my head, aware the air is suddenly denser and much harder to breathe.

She has stopped.

She never stops.

My heart leaps for joy.

Slowly, she turns around. Her natural, flawless beauty stuns me, as it does every time, disconnecting my feet from the ground. Gravity has become my enemy, freezing me in time, preventing me from catching up to her. Desire lifting me higher and higher, wave after wave, to the point I no longer recognise what the earth feels like beneath my feet.

She checks over her shoulder. First left, and then right, her eyes, wide and frightened like she's evading a predator. I've never seen her like this before. Scared. Vulnerable. Desperate. I want to help her. I want to protect her.

I beg for her name, like I've begged a thousand times before but it is wasted. She never speaks. She never hears my pleas.

But then her perfect lips part.

I hold my breath at the thought I might finally hear her voice.

'Help me. Someone, please help me,' she whispers, so timidly, so pathetically that in that one moment I know I will do anything for her, no matter the cost. Her voice abashed with innocence and in such sweet tones, leaves me gasping for air. Tears press out from eyes … run down my cheeks.

Outside of my dreams, I am neutral, colourless, impersonal – an empty vessel who feels nothing and cares for no one. Inside my dreams, I feel love and passion and intimacy and I would run to the furthest corners of the world just to see her smile, and I would lay down my life just to hear her voice, and sell my soul to the lowest bidder to simply hold her hand. I would give her everything and anything she asks for.

I mouth the words, 'what's your name?' As usual, my voice is mute and yet she tilts her head to one side as though she hears me. *Please*,' I beg, 'tell me your name?'

The sound of a large truck filters into my dreams.

I'm waking, I can feel it. I'm running out of time.

Please.

There is no smile on her lips as she mutters the sweetest name I've ever heard – Ember Riley.

Not the sun streaming through the window, almost blinding me, nor the clunking sounds of rubbish bins being emptied at five o'clock can possibly ruin my day.

I have her name.

Even the twist in my groin or the layers of ice needles under my skin, sewing pain into my muscles is easy enough to ignore.

I have her name.

A name I haven't simply conjured … in truth, I'm not that inventive, but a real name that reassures me that I haven't been making this whole thing up. I feel it in every inch of my being. The same way I can read emotions, the same way water has a calming effect on me, and the same way that I have this overpowering effect on women.

I waltz into the kitchen unable to wipe the smile off my face. 'Morning, Wally.'

Wally frowns at me. 'What did you get up to last night, or shouldn't I ask?'

Nothing is going to get me down today. 'She told me her name?' I blurt out without thinking.

Wally chokes on his coffee. 'Well, it is the decent thing to do, getting a girl's name before …' His laugh peeters out.

'NO, the girl from my dreams. I finally have her name.'

Wally stares back at me, his expression whitewashed. Although he has no newspaper this morning he still peers at me from over the top of his reading glasses. His mouth stretches downwards. He takes another sip of his coffee. 'Dare I ask?'

'You could sound a little more enthusiastic,' I grumble. I expected a tad more support from him.

'What … about a girl that doesn't exist? Please, River. Enough of this already.'

I take a breath. 'Her name is Ember Riley and when I find her, and show you that she's real, you are going to get down on your knees, dressed in a curly blonde wig and Hawaiian skirt and apologise to me for a whole hour.'

Wally simply nods his head, but I take his silence as his word. And I will stand by it. I will find her, and I *do* want that apology, but first, I have a four hour shift at the pool. And if I leave now, I'll be able to squeeze in a swim before I start.

By two-thirty that afternoon, my body is feeling less cage-like and I'm capable of having a reasonable conversation with a woman without wondering what her favourite position is.

I pull up a chair and sit in front of my laptop. I've been itching all day to start, and although it may be a long shot, I type Ember Riley into the search bar. The first three names come under a facebook heading which uncover three blondes and a ten year old girl from Missouri. The next few are under twitter, which also prove fruitless, and google images only reveals a cute, coloured actress with a curvy bod, even though her name is Amber and not Ember. Somehow, Ember Riley doesn't come across as someone who spends her time broadcasting her life to every soul on the planet and I'm only kidding myself if I think she is going to be that easy to find. I need to dig deeper, but where? Public records, the library, old newspapers … the list is endless. Maybe hiring a private investigator is the way to go, or perhaps now she is communicating in my dreams, she will give me her address too.

I shake my head realising that is the most pathetic thought I've ever had. If it has taken ten long years to find out her name, it might take just as long, if not longer, to find out where she lives. This is a job I need to take into my own hands.

For the next three months, every day I'm not working, I hang out at the district library, sifting through old newspapers. Natasha, the librarian, is more than accomodating, allowing me access to the back room where all their archived newspapers are stored. I sit here, day after day, hour after hour, scanning each page of the six biggest selling newspapers in the country, hoping to come across something, even it's only the same surname. A few times I thought I was on to something but it ended before it began and now, after searching through almost two years' worth of tales of woe, I'm beginning to lose hope.

I drop my head onto the desk.

The faint smell of ink from the Daily Telegraph makes my nose itch. I haven't resorted to the private investigator idea yet because it feels creepy and devious. I ask myself how would I feel if somebody was jotting down my every move and skulking in doorways taking photos of me.

The light fragrance of Yves St Laurent causes my head to lift. There's a light tap on the door. I know it's Natasha before she opens it.

'River,' she cooes. She pokes her head around the door. Natasha has a soft, caring face, no make up, which I like a lot about her, and mousey-brown hair that falls in curls around her shoulders. Her body isn't too bad either, clothes on or off.

'Come in,' I mutter.

Natasha pushes the door open, the tips of her fingers resting on the handle. 'I'm just about to close up. Did you have any luck today?' I run my hands over my head and leave them clasped against the back of my neck. I let out a sigh which doesn't require an explanation.

'Well, I might have something for you.' I wait for her to start to unbutton her white blouse with the tiny green leaves over it, but instead, she reaches into the pocket of her skirt and pulls out a slip of paper. This isn't the striptease that I've come to rely on.

I immediately sit up.

'It might be nothing, but I thought it was worth looking in to.' She smiles sweetly, her fingers sweeping across my skin as she passes me the note.

I unfold it. It's a newspaper article from one of the less known papers dated just over six months ago. It reads:

Tragedy struck a young family yesterday when a fuel tanker collided with their car on the eastern motorway around 3pm. The parents, Mr and Mrs Benjamin Riley were killed instantly, leaving their fifteen year old daughter, orphaned. Paramedics, who were called to the scene less than ten minutes later, said they were amazed that the child, who cannot be named, was uninjured in the accident.

There is no picture of the crash site, no car, no mangled number plate. I hold the article, unaware at first, that my hand is shaking. Something is familiar about this, as though I've read it before, or maybe dreamt it. My heart soars, bringing with it, another feeling.

Lust.

The beast awakens.

Take her.

I glance up at Natasha and her eyes glaze over instantly. The spell works like it always does. It doesn't matter that it's an illusion. It works, and I want her.

Now.

She stares back at me. Her lower lip trembles. Her mouth drops open.

She's putty in my hands.

She promptly closes the door behind her, leaving only the small lamp on my desk to light the room. She slides around the side of the desk until her thigh presses against mine. The same words filter through me as they do everytime I'm faced with sex –

Sink … Or …. Swim

They are the customary terms my brain asks me before I unleash my power. As usual, I'm too far away from water to swim and dull the sensation, therefore, my only option is to sink. It's this or pain and I know what I'd rather. I allow the good part of myself to sink into the murky depths of what I have become – a deceitful, manipulator of desire and go in for the kill.

I reach under her skirt, doing what I have to, to filter out the soft moan she makes as I pull down her knickers. She smiles seductively at me. 'Chair or table?'

'Chair,' I reply.

I drive home, hating myself more than ever.

Guilt is leaving it's mark on me, crumbling my once ruthless conscience. The decent person inside struggles with the consequences of the monster hidden beneath. I have become a Dr Jeykll and Mr Hyde character and the turmoil will not let up. I hate that Natasha has become one of my regulars. She isn't like other girls I *use*. She is gentle and warm and thinks of others before herself, except when she's with me and under my control. Maybe our time will be reduced now that I have a clue to go on with.

I hope so.

The upside to the incessant chaos inside my head is, I could be facing a real possibility that this families tragedy is my good fortune, and could lead me straight to Ember. The only problem is, I don't know where in England this fatality happened, and there is also the likelihood that she has moved away from that area if she's been orphaned. I have only one resource left to me.

I pull into the driveway and put the car in park. I need to make a phone call, one I don't want Wally listening to - one I don't want to make. My fingers shake as I punch in the number. A woman's voice answers.

'Freeman, Gladstone and Botch, can I help you?'

'Hey, Grace, it's River Fulton. I was wondering if I could speak to Mr Freeman?' Mr Freeman was my father's lawyer for fifteen years.

'River, how are you, lovey?' she purrs over the phone.

'Good, really good.' There's a brief pause.

'I'll check for you, honey. Just hold the line for a moment.' I've come to know Grace quite well during the time it took to settle my parents' estate. She is a motherly woman, nothing like my own mother, and gave me chocolate bars when I accompanied my parents to their twice yearly visit. I used to sit at the spare desk opposite her for hours on end drawing, and gazing at all the photos of her grandchildren. I wished for a long time that my parents would die and put me up for adoption so I could go and live with her.

'Just a second, love, and he'll be right with you,' she says.

'Great. Thanks, Grace.' The sound of a solo clarinet chimes through the earpiece.

I wait.

'River, m'lad. How are you? Are you phoning to make our next appointment?' Actually I'd forgotten about that. We're due to go over some stuff next month, just to make sure things are 'ticking along nicely' as Mr Freeman likes to call it. There's no reason why they shouldn't be.

'Umm not really, although we can do that too. I was wondering whether your firm hired any private investigators?' The sound of silence is more powerful now than that lonely clarinet.

'Has something happened? Are *you* in trouble?'

'No, it's not me,' I add quickly. 'I need to find a … an old friend that I lost contact with, and I thought a PI might be able to help.'

'Right,' says Mr Freeman. I detect the underlying suspicion in his voice. He's a well-educated man in his sixties and not lightly fooled. 'Did you loan this person some money?'

'What? No. It's a girl, actually.' I immediately know what his response will be. 'And no, she's not pregnant.'

I hear Mr Freeman sigh. 'Well, that's a relief. Old flame, is it?'

'A what?'

'A flame – old girlfriend, the one that got away.' He chuckles.

'Yeah, something like that.' I look up to see Wally peering through the window at me. I need to wrap this up. 'Could you recommend anyone?'

'We use a company called Iceberg Rose Investigation Services from time to time. They're good and we've had some quick, detailed responses from them.'

'Iceberg Rose? Okay. Great. I'll phone Grace in the next few days and schedule in that appointment.'

'Very good,' says Mr Freeman, 'and good luck locating her.'

'Thanks.'

I hang up and slide the phone into my pocket.

Wally is waiting behind the door as I enter. 'Secret phone calls, River, or should I call you Bond … James Bond.' I roll my eyes at his poor attempt at a Sean Connery accent. 'You're too suspicious, that's your trouble, Wal,' I say, grinning.

'With you, I have every reason to be.'

After a shower, I head down to the kitchen, rummage through the fridge and find a vegetable casserole hiding behind two jars of olives. I take it out, nuke it for a few minutes and then throw myself in front of the TV. Before I take the first mouthful, my phone beeps. It's a message from Serena. Same time, same place. That means 10pm at the Golden Finch Motel. I type back that I'll be there and go back to my food.

In all my time of watching adverts, I've never come across investigation companys' advertising their services, especially when that company happens to be the very one I'd made up my mind to phone tomorrow. The delicate

76

jingle and white rose at the end of the advert is all the sign I need to tell me I'm doing the right thing.

My decision is final.

Tomorrow, I'm starting my new life in preparation for meeting Ember, and I can't do that having sex with four girls per day.

I have to cull them one at a time.

Which means more time in the pool. I figure I'm in for some kind of withdrawal - a period when life can't get any worse, and what better time to do this when my life finally has a glimmer of light shining over it.

That night, and with all my appetites gorged, I lay awake thinking about Ember and the first time our eyes will meet. What will I say to her? Will I recognise her in the flesh? Where will this meeting take place? Will she be able to resist me where all others have failed? Her eyes are scorched into my soul, the colour of molten lava, mysterious, but innocent. They won't lie to me. I'm praying they won't lie to me.

The sound of my heart thundering away in my chest almost blocks out the voice of the beast that wants to consume her for its own needs. I only pray it remains that way. I pray, I'll be able to resist *her*.

Before I fall asleep, I make one vow – save none.

I will never have sex with her until I have total control over this wretched entity living inside my skin, no matter how much pain I have to endure or how much desire that floods through my veins.

I have to.

I have to believe I am capable of being a decent human being.

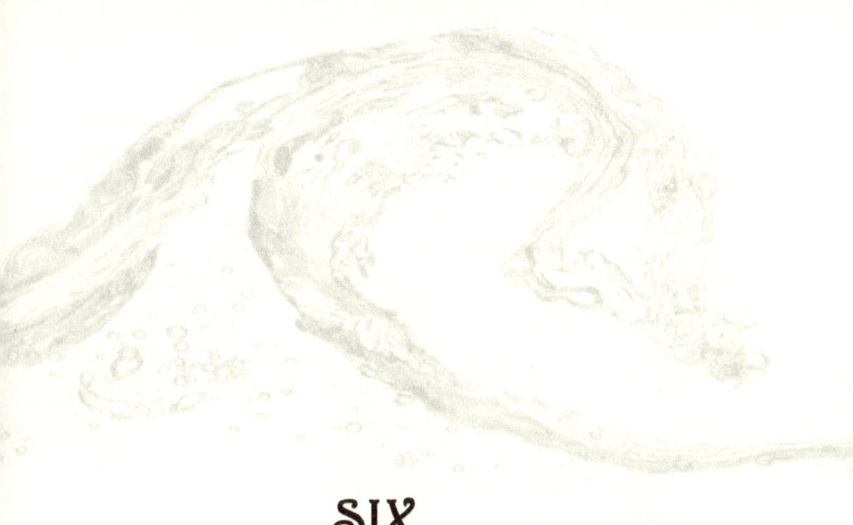

SIX

The next morning, I wake to the sound of voices outside my room.

'I still don't think he'll appreciate being woken up so early,' I hear Wally say.

The door flies open and Skye Buchannan bounds into my room and closes the door behind him. I'm half expecting him to comment on how big my bedroom is, and all the fancy décor my parents thought was necessary, but he doesn't.

'Fuck, dude, you've gotta help me,' he says, rushing to the window. He drags the curtains open with one fast flick, looks out and then yanks them closed again. His shoulders heave as he gathers his breath.

Confused, I push myself up as he perches himself on the end of my bed. His face is red, and sweat has stuck his perfectly styled hair to his forehead in straw-like clumps.

'What the hell are you doing here? What time is it?'

Skye stands and looks out the window once more before resuming his seat. 'I hate to come to you, but I don't have anyone else to turn to.'

I look over at the clock. It's only seven thirty and he's wearing his customary jeans and hoodie. From the smell of stale cigarettes and alcohol, they're last nights clothes. I also don't need my emotional magic wand to tell me he's anxious, his actions are clear enough. Regardless, a watered-down version finds it's way under my skin and trickles through my body.

I rub my eyes. 'Who have you pissed off now?'

'*What*? No-one.' He turns to look at me, his brows creasing.

'Then who are you running from?' Shock falls over Skye's face briefly before it's gone.

'How did you …'

'It doesn't take a genius,' I say interrupting. 'How often do you turn up at a friend's place at seven thirty in the morning, dripping in sweat and not wearing running gear.'

'More often than I'd like these days,' he mutters without looking at me. I lean forward not totally sure I heard right. He carries on. 'So, we *are* friend's, then?' Skye has a hopeful look on his face. He pushes his hair to one side.

I try his question on for size. We are new friends, even though I haven't seen him in the last few months, but friends nonetheless. 'Sure. How much do you need?'

Skye squints back at me. 'Who said it was anything to do with money?' I wait patiently. His posture, which had been stacked up tall, tumbles in. He lowers his eyes. 'Two hundred pounds.'

My immediate thought is drugs or betting debts. I'm wrong on both accounts.

'Don't look at me like that,' says Skye, lifting his gaze to meet mine. 'Some low-life piece of shit owes me money and when I asked him to pay up, he pulled a knife on me.'

'*What*?' I try to shake the confusion out of my sleepy head. "He owes *you* money?' He gets up and looks through the crack in the curtains again. 'Then why do you need two hundred quid? And what's the deal with the window?'

I slide across the bed to the window wearing nothing but a pair of boxer shorts. I pull back the curtains with a hearty tug.

Skye flinches, suddenly uncomfortable and legs it to the farside of the room.

There is no one there, which kind of surprises me. There's no posse. No gunman on the grassy knoll. Not even next doors golden retriever is padding around their garden yet.

I close the curtain again and Skye relaxes a little and find a spot on the end of my bed. I get back into bed but don't pull the sheets up, knees to chest, arms wrapped around. 'I need the money to buy his silence. He doubled crossed me, you see.' I open my mouth. 'And before you ask, I haven't murdered anyone, I haven't stolen anything and I haven't done anything illegal. Can we leave it at that?'

'And I'm just supposed to trust you?'

Skye shrugs. 'Sorry, I can't say anymore than that. It's for your own safety that you don't know. Believe me.'

I catch a glimpse of myself in the full length mirror at the end of the bed and smooth down a tuft of hair. 'Give me one good reason why I should.'

Skye drags his hand across his chin. It sounds as though he hasn't shaved in a week. 'Because you and I are the same, River, and the sooner you realise that and find that part of you which defines who you are, and separates you from everyone else, the sooner we can start talking on a level playing field.'

I open my mouth again, waiting for the *what the fuck are you on about* comment that tumbles over and over in my mind but somehow fails to come out. He *had* felt it too, that night, like I said, as though we were cut from the same cloth. I have so many questions about how he seems to know me better than I know myself, but how can I begin a conversation like that, especially when words won't even form in my brain.

'Can you loan me the money then?' asks Skye, angling his head to one side. Two hundred pounds is small change for me. I'm just about to say yes when, between the slit in the curtain, something small and black thumps against the window. Skye leaps off the bed so fast he lands on the floor two metres away.

I jump up and draw back the curtain.

A large black bird, either a crow or raven, I can't be sure, is sitting on my window sill. I look closely at it, wondering why it hasn't flown away.

'Have you got a shotgun?' His face is pale, and the sweat from before has returned by the bucketload. 'Plee-ase.'

'Yeah, I always carry a loaded firearm in my bedroom. It's only a fucking bird,' I say, banging on the window. It flies off.

'It's not just a bird,' says Skye, panting, his closed fist drumming against his chest. I don't hear the rest of what he says because he's rambling in low murmurs, but one word that doesn't quite fit alongside the word raven is 'stalking'.

Skye recovers himself and stands up, cautiously peering out of the window. 'The money?' he says.

I find myself going to the top of my wardrobe, pulling out an old leather satchel with a gold embossed logo of my old school on it, and take out a wad of notes.

'Whoa,' whispers Skye. I give him four fifty pound notes and put the satchel back. When Skye leaves I'll find a new hiding place for my stash.

'Thanks, man. You've just saved my life. If I can ever repay the favour, just call.'

I roll my eyes.

As if …

After driving down a couple of back streets and then onto a dead end road, I finally pull up in front of Iceberg Rose

Investigation Services. It isn't an easy place to find, being so far away from the centre of town. Part of me feels like I'm conducting illegal dealings of some kind. If it wasn't for the immaculate cream paintwork and modern window frames, a vast comparison to the grubby, vacated buildings either side, I wouldn't be stepping one foot inside. The green plaque on the wall says, I. Perkins, PI, Iceberg Rose Investigation Services, with a white rose beneath the writing, looks harmless enough.

I sit for a few minutes, contemplating going in. My appointment isn't until two. The receptionist sounded a bit offish when I phoned this morning, but the second I mentioned Mr Freeman, her tone changed and she slotted me into to see her boss at once.

I glance at my watch and then out of the window. The rain is still coming down in sheets and doesn't look like it's going to let up any time soon. I turn up the collar of my jacket and decide to make a run for it. It's only a few yards, but enough water to make me look like a drowned rat. Any other time, I'd take my time in the rain. The most wonderful place to be.

I open the panelled wooden door. Directly in front of me is a flight of stairs. The air is unusually musty and the tacky brown walls look dirty rather than deliberately painted that way. Again, a huge contrast to what I was expecting from the front of the building.

Before I clear the last few steps, I hear a woman's laughter and the sound of a phone ringing. The air lightens and the delicate scent of White Diamonds perfume hits me in the face. Suddenly, I have a bad feeling. I'm about to turn back when a woman speaks.

'Good afternoon. Mr Fulton, I presume.'

I look up to see a young woman, no more than thirty, dressed in a navy blue skirt that floats just above her knee and a fine knitted navy jumper that plunges a little low at the front. She runs her hands down the sides of her hips and my gut clenches, reminding me I have not swam or started my quota for the day. She walks towards me, extending her hand. Her eyes and hair are of the same shade of brown and the moment she shakes my hand, I know she has succumbed to my power. Her eyes mist over and her lips part as though she's about to speak but can't.

I withdraw my hand, taking a brief glance at the receptionist who is also staring at me, mouth agog.

'I'm Iris Perkins,' says the woman, smoothing back her hair seductively. My heart sinks as I register it's her who I'll be doing business with. Why couldn't it have been a man? It never occurred to me a woman might be running the show.

'River Fulton,' I say stiffly.

'Hold my calls for the next half an hour, Tania,' says Iris, addressing the receptionist.

'Sure,' mumbles Tania irritably.

'Shall we ...' says Iris, gesturing me into her office.

I grind my teeth, desperate not to fuck this up. If I can keep this wild cougar at bay, who is prowling around her desk likes she's on heat, and not be intimate with her, I will be able to separate our ties when the job is finished. All I have to do is keep my dick in my pants.

Easier said than done.

'Sit, please,' she says, wheeling her chair out from around her desk, before bringing it alongside mine. Her perfume prods at my inner animal as I sit back in the chair. It is amazingly hypnotic and isn't a brand I've come across before. Iris rises a little and leans across my body to pluck a tissue from the box on her table. The muscles in my legs bunch and tighten. I hold my breath.

'So,' begins Iris, 'what brings you into my lair?' My black magic is working extra quickly with her and I scoot my chair back an inch or so.

'I've lost touch with an old friend and I was hoping your firm might be able to track her down.'

Her warm brown eyes transform into black, bottomless pits. '*Her*?' Her voice sours. I know I should leave but I can get this to work in my favour. I relax my body and let the demon inside do its work.

A sense of calm touches her posture, loosens her muscles. Iris's eyes immediately soften. 'A family member, a sister perhaps?'

'No.'

'An ex-girlfriend then?'

'Not quite.' She crosses to her desk and with the sound of a key unlocking, takes out a leather bound journal from her drawer. She returns and begin to take notes.

'Well, Mr Fulton,' she purrs, rolling her tongue over my name, excentuating the L.

I want her now.

I want to take her and make her wish she'd never met me. Pleasure throbs below my waist, enticing me, tempting me to give in. She is so close. I can take her. It can all be over with in a few minutes and I could then carry on our conversation, making sure I give her all the information she needs that will lead me to Ember Riley, including the newspaper article that burns against my leg in my pocket. The very instant Ember's name flushes through my body, a new urge emerges.

My desire for her and only her.

She is the poison I'd die to have. She is the pleasure I want to feel in my bones. I have to be strong. I have to fight against the devil that demands I give in to what it wants.

Iris politely coughs.

I was miles away, stroking a beautiful girl's hair with my cheek. 'I will need something to go on with,' she says. She straightens her back and pulls her jumper down just far enough for me to see the black lace of her bra. The throb, ache, throb, doubles its rhythm, doubles its efforts. I casually place my hands in my lap, pressing down until the pulsing eases.

'Like what?' I mumble, struggling to gain control.

'A name would be a good start.' Her skirt sweeps past my leg as she moves over to the desk again. Instead of going around, like most would, she bends across the desk to reach for a pen, her skirt hitching up a little. My whole body lurches forward, not of my choosing.

Urgency dominates my body – for her, for Ember, for my sanity.

Iris is an exceptional creature, far more advanced than any of the bimbo's I'm used to. She has a way about her, that had it not been for Ember, I would have her as my first choice everytime and she'd already be on her knees with her hair tied back so I can watch.

My jaw clamps down as I draw on anything and everything I have to not seduce her right now. She would be a willing yet challenging conquest, a real test of my curse. Before I can make a move, Iris is back in her chair, her legs crossed, her shoe dangling on the tips of her toes and her heel caressing the outside of her lower leg. I blow out a breath and switch my thoughts to the only girl that can truly make me tremble.

'Her name is Ember Riley. I'm sorry I don't have a lot to go on, and I don't know what part of England she's currently living in, although I'm fairly sure she *is* still living in this country. She's between sixteen and twenty, although that's only a guess and she has red hair.'

'And how will you be paying for this?' Iris purses her lips and blows gently into my face. I'm beginning to wonder who is the predator and who is the prey.

'Cash,' I manage to say in mid-swallow.

She is within my reach.

Pornographic images of Iris posing on different pieces of furniture stain my mind, tempt me more. All I need to do is to give her the signal and she's mine for the taking. I reach into my pocket, the article still smouldering away against my thigh.

'This might help too.' She goes back to her journal and enters more notes.

Iris takes the slip of paper from me, her short manicured fingernails boldly trace over the back of my hand. I started to count – one, two three, four … It helps to distract me as she makes her way to where her Ipad is and takes a photo of it. She then hands it back to me as I head for the door.

'River, give Tania all your relevant details on your way out. I'd hate to find out something important and not be able to contact you.' The way she says it, sends a tremor through my chest. She is a game player, a professional and I knew it before I'd even stepped one foot inside her door.

'Of course.' I close the door behind me.

I've done it, and came out the other end with Ember in my thoughts, and completely guilt-free. That isn't to say, I've beaten the **beaSt** down entirely.

It's pissed.

It demands its fill.

Tania is watching me. Her head tilts to one side. 'All done, are we?' she asks in a pleasant voice. She is definitely my *release* type, but there is no way I want to hang around any longer. No strings, I remind myself. She passes me a clipboard over the chest high counter top and I scribble my personal details down so quickly I have trouble deciphering my own handwriting. Just as I give back the paperwork, Iris comes out of her office.

There is no personal barrier between us as she slides up next to me. 'One last thing, River, there will be an extra fee if this investigation goes past sixty days.' She then runs her palm slowly and purposefully around the curve of my buttocks.

Five minutes later, I'm in my car, reeling from the experience. I pick up the phone.

'Serena, are you at work?'

SEVEN

The brunette who works at the chemist is the reason I'm late for work this morning. Normally, I like to get to the pool half an hour before it opens to speed-swim fifty laps and prep the pool area, but when she saw me buying three boxes of condoms, she offered her services at once, her eyes the size of dinner plates. Pathetically, I didn't resist.

I pull into my regular car space to see Skye leaning over his motorbike, his head resting on his forearms. The skin beneath his eyes is darker than usual and his hair is dishevelled.

'You look like shit. Have you been here all night?'

Skye sighs. 'I was waiting for you,' he says, stretching and yawning. 'We need to talk.'

It's then I notice just how neglected he actually looks. His hands and face don't appear to have seen a bar of soap in a week and his clothes have that lived-in look only a homeless person would understand.

'I can't. I haven't got time.'

Skye tilts his head. So slightly. Like a dog tuning into a sound. 'The pool doesn't open for another ten minutes. You need to make time.' I squint at his comment.

Skye's jaw, normally loose and relaxed, clenches furiously beneath his skin. 'Fuck, River. When are you going to get it through your thick head ... we're different than everyone else.'

That gets my attention and our last conversation, which went something along the lines of *you need to find out what defines you from everyone else, so we can start to talk on a level playing field* plays back in my head.

My brain rants on like a crazy person in between locking my mouth and throwing away the key.

'Do me, and yourself, a favour, and go look up Elementars. It will all make sense to you then.'

I frown. 'What the hell is an Elementar? And what will make sense to me?' I ask, my voice gruff and unimpressed.

'Just go and do it,' he says in a tired voice. 'And when you come across the WaterLover, you'll understand.' He starts his bike and lethargically kicks out the stand. 'Otherwise we're never going to get anywhere.' He stares off into space. 'Otherwise, I might be homeless forever,' he mumbles to himself. His eyes come back to me for three long seconds before he speeds off, leaving me with more questions than a quizmaster.

The next four hours drag beyond belief. I can't get the word Elementar out of my mind. It hammers against my skull, temporarily drowning out the haunting whispers that have made my body its home, until I think I might scream it out loud or punch something. If I find out Skye is messing with me, I will struggle to tell him what I really think of him ...with my fists.

With two hours of swimming done and dusted, I head for home. My father's BMW makes light work of what would normally be a fifteen minute drive home, and eleven minutes later, I'm rushing through the front door, ignoring Wally's 'hey' and 'where's the fire' calls, as I fly up the stairs three at a time.

I turn on my laptop, impatiently clicking the mouse as I wait. The second I'm online, I type in Elementars. I'm half expecting an error to come up to tell me I've spelt the word wrong, but to my surprise, three items come up relating to Elementars. I click into the first, the same time my phone beeps. The message is from Skye. It says;

Don't bother checking the internet, you won't find the information you're looking for. Go to the library and search their section on philosophy and religion.

I stop.

My skin runs cold.

My body becomes ice and glass, a place where no life has ever existed. I glance over my shoulder expecting him to be there, but of course he's not. It still prompts me to get up and peer out of the window to satisfy my curiosity. Surely it's just another coincidence that he's text me as I'd logged on.

He's right though.

The three sites don't have much information, only stating that the four Elementars consist of a FlameMaker, a WaterLover, an AirWhisperer and an EarthLover and that they are mystical beings with powers that come from the four elements. The WaterLover part catches my attention and if I want to find out more, I will need to go to the library. And that means, seeing Natasha.

I grab my jacket from the hook behind the door and head back downstairs. 'I'll be back later,' I call out to Wally, not waiting for his reply.

Natasha heads straight for me as I enter the library. Her lips are sad for me today, her cheeks pinched. Her eyes fail her as they always do, trying so hard not to show how much she hungers for my hands on her body, for one kind word from my mouth or a single minute of my time next to her.

She is struggling.

She is slowly breaking.

'Hello, River.' The soft, scared tremble in her voice cuts into my flesh, exposing me. I quickly tell her what I'm looking for, saying it's for a project I'm working on, and she points me to the far right hand side of the library. I'm pretty sure she doesn't believe me.

'Will you be here long?' she asks, laying her hair over her shoulder as I start to walk away. The lucious curls gather at her neck.

I freeze.

I'm trying so hard.

So hard.

To walk away.

To protect her.

To be strong for both of us.

Instead, temptation and familiarity pull the rip cord inside me. I haven't indulged yet today and I feel my resolve slipping, force-feeding the guilt growing inside me. The beast attacks me from a different angle this time, reminding me of how smooth and velvety her skin is and how it shimmers with tiny goosebumps when I glide my fingers over her torso and down her thighs, how she whispers her longing in my ear. Her moans of pleasure echo around me …within me … miles from me, trying its hardest to drown out the yelling and screaming inside my head that says she also has *the most selfless heart. A kind and gentle heart.*

I bite back the anguish.

Teeth clenched, eyes close for a fraction of peace.

I can barely respond.

'I hope not.' The words are out before I realise I've said them and what is left of her hopeless smile dissolves into a thin line of sadness. 'I mean, it shouldn't take me too long to find what I'm looking for.' Her lips quiver. Her sunshine doesn't return.

I have hurt her.

Again.

And yet, I continue.

I'm worthless ...

She takes a sweeping view of the large split-levelled room.

We're the only ones left.

And as much as I hate to admit it, her naivety is intoxicating. 'I'll be finished in ten. You know where to find me,' I answer, without thinking. The monster rears its ugliness. It's winning. I want her right here, right now.

My body flinches as I take back control.

I take a step away from her.

My knees crack. My hips fracture. My neck splinters into a thousand sharp, angry pieces. My vision distorts, swirls, fights against me.

I steady myself against the wall.

Body swaying.

Beast rising.

I will myself to walk over to the floor-to-ceiling bookcases. The small white plaque I am aiming for, labelled myths and legends, is only twelve, tiny, agonising, mountainous steps away.

The first step is a knife twisting in my gut, the second … a spear through the heart.

I keep walking.

Step

By

Step

Until I'm far enough away to be able to take a breath without throwing up.

God, I'm some twisted excuse of a human!

I locate the book, large enough to be a small footstool. I run my finger down the index, disappointed to find only one reference to Elementars. When I finally sit down, my hands are shaking and my T-shirt is damp like I might have a fever.

Forehead slick with sweat, I pat it dry with the palm of my hand, flipping through pages until I reach what I'm looking for. I lean back in my chair for a moment wishing I'd brought a magnifying glass with me. The print is tiny.

It doesn't matter there are only a few pages relating to Elementars. There is enough text here to rival a novella.

I read quickly, skimping over the parts about origin of Elementars and how something called a FlameMaker first came to the earth, covering the entire surface with fire and flame. When the word WaterLover pops up, my mind slows. I read each word as though I'm learning English for the first time.

The WaterLover Elementar, Nereus, an immortal being, had a special affinity with the element of water. He used it to control and soothe his emotions when the heat of the FlameMaker was too much for him. He was her match in every way and was made for her and only her. He used water to sustain his ever-increasing thirst for her, slaking his desires, until his needs became uncontrollable. Unfulfilled, his lust finally overcame him, filling the earth with so much water, it dowsed the FlameMakers dominion, turning her to ash and the world to a watery mass.

I read and re-read that one passage over and over.

That's how I feel most of the time - that water can only hold me back for so long and that if I give in to the urge, I will spiral down a dark tunnel I have no hope of returning from. But, it's the first line which says the WaterLover has a special affinity with water that really takes me hostage.

This can't be real, can it?

I look at the spine on the book where it says Legends of the World. Why would Skye insist I look into this if it wasn't important and more to the point, what does he know about all this, that he isn't saying. The next time we are together, I'm not letting him go until I wring it out of him.

The once bright lights of the library, dim, and I glance up as Natasha flicks off the last switch.

I close the book.

Her hips sway as she comes for me. Her eyes are wide, desperate, aching, confused. The ogre stirs and fills my head with all the tantalising acts we could share. I try to push it away, but it's too strong. My strength is all but spent.

She sits on the edge of the desk, her skirt skimming the tops of her knees. A rush of pleasure empties into my blood. 'Find what you were looking for?' I push the book away and stare at her, wishing I had x-ray vision.

I try to shake off the hold it has over me.

I'm losing.

It almost has me.

'Kind of,' I mutter.

My urges rise and fall, leaving any decent fragments of me left to wallow in shame. Two very different sides of me fight for dominance, tearing the other to shreds. She looks at me longingly - a helpless, fragile spider caught in a web she has no chance of escaping from, completely oblivious to the torment going on inside me. I've seen this look all too many times, on the faces of my victims, yet this time, I'm powerless to save her.

She brushes her hair back from her face, releasing the sweet, fresh scent of Pears shampoo.

My body clenches.

My vision becomes white. Erasing anything good about me.

I am disappearing.

Fading into oblivion.

H e l p

This despicable curse battles it's way to the surface and peers over the brim of my sanity as her lips, lips that know me intimately, part.

My chest rips open. Killing my heart. Conquering me.

It's here.

It's free, calling champion and sneering at my weakness. I can't protect this sweet, naive girl anymore. I am beyond reason, beyond caring. The pain within, is too intense. Devour Her.

I have lost.

I swallow down hard. Not to catch my breath. Not to regain control. But because it's the only thing I know how to do.

I hate myself.

I hate myself more.

I hate myself for not fighting harder.

My chest crashes into my back. Lungs fill with concrete and knives and lead and dirt and any vile ingredient that manages to worm its way into my body.

The voices refuse to be quiet.

Won't leave me alone.

They laugh and tease and shout out to the world how utterly useless I am, how gutless and weak-willed I am. But worst of all how hollow I am.

I roll off her and pull up my trousers. I take one fleeting glance at Natasha, her face, all honesty and a pinch of hope.

It rips the skin from my bones.

'You know this isn't right, don't you?' she says, her voice so incredibly soft it's almost a whisper. 'For you, I mean. You deserve someone much better than me.'

She reaches out and runs her delicate fingertips down my chest to the waistband of my jeans as though she knows it will be the last time she'll ever touch me.

Her hand falls away. Her eyes close. She nibbles her lip. And sighs.

It's like looking at the sun.

She straightens her skirt and buttons up her blouse. 'And I know you don't love me.' She smiles but it doesn't touch her eyes. Not like before. Not like in the early days when we first met and she was totally infatuated with me, without knowing a reason why.

When she was a nobody.

When I didn't care about her.

'I've known for a while now,' she continues.

Her words punch into me. Collide with my heart, what's left of it. Smash into it a few more times just to make sure the message gets through.

It's the ultimate tragic conclusion.

They all end up like this ...eventually - moody, depressed, unable to find the joy in life because I have sucked them dry. The two-a-penny random girls with no integrity or self-respect are easy enough to forget. Natasha, I'm sure, will prowl the halls of my memory long after I die.

What can I say to her, after she's given herself to me wholeheartedly ... that she is merely a pawn in a terrible game I don't even want to be a part of anymore? How can I tell her that I've been in love with the same girl since I was seven years old and that she, Natasha, is only a means to an end? That is the brutal honesty and although my hunger has been sated and the beast driven away for now, I still can't honour her with the truth. I sink that much lower into the murk that I've become.

I can't look at her. 'I'm sorry.'

'It's okay,' she mutters. 'It's as much my fault as it yours.'

I look up at once.

Ashamed that she should shoulder any of the blame.

'I let myself believe that we actually stood half a chance, but I live in the real world, River. Deep down, I knew there was no way anyone like *you* would fall for someone like *me*. I was deluding myself to think otherwise.'

'Natasha ...'

'River. You have a lot to give someone, and she'll be one lucky, special girl, who will be everything you want her to be.' Her eyes fill up, but not a single tear falls. 'But that girl isn't me.'

For the third time in my life, I kiss a girl.

It isn't passionate. It isn't lust driven. It's sweet, simple and means more than I can ever say in words. Her lips are warm, supple and welcoming and I hear the heartfelt sobs inside her body like rain on a stormy night. Her amplified thoughts, too real, too honest, too goddam painful to bear witness to, take me apart, cut me, destroy me. I hear her telling herself not to love me, forget me, find someone new, but in my arms, her true self calls out to me saying I'm the only one she will ever love. Her emotions are raw. Her feelings are sincere. There is no spell. No forced lust. She knows it's the end. She knows I don't love her. But she doesn't care. She wants me anyway. I hate myself so much I could set myself on fire and burn for an eternity as penance.

I draw on any reserves and stand tall. 'I have to go.'

'I know,' she replies, pulling together the remnants of a smile. She adjusts the zip of my jacket. Just once. Places one hand against my cheek, fingers sliding down until her thumb brushes over my bottom lip. 'Goodbye, River.'

I leave, knowing I will never see her again.

I swing into the driveway to find Skye's motorbike parked under the porch. Regardless of how eager I am to speak to him, I'm not in the mood for his bullshit antics right now. Natasha's lips still smoulder against my own, the memory of her fingers gliding across my skin are now tight against my wrists like burning handcuffs, her sweet perfume has turned to acid in my lungs. I need a shower. I want to shut out the last few hours of my life.

I open the door to see Wally and Skye shaking hands and laughing.

'River, sorry mate, I came around to see if you wanted to go out, but I just got a text from this sexy redhead I've been trying to score with, and well, you drew the short straw.'

Wally laughs again and yet it's relief that blows through me. My enthusiasm to see him gone rises tenfold. 'I don't wanna keep you then.' I want to ask him about the redhead. What is the likeliness of him finding Ember before me when I've been searching for nine years? I'm dying to know about the Elementars too.

Skye's steely, grey eyes pierce into me, digging ... searching for more information.

He pauses.

Waiting for I don't know what.

'Right ...' he finally mumbles. 'Well, I'd better be off. We do need to catch up soon though, especially after today's new developments.'

The word stalked comes to mind, but I just need him gone. 'See ya then.'

I take off up the stairs, hearing the door bang shut after him. I throw myself onto my bed and lay there looking up at the ceiling, hearing the faint chink of cutlery from the kitchen. I'm not hungry. I can't even bring myself to sit with Wally and make small talk while he eats.

I close my eyes.

Natasha and Ember are waiting for me in my mind. Just like I knew they would be. One hurt, one soon to be hurt. How do I know this?

It's who I am,

I squeeze my eyes tighter, trying to purge the demon that mocks me, that instigates this torment. I'm not sure how much longer I can do this for.

After today, the effort to fight is waning. I am close to the end, ready to give up and go back to the old, selfish me and yet there's a tiny part of me that says there has to be something that explains this madness.

I'm on self-destruct.

My eyes open of their own accord and that's when I notice my wardrobe door ajar and the black suit I wore to my parents' funeral slumped on the floor. Someone has been in my room and even though it might have been Wally putting away clothes, which he rarely does, my gut tells me it was Skye Buchannan.

A new energy surges. I jump up and hang my head over the banister in the hallway, outside my room, and call down the stairs.

'Hey, Wal?'

'Yo,' Wally calls back almost immediately. His

footsteps come closer.

'Did Skye go in my room before?'

Wally's face grimaces. 'Oh yeah, sorry I forgot to tell you. He said he left his jacket on your chair the last time he was here. I didn't think it would be a big deal.'

Straight away I know it's a lie. Skye hadn't been wearing a jacket that morning.

'Is there a problem?' calls Wally.

My body becomes rock and stone and lead. My jaw clenches. 'No. It's okay,' I lie. I'm furious.

I go back to my room, hang up the suit and close the wardrobe door. The satchel of money was relocated the same day Skye was here, so I'm not worried about that.

What was he looking for?

Just to be sure, I open one of two bottom drawers hidden into the base on my bed and behind a pile of old jumpers, my fingers find the strap of the satchel I had pushed right to back. I tug the bag out and count the money inside. It's all there - £2300.

If he wasn't after money, why the need to come in here? I lay back down, reminiscing about the newspaper clipping of Ember's accident, feeling the need to reacquaint myself with it. I roll over and reach into the bedside drawer.

It is gone.

My breath catches in my throat, trying to strangle me, wanting to kill me. I get to my feet, reef the drawer wide open and dump the contents onto the bed. I surf through the contents of condoms and empty wrappers, magazines, and iPhone accessories. It was in the left-hand corner. I remember putting it there last night.

After searching my entire room, my suspicions are confirmed. Skye has taken it. My only question is … why?

I immediately pick up my phone and ring his number. It rings out to message bank.

You've reached Skye. I can't take your call at the moment because I have a life and you obviously don't. So, unless you've just discovered gold in your backyard, or are some kind of superhuman, then leave a message and I'll either bring a pick or we'll catch up for a coffee and some kryptonite. Ciao.

I try again, and another five times after that, finally leaving a message which says; *You thieving prick.*

Days crawl into May, casting off a colder than normal Spring. Random patches of rich blue sky finds its way through the collage of puffy clouds being tugged along by a breeze everyone is keen to wave goodbye to. A smudge of colour clings to the trees outside the window at Freeman, Gladstone and Botch Law Firm. I lose myself in their graceful dance, leaves being free to be just leaves and nothing else. I'm held by how simple life can be, wishing I was anywhere else rather than stuck in this red, wooden-clad office surrounded by the stench of old cigars and peppermints, and pictures of old railway stations, finalising the end of year audit on my parents' estate.

The last three weeks, I've sat by the phone, waiting.

Waiting in frustration.

Bound up in knots.

In negative thoughts.

Dying that little bit more every day, not hearing from Iris Perkins and whether she has unearthed any leads about Ember. That *extra* fee she spoke about has also kept me up most nights. Money isn't a problem for me, if that's what she's after. I've got heaps. But somehow I don't think that's her jam. It's clear she wants more, my concern is – how much more? Skye, on the other hand, has dropped off my irritation radar, for now, which I'm almost ok about, as far as things go. I'm still pissed at him for taking the newspaper clip, but it pales in comparison to living this fucked-up half-a-life shit that is slowly shovelling dirt over my head.

I've also cut back to two girls a day. I couldn't keep going on the way I was. I know that now. Every day was getting harder and harder to look at myself in the mirror and say what I was doing was okay … okay for *me* … okay for *Ember*. So something had to give.

But it has come at a cost.

I'm more moody than normal. Find myself more irritated at such small things that wouldn't have bothered me a month ago. Only yesterday, I screamed through the windscreen at a learner driver for going too slow.

Poor kid!

And don't get me started on the outbursts of anger I feel for no reason at all. Poor Wally is copping the brunt of that.

I'm slowly losing it …

It's a good thing I can swim as much as I want. I'm at the pool morning and night now. The one act keeping me sane … keeping the physical agony to a slow, choking strangle at knifepoint – the vicious blade slicing me at its leisure for seconds and minutes now instead of the long, lonely hours my soul has cried out to stop.

It's progress.

It's a massive feat for me.

God, I hope I can make it through this …

'So, you won't have anything to worry about.'

I come back into the room, not quite hearing what Mr Freeman said.

'Yep. Sure. Like I said, I've hardly spent a penny.'

Mr Freeman frowns, his cheek lifting slightly as his lips twitch upwards. 'You didn't hear me … did you, son?'

My cheeks redden. 'Sorry, Mr Freeman.'

'I know, son,' he says. His voice, layered in all kinds of sympathy. 'It's a hard time of year for you … being here … without them. I couldn't imagine losing my parents at such a young age. The anniversary of their death must be hard on you.' He pauses, prolonging the moment. I offer a fleeting smile, although I can't bring myself to tell him I hardly think about them. 'I lost my wife to cancer six years ago.' His hand is trembling slightly as he lifts if off the last document for me to sign. He reaches across the corner of his desk and pats my arm.

I should feel comforted or at least touched by the sentiment, but all I can see in front of me, on a sheet of paper, flashing in pink neon, is the date of my parents' death – 22 August 2017.

A rush of something hits me in the chest.

Seeing the date written down in text, awakens my brain, cramps my stomach. Skye's parents were killed on this day too, no real revelations there, but I'm positive it's the same date from the newspaper article. The same date Ember's parents were killed.

Fuck, if only I could check.

My life is amounting to nothing more than a bunch of coincidences I have zero explanation for.

EIGHT

No sexual urge.

No pain.

No desire.

Voices are but a whisper.

It's not silence. It's not even quite the peace I yearn for, but it's the closest thing I've been to in six years. I'm as close to heaven as I possibly can be without actually dying. And it feels amazing.

Eyes lightly shut.

Jaw relaxed.

Palms open.

Laying on the bank, sun beating down on my face, turning the insides of my eyelids into orbs of blood red, I couldn't imagine being anywhere else. Grass tickles the back of my neck as I shift to get more comfortable, my feet submerged in the coolest, cleanest water I've ever encountered.

It's actually Leo's idea I'm here. *Are you up for a little fishing and water-skiing at my parent's cabin on the lake for a few days* said his late-night text?

Of course, I'd jumped at it! What idiot wouldn't? A well-stocked cabin with plenty of booze to drown myself in if I want to disappear, a lake large enough to keep the beast at bay for a hundred years and no females.

Heaven!

Every nerve in my body had thanked me repeatedly those first two days I was here. Every urge, subdued, every fleeting thought that tried to anchor in, erased to a distant memory … until three girls gate-crashed our cosy little trio last night.

So their story went, the shack they'd rented on the other side of the lake, was *supposedly* overrun with cockroaches the size of gerbils. Leo, having his own agenda with the one called Denise, welcomed them with open arms.

It was then, I knew I was on borrowed time.

Denise and Steph are what I classify as cheap n bleached. Hair that has seen one too many bottles of peroxide, cheap tarty clothes and too much costume jewellery. Both have mouths like sailors too, and have been ridden more times than the London Underground.

I picked it straight away, that Leo was hot for Denise, when he sucked in his stomach and waddled over to her, stroking back his thinning hair, and flashing off his Star Wars collector cards at her. I should've packed my bags then and left.

I didn't.

Big mistake.

The girls story became more fabricated as the evening wore on, and I'm convinced now it was my hypnotic beacon that drew them in and not some bullshit insect infestation that they kept on insisting was the worst they'd ever seen. Since cutting back to two girls a day, my radar seems to have a much wider range than it used to. Another fucking problem to contend with, and so now I find

103

myself living in the second circle of hell with Denise, Steph and *Bronte*.

Another spiral of giggling laughter trills out, polluting the silence, turning my peace into torment. My serenity to anxiety. They're less than a few hundred yards away, lounging on deckchairs, drinking champagne from tin camping cups.

I refuse to look up.

Refuse to give them the pleasure of my attention. Why?

Because that's what they want me to do.

Because they've been doing it for two hours already.

Because when Leo and Daniel aren't looking, they act like dogs on heat around me. Just like I'd expect them to … blowing kisses. Nibbling bottom lips. Winking. Accidentally brushing me … touching me. Steph even grabbed my arse hard and whispered to meet her down by the lake after Daniel went to sleep.

Am I surprised?

No.

In all fairness, Steph and Denise are my typical go-to types.

Easy to cast away.

Easy to forget.

But, I wasn't that lucky. Leo and Daniel got in first, leaving me with Bronte. She's quieter than the other two and her sandy brown hair and absence of thick gluggy lipstick reminds me of Natasha, equalling more trouble for me. Bronte was trapped in my web the second she put her bags down, her eyes glazing over, her mouth open just a little. She never stood a chance.

She has those eyes that look up at you and say take me to bed and cuddle me afterwards. And I'd like to say I stayed on my side of the bed last night and didn't touch her at all, but that's not what happened. It was barely satisfying, but for her, shook her world … *apparently*, regardless if the water here is the best anti-hard on treatment. I hate to admit, it was out of habit rather than too tempting to pass up. I know … I'm a gutless waste of space – definition number sixty five.

She then admitted she'd only had sex once before with some nameless guy at a party, which made the guilt and torment circulating my blood ten thousand times more toxic than usual.

Fuck! I must have been the most deceitful prick in the universe to be punished with this curse.

I open one eye, my close to perfect peace shattered by another episode of whinnying laughter.

Except Bronte.

She is leaning forward, elbows on knees, staring at me. I turn up the volume on my phone and lose myself in music. It's going to be a long day and even longer night. For her sanity and mine, I've decided to leave first thing in the morning. The water has subdued my desire, but Bronte's seems to have intensified and if I'm not careful, I could have another pyschotic stalker on my hands.

Eyes closed.

Peace returning.

I still feel her staring at me.

'You've hardly said anything to me all day,' says Bronte, handing me a glass that night. I take it from her. It smells like scotch and coke. I kinda hum out some kind of an answer and look across the lake to where half a moon is settling above the treetops. Darkness has crept right up to the cabin porch, swallowing the edges of the bank where the tall reeds grow. A solitary frog croaks close by.

'You're not much of a talker either, are you?' The timber deck creaks as she pulls the chair out next to me and sits down.

I sigh. 'I have my moments,' I say around a tight smile.

'Everyone has gone to bed.' Her voice is shaky. 'Aren't you tired?'

I know what she's getting at and use it to my advantage. I scull my drink. 'You know what? Now that you mention it,' I let out an exaggerated yawn. 'I think I will turn in.' I get up and leave her on the front patio.

Ten minutes later, she crawls into bed next to me.

I don't turn over even though the beast is screaming NOW. NOW. NOW. I COMMAND it in my ears.

I ignore it.

Which I know is foolish. There's only one result that comes from not following orders.

Pain.

I am punished with torturous pain.

The blinding, white kind.

The kind that closes your eyes so tightly you see tiny blue stars. When your fists clench until every bone in your hands beg to be dust. It finds a way in, like it always does, and drowns me, suffocates me, strangles me until exhaustion takes me and I fall alseep.

Her beautiful face is there to greet me as always.

Ember.

I know I am dreaming.

I've trained myself to know.

I know by how weightless I feel. By how suddenly alive I feel. How emotional I feel. Feel everything. And it's so glorious and new and I'm not sure if I can hold so much love, so much tenderness in my body because I might just fall apart a little to make more room for her.

I call out her name.

She walks towards me. Tilts her head. Looks at me, as though she's really seeing me for the first time. Five steps away.

Now four.

She stops.

Looking at her is the most painful agony in the world and the most magnificent pleasure at the same time. She speaks – have we met before?

Many times, I say.

I want her to say more. I want to know everything about her, where she lives, what her favourite colour is, everything and anything, I don't care, even if she is talking in a language I don't understand. I just want to hear her. Breathe her in. Her voice, the sweetest lullaby.

She takes three more steps and I swear I could reach out and touch her she is so close. But even if I want to, I can't. My arms won't move, hands can't reach, fingers can't touch.

Ember, I whisper. She looks at me, eyes wide, confused, somehow happy to see me and yet a tear is freed to run down her cheek.

My body falls into ruin. She knows sadness. I know she does. I want to wipe the tear, the sorrow, this madness away. Instead, her hand lifts, coming towards me. Slowly, so painfully slowly. Like life has pulled on the brakes, fearful that any sudden movement might cause us to vanish.

Her fingertips brush against my bare shoulder.

Fire ignites in my blood.

Rushes to my head, my feet, my chest.

Turning my stone cold body into something new and exciting, the feeling surpassing lakes or rivers or streams or anything. Warmth, like I've never known before, spreads through me, filling me, touching every inch of me, calling to me. It's so completely overwhelming, I'm not sure I will ever recover from it.

She watches intently as her hand glides over my skin, tripping my senses, my off-switch, almost trance-like as though she can't quite believe what is happening.

When will you come for me, she whispers.

I am caught up. I am in chains. I want to pull her into my arms and tell her she is the only one and that I am coming. I am coming for her.

Her fingertips feel real against my skin, not a dream.

Not a dream.

Alive.

Her touch rips apart my broken world, lightly tracing circles into my shoulders and over my back.

River, she coos. River.

Confusion falls into my heart. She doesn't know my name. I've never told her. How does she know my name?

And that is when I realise, I am waking. It's not Ember's soft touch against my body, it's Bronte's.

Instantly, I become slices of cold metal. My arms and legs stiffen on their own accord.

'Are you awake,' says Bronte. 'You were mumbling in your sleep.'

I can't respond. I am so furious. Being woken from the most wonderful dream has ripped every shred of kindness from my body.

I grab a handful of blanket and drag it off her. 'Don't follow me.' My voice, only one shade of angry.

I contemplate resuming my spot on the patio, but I can't sleep now, even if I wanted to. I dump the blanket on the chair and sprint straight for the lake. I dive in off the dock.

The water cools me, untangles me, releases me from the pain. I power through the water, the moon my only companion. There's an irresistable sense of oneness as I dip below the surface. No-one watching. No judgements. No-one to count the minutes. It's a different kind of heaven. Familiar. Welcoming. A place I could call home.

I could stay here forever.

I breach the surface and swim towards the centre of the lake, suddenly aware of an increase in water temperature ... by some three or four degrees. My body automatically acclimatizes to the temperature upon entering the water, so this is something new.

I stop swimming, not needing to tread water, as my body has its own built-in buoyancy vest. For the strangest reason, my temperature isn't adjusting. In fact, I feel *too* warm.

The hairs on the back of my neck prickle against my skin as though I am being watched. I take a sweeping look around me, and yet I can barely make out the perimeter of the lake. No-one would be able to see me from there, even with a torch.

The feeling won't go away.

My breath comes faster.

Something swishes past my leg.

I duck below the surface. Have a quick look around.

It didn't feel fish-like.

It was warm. Warmer than the current water temperature and graceful, like … like …a mermaid.

'You're losing your goddam mind,' I mutter to the darkness.

And then …

My name …

Called out loud, and clear.

AND from under the water.

I dive beneath, my knee-jerk reaction to respond. 'Who wants to know?' As it happens, I don't ever recall speaking underwater before and yet my voice is crystal clear.

There is no answer … at first.

Learn, says the voice. *Trust*.

'Who. Are. You?' I ask again.

Nothing.

I burst through the surface, feeling a sudden need for breath.

The warmth disappears and the lake becomes my second favourite place again.

I'm in no huge rush to get home as I pack the car up the next afternoon, and yet the quicker I am out of here and on the road, the better. Leo had dialed in a favour and asked me to stay until lunchtime, which ended up turning into 3pm. He's never trusted Daniel to drive the boat, and wanted to get on the skii's one more time before I shot through, making it ten times more awkward with Bronte. She had sat in the corner of the kitchen this morning, her arms wrapped around her knees, watching my every move. I really can't tell if she's mad or sad, and to be completely honest, I don't give a fuck either way – all I know is I couldn't say goodbye to her. Definition number twenty-eight …spineless.

The second I turn on the ignition and glance over at my phone, my heart ceases to beat. Lungs fail to draw in air. I would bet my fathers Audi that the colour had drained from my face too when I registered that there was a message from Iris Perkins waiting to be read. When I finally find the nerve to open it, the message says: *I have some _interesting_ information for you. Swing by the office. I'll be here until 6:00pm.*

The next few hours of my life are the longest I've ever had. I can't decide between music or silence, talking to myself or keeping the thoughts inside my head. My concentration is minimal and I'm constantly being beeped at by passing motorists.

When I eventually pull up across the street from the Iceberg Rose building, the whole street appears more run down and deserted than before. Sinister looking shadows creep up walls and hide around corners, blackening roads and creating unnatural body shapes in darkened doorways. Fluttering newspapers and plastic bags race each other along the pavement, dodging lamp posts and getting caught by wire rubbish bins. A ginger cat smooches its' way against the crappy orangey-red brick wall of the building next to it. Two of the street lights aren't working and yet there's hardly any spaces to park. The roads are practically end to end in parked cars and I eventually find a space halfway down the street.

I check the digital clock on my dash before leaving. It says 6:18.

'Fuck,' I grumble, thumping the steering wheel.

The smell of mouldy food and wet cardboard gets stronger as I hurry up the street. It has rained in the last hour and the alleyway between Iceberg Rose and a rundown hardware store holds the culprit of the stench.

Four large rubbish bins have spewed their contents onto the ground, making the laneway almost impassable. I screw my nose up and push on.

'Hey, watch where ya goin'.' Hidden in the shadows, wrapped in a dark blue blanket, an old man, hair and beard of grey, clutches at his shoeless foot. He is quite a hulk of a man, now I've half-tripped over him which makes me wonder how the hell I didn't see him in the first place. 'Damn blind idiot,' he mumbles, snuggling back up to the wall.

I move on and pull in a deep breath as I stop in front of Iris's building. I try the door, expecting it to be locked. I'm surprised, and relieved, to find it open. Hope springs inside me as I mount the stairs two at a time.

A light tang of perfume greets me and although Tania isn't there filing her nails, the room is still filled with her perfume. The door to Iris's office is ajar and a subtle pink light entices me closer.

I pad across the thick burgundy carpet, my footsteps making no sound, and yet a foot away from the door, Iris suddenly appears.

'I was hoping that was you,' she says, casually leaning against the doorframe. 'Come in and make yourself comfortable. There's a cold beer in the fridge if you want one.'

'I'm good.' I squeeze past her as she steps towards me.

Her office feels different. The main overhead lights are off and a tall floor lamp throws an amber glow over a white leather lounge and matching chair which I hadn't noticed the last time I was here. Dressed in a tight-fitting mulberry coloured skirt, the tailored jacket, which isn't on for long, comes off as she waltzes past me wearing a cream satiny top that could easily pass for underwear. She sits down on one end of the sofa.

Last night's dip in the lake is starting to wear off in a big way, and the same desire I had for Iris the first time I met her, jumps up and grabs me around the balls. The monster is awake and it's hungry. My trousers stretch as the urge intensifies. I seem to have all the control of a pubescent choirboy. Something inside me says there's no way I'm getting out of here this time without dirtying my hands.

Iris rubs a slow circle on the seat next to her, and although I want her more than I've wanted any woman in a long time, other than Ember, I choose the chair instead. She doesn't look disappointed, but simply smiles and licks the corner of her lip. My body responds with a pulsating jolt to the groin.

I have to start this conversation before I lose control. I want this meeting to be quick and painless. Get the information and leave. If I delay any longer, things will become complicated. She is not a Bronte or a Natasha. Iris is a pro.

Fighting against the urge to unleash the devil tearing at me from within, I say between clenched teeth. 'So, you found out something?'

'I did,' she replies, crossing her legs. Her skirt rises up a little but it's the sound her stockings make that clenches my stomach and robs my brain of words and actions – the swish of sheer against sheer.

Like a hungry animal, my mouth fills with saliva. I realise what she is doing. She is controlling this situation for her own needs. She is the hunter and I am the rabbit, a novel experience and something that doesn't sit well with me. I am *always* the one who manipulates, not the other way around. This is a new game with a challenge attached. I need to turn this around in my favour.

Confidently, I sit back in the chair and fold my arms, giving the beast full permission to rise up and take a peek at her from under its pair of soulless lids.

Iris's eyes frost over with desire, her breasts heaving as she zeroes in on the obvious bulge in my trousers.

The ball is back in my court and although that's what I wanted, the control required to keep the beast at bay is like cutting a piss off in midstream after having a skinful of alcohol. 'And ... that was ...'

A fleeting ripple of confusion teases her eyebrows together as if she knows she is falling under my spell. She sits up a little straighter and rolls her lips over each other until they shimmer. 'How will you be paying for this?' She leaves my previous question hanging.

I lean forward, clasping my hands. 'Cash?' Her journal makes another appearance, and she pens down something I can't see.

Her eyes narrow. 'I don't want money.'

My jaw clenches. My worst fears are being recognised. 'What do you want then?'

'Time, River. I want your time.' Her words hang in the air, heavy and threatening. 'You owe me three hours and I want them repaid in six, half an hour increments.'

Iris pushes her knees together so that I can no longer see the inside of her thigh. She stands and crosses the room to her desk. Like before, she bends over to retrieve something, her skirt rising further up the back of her legs until I'm sure I can see satin. In my opinion, she takes an exceptionally long time to pick up a large white envelope from her bottom drawer, and pain finds a new home inside my hands as I pull up the reins of power.

Iris slowly walks over, fanning the envelope across her face. 'I did find something I think you might be interested in.'

Stupidly, I reach for the envelope only to have her withdraw it and hide it behind her back. She takes her seat, and again, pats the soft leather for me to join her. This backward and forward of control is making the beast grow stronger and more impatient and all I want is to unleash my full power on her, so I can get what I came for.

'Agree to my terms,' says Iris, slipping her finger under the flap. She looks up at me before removing a single sheet of paper and places it on the white coffee table between us. It is a contract. 'And then you can have the rest of the contents.' She shakes the envelope gently and I can hear the rustle of more documents inside.

I read it quickly, and basically, it equates to six half hour meetings, at a time and place specified by her, redeemable for the three hours she's spent on my case. I know exactly what she wants from me and for the first time in my life. I know I won't feel any guilt for what I'm about to do. Quid pro quo and all that. I was simply hoping it wasn't going to play out this way, but beggars can't be choosers.

I sign my signature at the bottom and push the paper towards her. She grins, her shiny pink lips glowing in the soft light. One copy goes into her journal, the other she leaves on the table for me. There is only one place that will see – the inside of a rubbish bin on the way out. I want no evidence of this happening.

'One thing left,' she says, gathering two glasses from the table. 'I like to toast all transactions with my favourite drink.' She pours out what looks like tomato juice, adding two to three drops of tabasco sauce.

She hands me a glass.

The smell makes me dry reach.

I've only ever had one Bloody Mary in my life and vowed never to again. 'Cheers,' she says and downs the lot. I look into the glass, hold my breath, and follow suit. She takes the glass from me as I focus on keeping down the vile liquid. 'Now that's all the business taken care of, I want the first half hour of your time, right now.' She places the envelope beside her and recrosses her legs, the swish of sheer, making the beast slaver even more. I know what I have to do. It's time to show her who I really am.

I blow out a slow, measured breath, relinquishing all holds, allowing HIM to emerge. Her eyes grow misty again and her control slips.

'Whatever you wish, Iris,' I whisper, turning up the heat.

Her mouth drops open as I draw closer, and the devil

crawls out of my skin and devours her.

Half an hour later, I am back outside her building, my body still tingling from the best sex I've had in years.

In. My. Life.

There is no hint of desire left anywhere inside me, which is strange considering even after screwing two or three girls in the same night, one after the other, a dull urge still remains.

The hobo is nowhere to be seen either as I pass the alleyway and I rip my contract into half a dozen pieces and stuff it into the rubbish bin. I half jog down the street and get in my car. The envelope, however, is a sharp reminder of who I am and what I've had to do to get it. It trembles in my hand. I close my eyes and say a quick prayer, begging for some kind of justice that what I've just done with Iris isn't for nothing.

I pull the contents out of the envelope and a photo falls face down into my lap. My body runs cold, as though I've been dead for a week. My fingers hover above it, deliberating whether I have the courage to turn it over or not. *What if it isn't her? Where will I go from here?* I can't bear the thought of looking at it and seeing the face of some random red-haired girl.

Slowly, so slowly I'm hardly moving, I pick up the photo and turn it over.

My breath spills out of me any way it can, while my heart thumps to a frantic new rhythm, unfamiliar to my body. I'm not even aware at one point that I'm actually panting until I close my mouth. I can't believe what I'm seeing.

It is her. Really her.

Such painful, painful joy.

I can't take my eyes off her face. The soft curves of her cheeks, the paleness of her skin in contrast to that vibrant red hair that looks like it would set me on fire if I touch it. Her lips are barely pink, and my first thought is how they would feel against mine if I were ever so lucky enough to kiss them. And it's true, her bronzy eyes *have* seen sadness, just like mine have, and yet they look at me as though we are friends.

She is real, just like I always knew she was, and having it confirmed only makes it all the more incredible. Left with no doubt in my mind, I know what I have to do. Getting Wally on-side is going to be difficult though.

All I can think of is, hold on, Ember, I'm coming for you.

NINE

I drive home, keeping the photo of Ember on my dashboard the whole way. A fear keeps welling up inside me that if I'm not looking at it, then it isn't real, and perhaps, the frantic scattering of paperwork off Iris's desk for my first down payment of deception, was only a dream.

In near total darkness, apart from two small candles almost burnt through, I find Wally sitting at the table, eating.

'Wasn't expecting you until Sunday night, lad,' says Wally swinging around in his seat, shocked to see me. I half stumble into the room. 'Yeah, I know. I came back early. Is there a power cut?'

Partially grinning, Wally presses his food onto his fork and pops it into his mouth. 'No. I *like* it this way,' he says, forcing the food to one side of his mouth. He finishes chewing. 'More intimate, don't you think?'

I flick on the light switch. 'Not really, considering you're alone. How much more intimate would you like to be with *yourself*?'

'Okay, you caught me. I do it to save electricity. I don't like saying anything because I get this huge spiel about how you've got more money than you know what to do with and that paying bills is the least of our worries.'

I shrug. 'It's true though.'

'But it isn't wise to take things for granted, River. One day it could all be gone.' He gestures to the contents of the dining room. The photo, clutched tightly in my hand, begs for another look but Wally's gaze holds me steadfast. As much as I want to share my news with him, something tells me he isn't in the mood to go another round of imaginary people from recurring dreams, as he puts it, regardless if I finally have the evidence.

He's missing his wife, I can tell.

'You're right, and so I'm going to leave you with your *intimate* dinner and slide off to bed.' I flip the light switch off as I go.

The second I'm out of the door, I bring the photo up to my face. A dull ache thumps in my chest. There isn't a smile on Ember's face, and as I re-acquaint myself with her more, I begin to wonder whether she was thinking about her parents at the time the photo was taken, to make her look so sad. The picture had obviously been taken in a park somewhere because the gnarly brown surface she's leaning against is a tree trunk. The book lying flat in her lap, with a flowy-dressed heroine on the front, looks to be fiction, and immediately tells me she has an inquisitive and imaginative mind and enjoys her own company. Her shirt is a little creased and her collar a tad crumpled, and her hair tangled by the wind, says she's not overly fussy about her looks, like most girls are. Her jeans are nicely faded which says she favours routine, and her sandals reveal no nail varnish on her toes, saying she doesn't feel the need to impress anyone. She wears minimal makeup that I can see and is exactly the way I remember her from my dreams. In my eyes, she is perfection.

My first questions to Iris Perkins will be, where was the photo taken, what else was Ember doing in the park and was anyone else there with her, and how long was she there watching her before the photo was taken? Whether or not Iris plans on giving me these details is irrelevant. I'm confident that with the right amount of persuasion, she'll willingly unfold like the first flower of spring.

That night, with Ember lying next to me on my pillow, I fall asleep with her beautiful face etched into my mind forever.

The next morning, I find Wally at the kitchen sink, whistling. I take it as a good sign.

I load up the toaster with four pieces of bread, knowing he only eats Bovril on toast for breakfast and test the kettle with the back of my hand. It has recently boiled.

'Tea?'

Wally frowns but nods. 'What's up with you this morning?' In my peripheral vision, I see Wally turn his head sideways, angling it to look under my downward gaze. 'Last time you made me tea, you asked if you could have a girl sleepover.'

My head bolts upright. 'Christ, Wal, you're never going to let me forget that, are you? I was seventeen when that happened. I've made you tea since then.' My parents had been in the ground a few months, when this girl followed me home from a party. I don't remember her name or what she looked like, only that we were pretty drunk. It was bad timing, on her part and I was desperate to purge the remnants of the beast that already had four girls that night. I offered to send this girl home in a taxi, at my own cost, but when she broke down saying how she always felt rejected and no good, the sinister villain that I was back then, swept her upstairs and screwed her until we both passed out.

'I didn't make you tea then, *anyway*,' I say, recalling the fragments of that night. Wally laughs.

'Well, are you going to let it stew all day?' he says,

119

gesturing to the teapot. The toast pops up and I make several trips to the table until everything is set.

Wally butters his toast. 'By the way, you forgot the Bovril.' He smirks. I rise one final time and return, sitting down with a huff. The photo falls out of my pocket, catching Wally's eye as it flutters to the ground.

'What's this?' He reaches for it the same time I do. I manage to get there before him.

'It's a photo,' I say, dusting my sleeve over it.

Wally picks up his cup, holds it to his mouth and blows into it. 'Of whom?'

I grind my teeth as he takes a swig of his tea. This isn't how I'd envisioned this conversation starting. I was going to wind up to it. Bring the dream in slowly and ease into the possibilities of what dreams really mean. But I'm out of time and out of answers.

'Ember Riley.'

Clouds cover Wally's eyes and his head tilts as though it should mean something to him. I wait for him to remember and when he shakes his head and his shoulders heave in defeat, I know he hasn't really been listening when I'd mentioned her name. Agitation creeps beneath my game face.

'Ember Riley – the girl I've been dreaming about.' The second the words are out; I wish I could take them back and wash the sourness out of my tone too. Wally's posture slackens.

'River …'

'I know what you're going to say,' I interrupt, 'but it's *her*. I know it's her. I've had a private investigator looking into it for me and everything …' My voice trails away to nothing. This is the first time I'd mentioned the PI, and crumpling further, Wally folds back into his chair. He suddenly looks weary as if *he's* been the one up, night after night, with images of a strange girl calling to him in his dreams.

'Please, Wally. She's real. Don't try and change my mind or tell me it's all in my head. She lives in

Gloucestershire and she is the girl I've dreamt about every night since I was ten years old.' I pause and wait until he looks at me. 'She's real.'

With a slow nod of his head Wally manages to conjure a smile. It's weak and a little pathetic, but it's a start. 'And what do you plan on doing about this girl? Go down to Gloucestershire and tell her that you've been dreaming about her for years? My guess is she'll slap you in the chops and tell you to go drown yourself.' The same thought had crossed my mind too. 'And she'd have every right to.'

'Not quite, but I do want to see her.' I don't have the heart to tell him I am prepared to do anything and everything just to be near her. I can't tell him just yet that I want to move to Gloucestershire so that I can see her every day, even if she doesn't know I exist. How retarded would that sound to him? How utterly, mind-blowing, ridiculous would it be to uproot my life here all because of a girl I've never met before, and yet, deep down, I know that's what I have to do.

For now, that particular conversation will have to wait. Wally is a seagull, and feeding him little bits over a period of time rather than allowing him to gorge is the best way, otherwise he'll overload and explode.

I pick up my plate and glass and take it to the sink. Wally has his head in his hands when I return, and his fingers slide down his face as he looks up. 'I hope you know what you're doing, lad. I'd hate for you to make a big mistake and have your heart broken.'

My body shudders from within as though all the warmth has run out of me. 'My heart's already broken, being without her.' I leave it at that and go and change for work.

Sitting two metres above the pool in a chair that could double as a method of chinese torture for me, I gaze at the water, not really observing the fifteen swimmers who look up to me to save their lives if they get into trouble.

121

My mind isn't on the job because coming up with the different ways of convincing Wally to pack up and move to Gloucestershire takes up every available space in my head.

Four hours later and still with no strategy in place, I'm thankful that my shift is finally over. I complete my customary two hundred laps, ten minutes faster than I normally do and stop by the kiosk. I tune out to Serena prattling on about why Sophie hasn't washed up her plate from lunch, and grab a Coke for the trip home.

It's still warm outside and I take a leisurely stroll across the car park, letting the last of the sun shine some sort of happiness into my body. It vanishes the second I see Skye sitting on the bonnet of my car.

I pick up the pace, my fury right alongside. There is still the little matter of my newspaper article.

'Didn't realise you were at the lake. Was it an enlightening trip?' calls out Skye. I'm still a few yards away.

I frown. *You didn't realise because I didn't tell you, you twat.* Something in the way he says it makes me think he isn't just asking about whether I had a good time or not. And how the hell did he know?

'Where the fuck is it?'

Skye's jeans making a squeaking sound as he slides off the front of my car. He holds his hands up in surrender. There is no fear in his eyes, only humour, which iritates me more as I front him. He has confidence, I'll give him that, even though I'm much broader in the shoulders and chest than he is, and a few inches taller.

'Where's what?'

I clench my teeth together until I feel my jaw begin to ache. 'Don't fuck with me, Skye. I know you took it.'

A smile waits at the corners of his mouth and my fist tightens, dying to replace his smirk with a mouthful of blood.

'*What*? I was interested in her, that's all.' Casually, Skye raises his hand and runs his fingers through his hair.

Just like Daniel's perfectly quaffed hair, it falls back into place as though he hasn't even touched it.

'Why?'

'For my own reasons.' Skye reaches into his pocket and produces a creased up piece of paper and dangles it in the air between us. I snatch it away, too hastely, tearing off the corner. I smooth the newspaper clipping out as though it's made from the most precious of silks.

'Why didn't you tell me about her?' Skye repositions his hands on the bonnet. I scowl as he takes liberty after liberty as though no boundaries exist between us.

My anger bumps up a notch. 'What has it got to do with you? And get your frigging hands off my car.'

'Oooh, testy,' says Skye, removing his hands. 'Sounds like somebody needs to get laid. But you know what, I like this stronger side to you. The pussy, emotional shit was really getting under my skin.'

My mouth opens to retaliate but I still can't believe he has hit the nail on the head ... again. I say the first thing that comes into my head. 'Go fuck yourself.'

Skye smirks. 'Come on now, I know you don't mean that. I just thought the story might have something to do with ...'

He pauses.

His eyes probe me and his head tilts before a frown puckers at his brow. 'Did you end up going to the library like I suggested?' His hands find the bonnet again.

I don't have to say yes to let him know I had.

'Mmm, thought you wouldn't be able to resist,' he says, showing off his wide grin. *God, he has really white teeth.* 'And did it make sense to you?'

I shrug, not wanting to give him the satisfaction. What I'm more interested in, is why he took the newspaper clipping in the first place.

The lightness disappears from his face. 'Is she red?'

'What?'

'Does she have red hair?'

My jaw tightens, my teeth grind solidly against each

123

other. I feel a headache coming on.

'Oh, I get it. You think she might go for me rather than you?' Again, perception is by far Skye's greatest skill. That *is* my biggest fear, and again, as though he's tweezerd it from my mind, he uses it against me.

Without thinking it through or worrying about the consequences, I swing my fist at him. I'm not, however, expecting my hand, which throbs with power, to stop inches from his face as though I've hit an invisible wall. A smart arse grin takes over his facial features, making his eyes squint and his nostrils flare. The beginning of a chuckle rumbles in his throat. I retract my arm, determined to inflict more damage this time, but the same thing happens. Some kind of magical barrier, as stupid as that is to say, prevents me from delivering a deserved blow to his chin.

Skye bursts into laughter. 'Frustrating, isn't it?' My fury forbids me to answer. 'Look, I don't want to fall out with you, stud, but until you've discovered who you are and what you can do, I can't help you.' He doesn't give me the chance to respond. 'Tell you what, Harry Potter, go home, run a bath and soak there a while. It might surprise you to discover what secrets lies within that thick, watery skin of yours.'

'Does this have anything to do with the WaterLover Elementar?'

'There you go,' says Skye. There is a condescending tone to his voice. 'You're almost there. I knew you'd come around, but I don't want to spoil it for you, so when you've figured it out, text me and we'll talk.' He cuffs me against the shoulder as though we've been friends for years. 'Have to say, Riv, it's been a long time coming.'

That night, I head into the bathroom and lock the door. I can't remember the last time I took a bath in this house and the large room with its square brown tiles, flecked with golds and bronzes are even more foreign to me as I sit on the edge of the bath and wait for the huge tub to fill.

I don't understand why my parents had something so elaborate and yet never bothered to use it. It's big enough to fit six people.

Water gushes out of both taps, taking fifteen minutes for it to reach an acceptable depth before I can submerge my shoulders under with comfort. Stretching my feet out, I can't touch the end of the tub, regardless of being over six foot in height. I rest my head against the curved out headrest and close my eyes.

Like a thirsty coral sponge, left exposed at high tide, my body eagerly soaks up the water until complete saturation takes place. My whole essence takes on all the familiarities of a marine creature, ceasing to be the land dweller, I know in my heart, I'd mistakenly been born to be. I have no explanation why I feel the way I do, no more than a girl growing into a woman does, or a dog instinctively knows when to wag its' tail when it's happy. And it isn't the need or desire that lures me into its watery depths trying to free me from turmoil either. It's so much more than that. I sink further beneath the surface until the warm water laps against my chin.

I lay there, reflecting inwards, sensing a turning point in my life. And in those brief moments that creep up on you and change your life forever, I discover it's a harmony that water and I share – not giving or taking from the other, but a perfect partnership of balance and truth.

As if nature itself whispers gently in my ear, I give way to the air. The water rises above my chin and lips, past my nose and eyes until I'm completely submerged. The gloriously warm liquid swaddles my body, and even though my lungs feel tight they aren't craving for oxygen. I thought swimming a whole length of the pool underwater was something not of this world, but something reachable and probable for a large number of people, and yet the longer I hold my breath, the more my identity as a WaterLover is all the more credible.

I begin to wonder how long I *can* hold my breath for

125

… forever?

Eventually, when the water grows cold, not that it worries me too much, do I realise forever is a very real possibility. I feel like I'm finally home.

'Have you drowned in there?' Wally's voice follows three sharp taps at the door. Reluctantly, I pull the plug and get out, returning to a world of pain and unrealistic expectations.

Crossing the landing to my bedroom, I hear the theme tune to Top Gear coming from the TV downstairs. It's Wally's favourite show and if I time this right, I can use his good mood to share my plans.

I grab the first pair of shorts and t-shirt from the pile of fresh linen on the top of my chest of drawers and get dressed. I bundle up the wet towels and head downstairs. It's only as I dump the load off in the laundry do I take a passing glance at my mother's grandfather clock in the hall. I'd been in the bath for an hour, with forty to fifty minutes of that being fully submerged. That is definitely something I can't tell Wally about, but showing him, however, is another story.

I slump down onto the sofa next to him. 'Oh, River, you've gotta watch this. Hugh Jackman is taking the driving challenge tonight. If he can hit the notes from Les Misérables, then he should do well at this.' I don't know what singing has to do with driving, but that's Wally in a nutshell. His analogies are more than a little odd.

'Sweet,' I reply, not particularly interested. 'Give me Wolverine or Van Helsing any day of the week.' I sit through ten minutes of car talk, patiently waiting for the adverts, mindful to keep my voice steady and composed.

'What are you up to tomorrow?'

'Why?' His left eyebrow turns up at the end.

'I was wondering if you could help me with something at the pool.' Wally's expression changes from one of suspicion to interest.

'Help you out with what?'

'I need you to hold a stopwatch.' *Keep it plain and*

126

simple River, and don't use freaky words like breath holding or drowning.

His eyes flash with excitement. 'Are you back racing again?' His interest channels back to the TV as Top Gear returns.

'No. Could you lend us a hand anyway?' Wally's smile grows as Jeremy Clarkson cracks a joke. I might as well have turned to dust.

'Wal?'

'What? Yep, sure. Stopwatch.'

That is as good as I'm going to get out of him, but that's fine by me. I get up and retrace my steps to my room, grinning the whole way. Wally has no idea what he's let himself in for.

The next morning, Wally and I turn up at the pool early, allowing plenty of time before my shift starts. Serena is already here making sandwiches for the day and accepting the occasional food delivery. She willingly lets us in on the proviso that we get together later on. She flashes me a smile and smacks me on the arse as I head into the changing rooms.

Less than five minutes later, I'm ready.

Only a glass wall separates the main kiosk from the pool and I grimace as I watch Serena flitting back and forth from the kitchen carrying salad rolls and cupcakes. Seeing me on the bottom of the pool for longer than is humanly possible is one secret she doesn't need to know about. She has a tendency to gossip, evident by the way Sophie and Siobhan are always in a three-ringed catfight with her. But I can't think about that now. This is about Wally and convincing him I'm more than simply *normal*.

Positioned at the edge of the pool, Wally folds up my towel and sits on it. He looks happy and unsuspecting of what's to come. He rolls his trousers up to his calves and swishes his feet about in the water. The stopwatch he's holding, is already getting a good workout too.

'So, tell me what we're doing here again?' Wally

looks up at me.

Plain and simple, I tell myself. Just keep it plain and simple for him. 'All you need to do is click the stopwatch the second I hit the water and don't turn it off until I come up.'

'I thought you said this wasn't a race,' he grumbles.

I feel a smile flicker over my lips. 'It's not.'

'What are you doing then? Planning on setting a new world record for holding your breath?'

'Hmph. Something like that. But promise me one thing, no matter how long I'm down there for, *do not* jump in and pull me out.' I pause as Wally lowers the stopwatch, his eyes wide and confused. 'It's like I've been saying all along, I'm different and you need to see this once and for all.'

Wally's amused expression falls away. 'But what if ...'

'Wal, please. Promise you'll sit here and keep the timer on me. I'll be okay.'

Wally nods and before any other discussion can be entered in to, I blow out my breath and dive in.

My body, totally airless, sinks like a stone. I swim around beneath the surface for a minute or so, just to let Wally know I'm alive and not in any trouble. I then positioned myself crossed legged on the bottom of the pool, just beneath his feet, constantly looking up and waving to him, giving him assurance.

I see him peer down at me several times and although I can't make out the expression on his face, I can only imagine it's somewhere between shock and amazement.

After the first few frantic minutes pass, I begin to count in my head. When two thousand seconds pass, I know I've spent just over half an hour down. I uncross my legs and float to the surface.

I hear the click of the stopwatch as my ears breach the air/water barrier. 'Thirty six minutes and forty two seconds,' says Wally. There's a slight wobble to his voice.

Water runs down my face and into my smile. 'You okay?'

Wally sighs and rubs his hand over his chest. 'The first few minutes I thought I was going to pass out or have a heart attack, but it got easier.' There's a look in his eyes which tells me he finally understands what I've been talking about all these years. 'How ...?'

Water drains off my shoulders as I shrug. 'I don't know. The weird thing is, I could've stayed down there all day. I'm not even slightly out of breath ...'

'What does it feel like?' interrupts Wally. I swim over to the steps and get out. I turn back to him, not even having to think of a response. 'Like I finally belong.'

A hum of acknowledgement sounds in Wally's throat, and I can tell in his eyes, he genuinely believes me. 'It's like my life on land has been some kind of mistake.'

Wally rises and launches a towel at me. 'Give me your hands a minute.' I hold my hands out and he turns them palm up, inspecting my fingertips. 'Doesn't even look like you've been in the water? Your fingers aren't pruned.' He drops my hands. 'Is all of your skin like that?'

'What? *Waterproof*?' It's a strange thing to say, especially when bodies are generally waterproof, unless of course they've be submerged for considerable amounts of time like in the instances of dead bodies disposed in rivers.

'Yeah,' mutters Wally.

'I guess so, and that's not the longest I've stayed under either. Last night in the bathroom was close to an hour and I don't think this is the extent of it either,' I say, towelling off.

Wally's curious looking brow shifts into a frown. 'How do you mean?'

I drape the towel over my shoulders and help Wally to his feet. 'Put it down to intuition. But I feel something coming, and it's got nothing to do with holding my breath and everything to do with Ember Riley.'

TEN

'WHY don't we ever go out on dates?' asks Serena. She's sitting on the edge of her bed, detangling her hair with her fingers. 'Are you embarrassed to be seen with me?'

It's the first time Serena has ever questioned our purely sexual relationship, which means only one thing. Our little arrangement is coming to an end. She's fallen in love with me and that isn't healthy for either of us.

Laying on her double bed, listening to the rhythmic purrs of the semi-soothed beast inside my chest, I reach for my t-shirt only to have her pick it up and sling it over her shoulder. 'Leave it off,' she says, gathering her wavy, blonde hair into a ponytail. She ties it back with an orange hairband.

'No, I'm not embarrassed to be seen with you,' I respond. I wish I had the comfort of my clothes. 'Where has this come from?'

Stretching out next to me, she reaches over and traces the midline of my chest and then down to my stomach, marking out each individual abdominal muscle with her finger. I don't do the snuggly cuddly thing afterwards and she knows it.

I pull away from her and swing my legs over the side of the bed, snatching the t-shirt as I go. I have zero experience of a girl's bedroom and don't understand how at twenty-one, Serena can still be living at home. I would have been long gone at eighteen if it wasn't for my parents' premature death.

A few stuffed toys linger around her room with a bundle of them staring at me from a white chair in the corner. There is a poster of some boy band I can't remember the name of, hanging above a girlie cluttered dressing table, and her purple and green flowered duvet and matching curtains aren't that dissimilar from the wallpaper. But it's the smell of cheap perfumes that turn me off. To me, perfume says a lot about a girl – who she is, what she wants, how she expects to be treated, but more so, how I will treat her. Yes, it sounds somewhat shallow, and isn't always so, but that's what my experiences have taught me, being emotionally sterile as I am.

'Then what is it, River?' Her voice softens and even though her eyes fill with water, her lips turn upwards into a smile. 'You won't hurt my feeling, honestly. I'd just really like to know.' She finds a pair of striped pyjama bottoms under her pillow, slips them on, and resumes her position. On top, she is wearing *my* favourite aqua and black bra.

'Can we just put it down to … that I'm not the dating type?' I partially have my back to her but have the decency to turn around as she speaks to me. I know it isn't the answer she's looking for because she sits up and her gaze drops to her hands, busily teasing a loose thread on the seam of her PJ's.

'I thought you were going to say something like that.' As hard as it is to admit, I need her. And I need her *not* to give a shit about me and resume our casual relationship the way it was before. I have another three months in this town, *at least*, before venturing south to Ember, and having Serena on hand is more than just convenient, it *used* to be guilt-free. That may change now and the thought of breaking another girl's heart is more than I can stand. I need to repair this but I'm not sure how.

I get up and walk around the other side of the bed. I sit beside her, sensing her apprehension. My arm feels unnaturally heavy, *and* unwilling to move as I place it across her shoulders. It doesn't feel right to be there, and I almost retract it until she reaches up and weaves her fingers through mine, holding me prisoner. I feel really out of my comfort zone to be so outwardly affectionate and the very idea of what I'm doing turns my insides to milk and orange juice.

Needing help, I cowardly summon the beast from its slumber to do the work for me. I can't see what Serena sees, but when her mouth drops open and she stares at my lips, she is just where I want her. It's not in her best interests, or mine, to discuss any emotional concerns.

I know that she wants me to kiss her.

But that is never going to happen, not now, not ever.

These lips are reserved for one girl only and even then, I'm not a hundred per cent sure if I would be so bold.

I go in for my killer line. 'Do you want me to leave because if it's getting too hard for you, we can end it, no hard feelings?' My words are drizzled in chocolate syrup, and just like I know she will, she laps up every sticky drop.

'No, I don't want you to leave. I love having you here. I love …' She pauses and runs her tongue over the length of her top lip.

I cringe. I can't bear to hear her say she loves me. 'Sshh,' I say, placing my finger against her lips. Breath trembles out of her mouth and I know she wants me again.

I push her back onto the bed and rip off my t-shirt. Her breasts heave from under her bra and I feel myself coming apart, readying the beast for action. Her hands reach up

132

for my neck and she pulls me down, crushing my body against hers. Her lips find my ear.

'River,' she says breathlessly.

I draw back a little to look at her face, expecting, *I love you* or *shake this room apart.* But it isn't either.

'And don't want you to worry. Even if we *do* break up, I won't tell anyone how long you can hold your breath for. Your secret is safe with me.'

And there it is ... her hook is attached.

Wally and I sit in a secluded area of the pub away from the bistro and it's tempting aromas of roast beef and potatoes. I don't know why I picked this place, not when we could be at home having a quiet cup of tea. I figured getting a few scotches down Wally's throat might ease the pain when I ask him to upend his life and move to Gloucestershire with me.

'So, what's this all about then?' Wally takes a sip of his drink. The only way to do this is to rip the plaster straight off.

'I'm moving to Gloucestershire and I want you to come with me.'

'It's because of this girl, Amber ...'

'Ember,' I correct. 'And yes. It's because of her.'

'Why?' He knocks back the rest of his drink. 'You're a man in your own right. What do you need me for?'

'She's only seventeen, probably still at school. It will just sound more plausible if I pretend to be her age and live at home with ...' The last word doesn't make it out of my mouth. How am I going to tell him that my plan is to lie *twice* to this girl who has stolen my heart and say that I really live with my uncle and aunt, who are on a photo shoot up in the Lake District and that I'm being minded by none other than the *butler*. For the first time in my life, I feel myself drowning.

'And you think by introducing yourself as a seventeen year old that will make her more available to you? You're starting this friendship based on a lie, and call me over-cautious, but it'll come back and bite you on the arse. Lies always do.'

'I know. It's either this way or stalking her.'

Wally lets out a laugh. 'But it's okay to hire someone to do the dirty work for you.' He takes a breath. 'I need another drink for this.' He gets up and walks over to the bar. I stare into my scotch and coke, knowing Wally speaks the truth. As much as it pains me to come across as a sap, I have to go a little deeper and let him in.

Wally sits down and I pick up from where he left off from. 'When we were at the pool the other day, and I showed you that freakish ability ...'

'Sshhh,' says Wally, nervously checking over both shoulders. I lower my voice.

'When I showed you what I can do, you might also recall me saying something about Ember being part of it.'

'Yeah, I do. But why not take a holiday for a few weeks and go down to Gloucestershire and orchestrate a chance meeting for the two of you. Get to know her first. How do you know she isn't deliriously happy and has a boyfriend?'

It's a fair point and something I had deliberately pushed out of my head. 'I don't, and I can't.'

'Why not?'

My body pulls me in all the wrong directions. 'Because I know when I get there, I won't be able to leave her, even if it's to pack up the house and move. It's why I haven't driven down there to see her. I don't think I could ...' I drop my head into my hands, massaging my temples as each of my rationalisations is left floundering. I drag my face through my hands, leaving my fingertips covering my mouth. 'It's hard to explain, but it's like a force I have no control over, like we share the same gravitational pull or something. I know if I see her, I won't be able to leave. It's all or nothing, come what may.' *Come what may* is another term my father used a lot and Wally stares at me, a knowing look on his face.

'And what if she doesn't feel the same way about you,

River? What then?'

'I don't know.' Strangling in my throat, my words choke off. As egotistical as it is to say, I don't think that is what fate has in store for me. *God, I hope that's not what'll happen.*

'And you're willing to uproot your life *and* mine, on a *maybe*?' Yes, I am, although I don't say it aloud.

Silence sits between us.

Air is as willing to fill my lungs as it was before and yet I can't breathe. If it wasn't for the sound of glasses chinking across the bar, the low chatter of voices and the occasional boom of laughter coming from the bistro, this room of black tables and chairs and thick bottle green curtains, would seem as dark and oppressive as a tomb.

Say something, Wal. Please say something. He fiddles with his glass, twisting it this way and that. His breathing is shallow too, his teeth gnaw repetitively over his bottom lip and his eyes are misty and lost. I brace for bad news. He needs time.

Eventually, Wally glances up at me 'If I say yes, when do you propose for all this to take place?'

I can't help the smile that pulls at the corners of my mouth. 'The sooner the better.'

Wally's eyebrows rise. No words are needed.

'Two months, maybe three,' I answer. 'I want to start the new school year in September.'

Wally takes a small sip first, stares into his glass and then downs the rest. 'I don't know, River. I just don't know. I need time to think this over. It's a huge step, relocating, as you know …'

'I'm not going to sell the house just in case it doesn't work out.' The words taste sour coming out of my mouth. 'I've already spoken to Mr Freeman. He thinks investing in real estate is the way to go.' The scratch at the back of my throat tries to convince me what I said was a lie, but technically, it isn't. The last time I went to see him, real estate had come up in conversation, and he had said that investing in property was a smart thing to do.

135

'Mmm, nevertheless, I need time to think about it.'

'Sure.'

As much as I want to stay and re-state my case, Wally needs to be alone, perhaps with another scotch, and I need to leave right now.

Recklessly, I'd left the pool in a rush, with no swim and no sex under my belt. 'I'll leave you to it, then,' I say, pushing the rest of my drink away and getting up.

Pain grips me.

Hard and fast.

A punch to the stomach. Uppercut to the jaw.

Gingerly, I reach up and wipe a light film of sweat from my forehead, steadying myself against the table.

'You alright, River?'

'Yeah,' I say, but I won't be if I don't get out of here. It wouldn't have mattered if I'd been ten minutes late. Wally wouldn't have minded, and I wouldn't be in the state I'm in right now. Ten minutes is all it takes for one of the S girls to place the OUT OF ORDER sign over the girls toilet door and we're done.

But I wasn't thinking straight when I left the pool.

My head was full of all the ways Wally would reject my plan. How he would harp on about why moving was a stupid idea. And I was right.

I scan the pub on my way out, hoping to catch the eye of a willing victim. As fate would have it, there are only three females in the room. Two of them are old enough to be my grandmother and as horny as I've been, resorting to 'banging a granny' never *ever* crosses my mind regardless of how desperate I am. And I'm definitely not about to start now. The other female is a waitress. Short black skirt and shoulder length blonde hair. Perfect. She reminds me a little of Sophie from the back. I watch as she carries plates to and from the kitchen, and not once does she look over at me. I smirk inwardly, wondering if I'm losing my touch.

My amusement doesn't last long.

Panic sets in.

I head out of the pub and onto the busy high street, needing some air. I've no idea where I'm going.

I'm about to cross the street when I spy a redhead on the other side. The tone and texture of her hair is a perfect match.

My chest is about to collapse.

My legs decaying beneath me.

What if it's her ... come to seek me out?

My heart takes off at a million miles an hour. I strengthen my concentration, demanding she turn around. I need to see her face. Need to see if it's her.

She stands fast and continues to stare through the shop window. I balance on the edge of the pavement, eager to cross, my mind not where it should be. I blindly step out onto the street. That one second, when you realise you're in trouble, and time slows down, is the moment when life becomes the clearest. I see the bus heading towards me in slow motion. I see my feet step off the kerb and onto the road. I know what is going to happen but I can't do a single thing to stop it. The sudden wallop of a bus's wing mirror slams against the side of my face, knocking me senselessly to the ground.

I must have blacked out because when I come to, all I can make out are the hazy legs of shoppers sauntering past me. Something trickles down my left cheek and I reach up to touch it. The pain is coming from somewhere near my eyebrow.

'Don't.' A hand, firm and cold, forces my own hand back into my lap. Of all people to find me like this, it's Iris Perkins. 'Come on. Let's get you cleaned up.' I'm surprised by her strength as she helps me to my feet.

'Lean against me,' she says firmly. Forever the control freak. 'My car's just there.'

I don't recall walking or getting into her car. I do feel her tits pressing into my chest as she reaches over to buckle up the seatbelt.

'I live at ...' I begin.

'I'm taking you to my place.'

I mumble a response.

I'm suddenly very tired. I can't keep my eyes open.

My head lolls back onto the headrest.

'Don't go to sleep. You probably have a concussion,' I think I hear her say, but I'm not sure. It could be a dream.

Her voice wakes me every now and then, and I catch glimpses, flashes of buildings from the east side of town. I'm sure she is talking to me, but nothing is registering.

I don't start to sober up until I find myself propped up against a wall in what looks like the foyer of a posh hotel.

'You live here?' I manage to say.

She doesn't reply, only turns her back on me.

'Lawrence, do you have any first aid in that little box of magic tricks you have hidden back there.' Her voice is like treacle.

A tall, fair-haired guy, twenty-five tops and fresh off the farm, beams back at her. 'I'll see what I can do.' He disappears from behind the desk into a room which says private and returns a few minutes later carrying a first aid box. 'Take it. I'll get it back off you later.' Knowing what the interaction between two people who have been intimate looks like, I'd bet my life that Lawrence is another submissive plaything for Iris.

'Thank you, Lawrence.'

Iris ushers me into the elevators and presses the button for floor eighteen. Several times, she glances up at my cut, which has slowed.

'After you,' she says as the doors open at floor eighteen. A wooden side table with a bunch of long-stemmed lilies steal my gaze. I stare back, seeing my reflection in a massive rectangular mirror behind it. *God, I look a mess.* The neck of my t-shirt is stained red and my face looks as though I've been five rounds with Connor McGregor.

'Nice place,' I say, wishing I hadn't looked down. My vision zigzags sharply, just like the patterns that have

138

been woven into the navy-blue carpet.

She smiles. 'Not quite as nice as yours though.' I'd forgotten I'd given my personal details to her secretary that first day in her office, but that doesn't dismiss the concern that's building inside my chest. Iris had gone out of her way to see where I lived. The question I want to know is ... *why*?

'Sit down,' she says, waving me into her apartment. Two ergonomic designer chairs, one red, one white sit lonely and waiting in a room with a glass table and a huge plasma TV. It reflects back what I know of Iris – particular, orderly, and cold. Everything around me is either made from plastic, glass or metal. No rugs or curtains, not one plush cushion. Bold colours, red, white and black adorn the things around her– voguish art pieces of symmetrical shapes that wouldn't look out of place in a gallery, along with sharp lighting that beams upwards, drawing attention to a magnificent mural on the ceiling – an optical illusion - the apex of a glass roof.

I let out a low whistle.

'Don't be impressed,' she says rudely. 'I don't need the flattery.' She disappears and comes out a few minutes later, changing out of her matching grey pants and jacket into a dress that would stop traffic – a killer red mini. One arm and shoulder is totally exposed, the other clad in tight, red spandex.

'Thanks, but I'm ok, and you look like ...' She walks past me without answering, carrying a bowl of water and the first aid kit under her arm.

'Sit,' she orders. 'Don't make me ask you again.' I opt for the white chair, being the closest, then think twice, hoping I won't get blood on it. She kneels down, spreads my knees wide and wriggles her body in so her waist presses against my inner thighs. She places the bowl at my feet.

'Let's have a look at you,' she says. As much as she looks exceptionally appetising in that dress, the condescending tone in her voice keeps me, and the beast,

139

in check. I shift in my seat trying to outmanoeuvre the stomach cramps that are getting worse by the second.

I'm surprised by how delicate Iris's touch is, but even more so, that she makes a point of only washing the blood from my cheek and completely avoiding the wound. Then, very carefully, she cut three strips of white tape, each one the exact same width and length, and then fastens them to my eyebrow. All this done in complete silence. After ten minutes, I feel compelled to speak.

'Can I ask you a few questions about the girl I asked you to find for me?'

Her face sours. 'I don't talk business out of the office.' She sits back on her heels for a moment, pushing the bowl and other materials aside. The hem of her dress rides up as she rests her hands on the floor behind her. Her thighs, like sponge cake, make my mouth water. I can almost see her knickers. The pain subsides as the beast surges forward.

'How do you feel?' Her eyes catch me looking at her legs.

'Good. Doesn't hurt a bit,' I say, reaching up to inspect her handiwork. Like a cobra, she strikes with lightning speed. She slaps my hand away, forbidding me to touch it. I gasp, surprised and shocked by her actions. She smiles sweetly as though nothing has occurred and presses her hands into my knees. She leans in closer, her lips inches from mine. I'm just about to say, I don't kiss, when she speaks.

'I want you to give me your next half an hour. NOW.' I knew this was coming. The pain is slipping away in response, and every animal instinct I have, surfaces. Her journal also makes a surprised entrance and she flips over a few pages and begins to write.

'And this time, I want you to kiss me.'

'No.'

The word is out before I know I've said it.

She looks a little amused that I'm so direct. 'Just like that. No.'

I can't falter. 'That's right.'

'So, there's nothing you want, nothing I can give you in return.' Her eyes widen.

This is how it works for her. You give a little, you get a little. What she doesn't know, is I get a lot and give very little. All I have to do is be myself and she'll be at the mercy of the beast who simply wants to put her in her place once and for all and show her who's boss. I could easily take her and be out of here without thinking twice about it, but with Iris, it's complicated and dangerous.

'Information. I want some information.'

A self-satisfied smile plays around Iris's lips, and I grin back feeling more superior than I've ever felt.

'Okay. What do you want to know?'

'What Ember was doing at the time of the photo and where was it taken, and also, how long did you spend watching her before you took it?'

'You are a curious little bean, aren't you? She must have done a real number on you.' She smiles spitefully and enters more into her journal.

'She hasn't done *anything* to me,' I snap. 'Are you going to tell me or what?'

Iris purses her lips and stares at me for a long time. 'The photo was taken in the park just around the corner from where she lives, and I watched her for about an hour as she sat under the shade of a tree, reading a book.' I want to know what she was reading, and Iris picks up on it. 'I didn't have an ultra-zoom lens on my camera so I'm sorry I can't enlighten you what that book was.' She takes great pleasure in letting me know this. 'Quite ordinary in the looks department, but I suppose if you like that kind of thing.' The more Iris speaks, especially regarding Ember, the less I want to hear.

'Ember is more than *ordinary*,' I say defensively.

'Mmmhmm,' mutters Iris offhandedly. Her eyes narrow and I know her part of the deal has been met.

'Now then, where were we?'

My eyebrow arches at her response. I'm not going to

say that dreaded word for her - kiss. I sit back in the chair and turn up the heat. The **beast**, waiting in the wings, is willing to play. I envision talons of black mist edging towards her, drawing her, luring her, as though she has no control over thought or reason.

Her dewy eyes are a dead giveaway.

It's working.

Her lips part. She leans in slowly, deliberately, calculating every move. Her breath is hot against my lips. She is waiting for me to come that extra few inches, but I resist. I am in control. I am manipulating this game. I wrote the rules and know when to change them.

'Well,' she whispers.

I smile. 'I'm right here.'

She nibbles the corner of her lip before kissing me. It's my plan from the start – her initiating the urge to kiss me, and with a little help from my dark side, she has now been part of my greatest triumph.

The kiss does nothing for me and will go down in history as the biggest snowflake ever – cold, bland, but most of all, leaving no trace it had ever been there. As though she was dead. There is no passion or hunger behind it, regardless of how super-hot and sexy she can be. There is no excitement, no energy, nothing that raises the slightest pulse in my body and yet I still throb for that release. No brainer there. For the first time in a long while, I feel as if I can get up and leave and not feel the worst for it. The kiss, however, allowed me to see something more of what I already know about her - her cunning nature, her love of secrets and her desire to control all things wrapped up in a blanket of blackness. But something else. Something far more intriguing. A scared, timid voice, begging for mercy, begging for release. I don't understand what it means.

'That wasn't too bad, was it?' she says, lowering her eyes at me.

I lie. 'No.' And now that I'm here, it isn't that I want sex. I just want to be out of her debt and devoting the next half an hour to Iris means I'm two sessions down with only four to go.

The voice in my head, as clear as if it's my own thought, whispers very slowly. *Trust yourself. Learn what you can from her. She holds all the answers. Beware of the beast.*

It's the same voice from the lake. I want to take the time to ask more questions, unravel what it means, but there just isn't time. I know what I must do.

'You are in so much trouble,' I say, lunging at her. She lands on the cold, tiled floor and I take pleasure in knowing she'll feel right at home with the temperature.

ELEVEN

FORTY minutes later, I reach for my phone.

And a mint.

I need to get rid of the damn taste of tomato juice that Iris loves to finish up with.

'Skye?'

'Who wants to know?'

I scowl.

He fucking knows it's me. My number would have come up. 'Don't be a twat. It's me, River. Can you pick me up?' My car is still parked opposite the pub where I met Wally for lunch.

'Where are you?'

'On Harrington Street, next to the bingo hall.'

Half an hour later, the sound of Skye's bike blisters up the road.

'What took you so long?' I ask, impatiently flipping up the visor of his helmet. I've no idea why I'm so irritated with him, especially as my second session with Iris was better than the first. I just can't understand why I left her place with a pounding headache and in a shitty mood.

It was weird.

I can't quite explain it.

Other than her apartment seemed to grow ears and eyes the minute she ripped off that red dress. I felt watched, not that it would surprise me at all if she had a hidden camera set up somewhere. But on edge … wary. Like I was waiting to be pounced on by an irate husband. And for a new building, there were way too many creaks and groans from the floorboards and walls.

Then there was this *other* sensation that seemed to be *living* in the room.

I can't describe it because I've never felt anything like it in my life before. But heavy, claustrophobic, like the air was being squeezed out of the room to make way for something that didn't need air. Like I said, weird.

Skye tilts his head at me, inspecting me.

'What?' I snap. 'Don't look at me like that. Where the hell were you?'

A wry smile pulls at Skye's lips. 'I stopped for a coffee,' he says sarcastically. I roll my eyes. Take a breath to calm myself. 'And a Bakewell Tart.' I grit my teeth and feel my fists ball up.

'Dude, you need to take a chill pill before you explode. It takes me twenty minutes to get here from my place. I came as soon as I could.' He leans in closer and pats my shoulder.

Instead of being irater, his friendly gesture takes the edge of my mood. 'Thanks for coming.'

Skye then spots the three horizontal strips of plaster on my forehead.

'Bar brawl bonanza?'

I frown, the skin pulling against the tape. 'Not quite.'

'Jelly wrestling then,' says Skye with a smirk.

'Not even close. Just give me the damn helmet.' Skye bowls the spare helmet under arm and I catch it. I slip it over my head, wincing as a warm dribble of blood trickles down my cheek.

It has never bothered me to know where Skye lives, but as we head south east, past the gas works and into the lower-class part of town, I realise his digs aren't going to come with a cottage garden and a bird feeder. We stop in front of a tall, grey block of flats, the bottom level strewn with graffiti. I don't say anything but that doesn't stop Skye from interpreting the look on my face.

'We can't *all* afford mansions, you know.'

Two drunks prop up the doorway to the main entrance and Skye reefs the door open, ignoring their slurred grumbles as he wedges his foot in front of the door. I make a beeline for the elevator.

'Good luck. They haven't worked since I got here,' says Skye. I cringe at the smell of stale piss as he heads towards the stairs.

Skye smirks. 'You gonna love this then,' he says, turning onto the first landing. I follow behind him, not fully comprehending what he means until the smell changes to vomit. 'Watch that,' he says, negotiating two steps at a time. I step over someones unwanted lunch and trudge on. The spiral goes up and up. My legs burn and my breath heaves. I take down shallow sips to avoid large lungfuls of the foul tasting air.

'How do you put up with the smell?' I manage to mumble through clenched teeth.

'What smell?' he says and laughs.

The higher up we go, fifteen flights to be precise, the denser and more putrid the air is.

'Last floor.'

'Urgh. Did someone die here?'

'I'd say more than one.' He laughs again, much louder this time. 'No ventilation up here. You know, the penthouse suite is totally overrated.'

We finally stop and I lean against the wall. A ring of daisies has been drawn and coloured in around a faded black number fourteen. Skye reaches into his pocket and pulls out a set of keys, clipped to a plastic daisy keyring.

I shake my head but say nothing. I realise I actually don't know the guy with his back to me at all.

The door swings open and the aroma is the first thing to hit me – citrusy, fresh and crisp. I take in a hearty breath as Skye closes the door behind him.

'Better?'

'Much.'

'Don't worry about that,' he says, waving towards a lounge room he has no intention of going into. I pause for a minute before I pass. The room is small but surprisingly clean and the mismatch furniture, a green sofa, a mauve chair and three brown footstools, which have seen too many decades come and go, work remarkably well. The pile of surfing magazines stacked up on the coffee table look as if they've been straightened with a set square. The surfboard, propped up in the corner of the room, might seem out of place next to a mantelpiece full of precisely placed motorbike trophies, and yet doesn't and even the oversized window taking up most of the northern wall laden with crystals of every colour and shape has an orderly and structured purpose. Taking a sneak peek into Skye's world makes me more aware of how different we both are.

I stare blindly into the room, the sun glinting against each gemstone, setting the whole area alight with colour. I feel the sudden urge to go in and explore, but don't.

I look around for a female presence. 'You live here alone?'

'Yeah, mostly.' I notice the lengthy pause. 'Except when my brother stays over.'

I'm sure he told me he had a brother, although I can't recall his name. 'And does he have a name?'

Skye's gaze darkens. 'Not this week.' I want to ask more, but the look on his face changes my mind … for the moment.

'That looks a mess,' he says. He lifts his chin to look at my eye. My face feels tight from the blood that has dried against my cheek. Skye shakes his head. 'You really

147

are so green about all this, aren't you?'

I'm over his riddles. 'Do you wanna tell me what the fuck is going on, or do I have to beat the shit out of you to find it?'

'Is that how you got this?' he asks grinning and gesturing to my face, 'looking for information.'

'No,' I retort sharply.

'Right,' says Skye, drawling the word out. 'Stupid me. I forgot you are Mr Calm and non-emotional.' My eyes widen. My jaw clamps together, biting a chunk from the inside of my cheek. 'We'll get to that later. This way.'

He stands in the doorway of the bathroom. 'Come on, if water won't come to Mohammed, then Mohammed must come to the water.'

'That's mountain, you dick,' I say, getting up.

'Whatever. I don't care. It got you moving, didn't it?'

I follow him into an olive-green bathroom and sit when he points to the toilet.

'What's this ... first aid 101?'

Skye sniggers. 'More like Elementar 101.' My heart registers the word, sending several heavy thumps into my throat.

He rips the remaining two strips off my eye, catching my eyebrow hairs in the process.

'Easy,' I groan. I glare at him, but he simply smiles. He thrusts a plastic jug under the tap and begins to fill it. He whistles too, which is just as annoying, his head bobbing from side to side. Skye turns off the tap, the water slopping over at the side of the jug.

He cradles it gently. 'Ready?'

I open my mouth to say, 'ready for what', when he throws the entire contents in my face. 'What the fuck. I'm gonna beat the living shit out of you,' I yell at him. I stand up and grab him by his shirt, fist at the ready ... again.

His eyebrows rise and a smile flickers across his face. 'Are we doing this again?' he asks.

I remember the invisible barrier. 'You're a complete wanker, do you know that? I don't know what you're up to …'

Skye interrupts me. 'You've still got no idea, have you?'.

'*What*?' I manage to spit through my teeth.

'What you're capable of.'

It's then I notice the throb of the cut is gone.

'Look,' says Skye, gazing at something beyond my shoulder.

I turn to see a wide mirror on the wall behind me. At first, all I see is my face, shiny and wet ... beads of water trapped in my hair, the front of my t-shirt soaked, turning the blood red to a washed out pink. It takes a moment to realise what I should be looking at. The blood is gone from my face, that is no surprise, but so is the gaping cut. All that's left is a thin, white line.

I lean forward, peering closer at my reflection. I run my fingers over the freshly healed scar.

'How …' is the only word my brain allows me to say.

'It's like I've been saying all this time. You've got powers, man, and the sooner you realise you're not just some over-sexed, walking boner, the quicker we can get down to what's really going on.'

There are so many questions buzzing in my head, but I'm still playing catch up with this strange phenomenon.

I'm healed.

The cut is gone.

The anger has gone. 'You could've asked me to put my head over the sink and …'

'I'm not a fucking hairdresser, bro, besides where's the fun in that?' Still gawping into the mirror, I see Skye smirk. 'You should have seen your face.'

He breaks into hysterics.

I suppose it was mildly amusing. It would have been something that would've made me laugh if I was on the other end of the prank.

'How did you know that would work?'

'I didn't,' he says, still laughing. 'It was just a guess.'

After Skye mops the water off the floor, toilet seat and walls, he then pulls out a chamois from under the sink and buffs off the spots left on the mirror. He throws me a towel from the airing cupboard, and I follow him into the kitchen.

'You've gotta give me more,' I say, leaning up against the kitchen cupboards. I wipe my face and rub my hair dry.

'Like you said, seeing is believing.'

Wait a minute – I didn't say that. I'd *thought* that, *and* I don't remember saying the words out loud, certainly not to him anyway. All this time, I was trying to convince Wally that I was different and Skye, it seems, was doing the same.

I dump the towel onto the chipped bench top and without hesitation, Skye picks it up and folds it neatly. He then lifts the lid off a wicker basket that I'd mistaken as a rubbish bin, and places it on top of a stack of other folded items. I stare at him, confused.

'Dirty washing,' he says, very matter of fact.

I let out a laugh. 'Who folds dirty washing?'

Skye seems put out by the very implication that something he's done is wrong. 'I do. Do you have a problem with that?' *No*, I think, *not nearly as much as you do*.

'Whatever blows your hair back, man,' I say, shrugging. Okay, Skye is some OCD smart-mouthed enigma, who lives in a world of riddles and unanswered explanations, but what does that say about me – who can heal wounds from applying water, hold his breath indefinitely and shag any female I choose. Who am I to judge?

I wait for him to begin a sentence that goes something along the lines of *the reason you are the way you are ...* but he doesn't. Instead, he wipes down the spotlessly clean bench, again, hangs up the tea towel, and places it on the rack. He then turns to me with hopeful eyes.

'What are you doing tomorrow? Can you get a couple

of days off work?' It's Wednesday, and coincidentally I only work Saturday, Sunday, Monday and Tuesday.

'What for?'

Skye lifts the sleeve of his hoodie and checks his watch. 'Can you get the time off or not?'

'Shouldn't be a problem. Why?'

Skye checks his watch again. His jaw tenses. 'I have to go now but be here tomorrow at nine thirty and all will be revealed.'

'Why can't you just tell me? Why the big fucking surprise.'

'You'll see. We need time to go through this, and I need to be somewhere.'

'Where?'

He clears his throat, picks up his keys and ushers me out of his apartment.

When I get home, I find a note on the hall table from Wally. It reads:

I've gone to my sisters for a few days to think things over. Look after yourself. There's plenty of food in the fridge.

TWELVE

SITTING by the lake, the same lake coincidentally that I'd visited a couple of weeks ago, I'm back to that same old feeling of total surrender and serenity. There is no place on earth quite like it and from the boat ramp, I can make out Leo's grandparents cabin across the lake. All looks quiet over there now, unlike here. Skye is up and down every few minutes adjusting poles and pegs, regardless that we'd set the two A-framed tents up over an hour ago. These digs aren't as sweet as the cabin, but truth be told, I've slept in worse places. Much worse.

I'm just glad to be here, and no longer in the car with him. A good portion of the two hour trip was spent with me asking what this was all about and where were we going. The words s*eeing is believing* are etched into my brain forever as he customised every song that played to those three stupid words until I finally quit asking. The rest of the journey played out in silence with Skye plugged into his iPhone, tapping his foot annoyingly against my car door.

I open one eye. 'You haven't been camping much, have you?' I say, relaxing on a make-shift sun lounger.

'Yeah, course. All the time.' He sniffs. 'Australia is one long camping holiday, didn't you know. Except we're not pussy like you guys here.' I raise my eyebrow. 'We don't have to put up these dumb-arse contraptions. We use swags.'

'Swags?'

'Exactly my point. Who doesn't know what a swag is?' He re-adjusts the guide wire again. 'You know, a *sleeping* bag.' His tone changes. 'But not just a sleeping bag. It's heavy duty, for the serious camper, and what the fuck is a sleeping bag anyway. Who sleeps when they go camping, especially if girls are there.'

'But there aren't any girls here,' I add. My peace and serenity slips into irritation. I prop myself against my elbows and look back towards the water.

The sun is level with the mountain tops, still warm enough to swim but casting shadows over parts of the lake where Loch Ness monsters might lurk. I try to focus on the words Skye had suggested; *become one with the water*, but nothing is making any sense other than how Ember is real and no longer a figment of my imagination.

Frustrated, I strip off my t-shirt and dive in.

The water, cool at first, takes less than a second to acclimatise to. The silky liquid wraps itself around me as though I am the centre of its universe. I dip beneath the surface, without giving a single thought to whether I should hold my breath or not.

One blink and my whole world changes.

It's a place I could call home. Where life can be anything I want it to be. No one to answer to, no one to hurt or cause pain to. No one to please other than myself. A world according to me, where guilt washes clean, where lust sinks to the bottom and disappears into the loamy bottom, and voices are silenced.

The first three feet are relatively clear, and as I swim down further, the lack of sunlight and thicker sediment makes the water slightly murkier. But for me, it poses no problem.

My eyes adjust to the cloudy conditions quicker than it takes to wink. Fish take cover as I swim past, darting in and out of reeds and grasses that have found a home here. My eyes pick up a huge pike fifty yards away. It should be unnerving that I can see at such a distance but I can't help being in awe of such a gift. My vision is almost *too* perfect.

I feel no pressure inside my chest as I venture deeper and there is no buoyancy trying to float me back to the surface. The simplicity of life is overwhelming. I feel no hunger or thirst even though we missed lunch. The voices in my head have become slivers of old memories that have forgotten they belong to me, allowing me to finally feel at peace.

Smaller fish, startled by my size, zip out of my way as I swim further out. The inbuilt compass, I never knew I had, informs me I'm close to the centre of the lake - almost half a mile from shore. I turn around and head back, taking my time to investigate this new watery world that invited me into its warm and welcoming domain.

I decide, I *am* one with the water. Just being in it.

And it is one with me.

Believe whispers a familiar voice. *You must believe. She needs you.*

I now understand what Skye meant. I permit one solitary question to touch the edges of my thoughts though - *how the hell did he know to even say that*.

'I'm impressed,' I hear Skye call out as I resurface a few feet away from him. He is sitting on the bank, his legs stretched out in front of him, clapping his hands. I swim to the wooden dock and heave my body out of the water. 'And they're some killer eyes you've got there, too.' I take his word for it. 'You were down for well over an hour, did you know? Is that your longest time?' I shrug my shoulders and drag my hands through my hair to

154

remove the water. 'Did you manage to find that magical ingredient yet?' he asks.

I have, but I say nothing. The more questions I ask him these days, the quicker he clams up. I want to see what else he knows.

Skye sighs and gets up. 'I think we need to scale down a little then.'

I frown. 'Scale down *what*?'

It looks like he's been busy whilst I was exploring. A stump from a recently sawn-off tree has been placed near the bank of the lake and sitting on top is an old metal bucket.

'Come,' he says, walking over to it. Hesitantly, I follow, refusing to take my eyes off him as he scoops the bucket into the lake and places it back on the stump.

'Don't even *think* about throwing it on me,' I say, raising my eyebrows. Sure, I'm already wet, but I'm not about to let him make a fool out of me again.

'*Chill out*,' says Skye. 'I'm not gonna chuck it over you. Geez!' He gestures to himself and then to me a few times with his hand. 'We *really* need to work on our trust.'

He's smirking again and I feel my temper flare for all the wrong reasons. 'It's just, I found that when I focussed all my attention on the element, it worked much better.' There's another of those ambiguous statements.

'*Worked* for you?'

He grins. 'Just trust me, bro. Seriously. God, it sounds like someone did a real number on you.' My father is the first to spring to mind, then my mother, then myself. 'Have you ever trusted anyone in your life?'

'Yes,' I snap. Wally. But we are heading off topic. 'Focus, how?'

'I don't know. You're the one with the power, Clark Kent. Zap it with your mind or something.'

I scowl.

'Dude, don't get all dark on me. I'm not you.' He sighs loudly. 'I can't believe that you didn't figure this out

155

years ago. Control it. Make it disappear. Make it move. Part the sea like Moses.' His stupid, lopsided grin grates against my nerves.

I turn my focus to the pail and stare into the bucket. I try to make something happen. I push and pull with my mind until my brain throbs, my head aching so damn much that it feels like it's going to fracture into a thousand tiny pieces. I concentrate harder, ignoring his child-like laughter, willing and pleading with it. No matter what I do, the water doesn't even swirl, let alone create a ripple.

Twenty minutes pass. 'I've got nothing.'

'It worked for me,' says Skye smugly, 'but then again, I suppose we *are* all different.'

I glance up at him, wishing I could stick his diversities up his arse. 'Tell you what, champ. Let's blow off the lessons for a bit. How about a race?' I don't answer.

'You see that pontoon over there?' I look up to see a white platform, floating about three hundred metres off shore.

'Yeah.'

'First one there ... wins. I'll even give you a head start,' says Skye.

This is one bet I can't lose. 'No need,' I say, getting up and standing at the edge of the lake.

An electrifying buzz still lingers in my skin from my first dip. I know I have this one in the bag. I wait for him to say go and then hit the water with such a speed, the very second my body comes into contact with it, my legs are powering me forward beneath the surface. I head in the general direction, using my internal compass so I don't have to break the surface and slow down.

At one point, the water pulls me along, separating a smooth channel ahead, just for me to swim in, reducing the effort I have to put in and allowing me to go harder and faster. I look through the clear water as the shiny white bottom of the pontoon comes into view, confident that I'd won.

Thrusting my hand out of the water, I grab the slippery

edge and haul my body onto the floating surface calling victory.

'Never mind, champ. Better luck next time.'

I look up to see Skye standing over me. It takes a moment to realise he isn't even wet. I feel cheated and the look on his face as I sweep his feet from under him, catching him unaware, is something I've wanted to see since I first met him. He falls backwards into the water with a huge splash.

'I suppose I deserved that,' he says, pushing his wet hair out of his eyes and resting his arms against the lip of the pontoon.

Being here, firmly establishes one thing – I have no idea who Skye Buchannan really is. I've watched him many times, studied him, even when he thinks I'm not looking, trying to piece together an ounce of who he might be and how he seems to know everything about my life and still, I know absolutely zilch about his. My emotional radar picks up nothing with him either, which is kind of odd because it generally connects in with a simple handshake. A dull hum is all I get.

Staring at him from across the small campfire, the night air sweet, like rain has just fallen and the sound of a hundred crickets pulsing around us, I can't begin to wonder what he is thinking and whether he's going to let me in on it. He looks relaxed, leaning back on his elbows, his legs outstretched, feet crossed at the ankles, a curious smile making a home around his lips. We've barely spoken since this afternoon. And I'm beginning to think it was a big mistake coming here.

'Have you ever heard of a book called Peri Phuseôs tôn Ontôn?' he says, totally out of the blue.

I shake my head. 'No … should I?'

Skye's lips twitch one way and then the other, contemplating my question. 'In the light of recent discoveries, probably not. It translates to 'On the Nature of Things that Exist'.'

157

Again, I wait.

I lean forward, curious.

'It's a book that changed my life.' In the firelight, Skye's eyes burn like smelting silver. A memory catches his attention, stalls his words, pulls playfully at his lips. It bugs me to ask, but I can't hold back any longer.

'How?'

'It told me who I was and why I was different from everyone else.' He looks up at me, re-igniting that same brotherly connection I'd felt as he dived off the ten metre platform at Gattling Aquatics. 'And that I wouldn't have to do this alone.'

I feel a strong pull in my chest. Like a desperate feeling trying to tear its way out. Trying to make itself known. Be recognised. Be free. Be part of something other than just myself. Almost begging me to sit with it awhile and understand its simple form. It's like nothing I've felt before. For the first time in my life, I wonder if it's fear. Is this what being scared feels like? Not of Skye, but actually permitting myself to feel, to connect with another human other than Ember and Wally - the two people who show up for me every time without question.

'You must know, by now, who you are …'

The word WaterLover sits in the back of my throat and yet it feels too weird to say it aloud. Instead, I nod.

'Why do you find it so hard to believe?' he asks.

'I don't know. It sounds … too … incredible.'

'You *are* incredible. How many people can hold their breath under water for an hour like that or heal their skin? How could you not think you are something more than … *human*?' Glinting at me from across the fire, the wondrous smile on Skye's face matches my own.

'Do you realise what you're saying? It sounds worse than vampires or werewolves for Christ's sake.'

Skye laughs. 'Yeah, I know. Wild, right? It took me a long time too, to admit that I possess all the traits of the AirWhisperer, although I was fortunate to have the book from an early age. Suppose that counts for something.' A force of recognition tugs at the core of me. 'We are brothers, River.'

The pulling in my chest ceases.

Something suddenly shifts. Feels different in my body, under my ribcage, inside my heart. Warmth moves in, letting the cold out with it. A humming of something wonderful and frightening is happening to me.

My breath comes faster.

The ground slopes away from me, flashes of stars bursting in and out of my vision. I twist my fingers through the grass, trying to fend off this impossible vertigo. And then balance returns as though it never left, as though it's always had a home within me.

I want to ask, what was that? What just happened to me? A sensation I'm not familiar with seems to have slipped beneath my skin, through my bones and into my heart. Snuck in, under my radar, when I wasn't looking or trying hard to keep everything out. It's totally foreign to me to try and describe because I've never known what oneness has meant.

I still don't.

And yet, it is the only word that knocks against my skull, tattooing meaning into my flesh. I feel a sense of belonging, of kinship, open to feeling anything I want, whatever that might look like.

I repeat his words silently. *We are brothers.*

My heart beats confidently, resolutely, to a newer, brighter rhythm than it's ever known before. A beat that brings a smile to my lips for no other reason than I want to, and I can, and it doesn't matter who sees it or why. I find my mind wandering, dreaming of a lifetime of companionship. Possibilities come at me in a rush of images, of fishing trips and camping, of boys nights out, and of family gatherings, of having a best man at my side and watching our own children run about in the park at birthday parties.

'Hey, are you still with me?' Skye says.

Half-dazed, I return to feel the cold ground pressing

into my legs. I shuffle closer to the fire, the night air nipping at my back. Skye moves closer too and rubs his hands together. His face, no longer tired, his get-up-and-go energy, that seemed so exhausting, has now faded considerably.

'This book?' I say, 'how did you come across it?'

Skye half-laughs. 'In Australia, would you believe? Who said nothing exciting ever happens down there?'

One of my shoulders shrugs. 'I would just about believe anything these days.'

'Yeah, well, I was thirteen years old, and living in an outback town in North Queensland.' Skye crosses his legs and rests his arms loosely in his lap. 'A number of strange things happened to me the few years preceding it ...'

'Like what?' I butt in.

'Like hearing radio static as though someone was trying to tune into my head, to moments when I would see myself hovering above my bed, watching myself sleep.' He stops to scratch his head, the humorous, puzzled look on his face makes me smile. 'But the weirdest thing ... was this high-pitched whistle in my head that no matter what I did or said, it drowned out everything. Mum took me to doctors and ear specialists, but they never found anything. That was the weirdest.'

'I'd say looking down on yourself asleep tops that.'

Skye sniggers to himself. 'Actually, it was more like a hum – a heartbeat of a hum that acted something like a homing beacon. The further south I walked the softer it got, the further north, the louder.'

'How long did it take you to figure that out?' I ask.

Skye nods his head and keeps nodding, as though he is remembering like it was yesterday. 'A while. A while.' He laughs a little. 'And being born into a family of adrenaline junkies isn't all it's cracked up to be either, you know? It made me exceptionally curious and a little crazy at times.'

'I understand the crazy part,' I mumble. Skye looks up, shocked, and it's only then that I realise I'd spoken the words out loud.

'Well, for me, I developed a healthy attraction for adventure and anything off-limits. Even at a young age, I told myself this humming in my head was some bizarre quest, the adrenaline alone, urged me on.' It made sense why he was so flippant about everything and why there didn't seem to be a serious bone in his body. 'I had to see it through to the end and to be honest, my best friend at the time, Todd, convinced me it could lead to treasure.' Skye chuckles to himself again. 'How naïve I was back then. But little did I know ... Todd was right.'

I throw another log on the fire and inch closer.

'So Todd and I set out that morning in search of this sound that progressively grew louder the further north we went. I won't bore you with the details, but the long and the short of it was, after four hours, it led us to some old fella's backyard on the outskirts of town. By now, the buzzing in my head was so loud, I could hardly see his stone path that led to this dodgy-looking birdbath in his back garden. The dizziness finally got the better of me. I slumped down and the second I hit the deck, the terracotta paver beneath me cracked in two as though it had been struck with a sledgehammer. The racket in my head stopped immediately.'

He stops talking, picks up the sleeping bag behind him and wraps himself in it. 'Do you know what eternal peace feels like, River?'

I nod and get him to throw the other sleeping bag over too. 'Go on, what happened.'

'Beneath the paver was a grey, glossy looking stone, which resembled polished granite. The stone had a four pointed star on it, each pointing to a different colour – red, yellow, green and blue. But the colours were washed out, all faded, like they'd been painted a thousand years ago and were hardly there at all, until I placed my hand over it.'

I wait, not wanting to interrupt. Instead, I look over at him and raise my eyebrows.

'The dull shades burst into vibrant colour, almost blinding me. I knew it was not of this world when I traced my finger over the marble and watched the stone dissolve before my eyes. In its place ...' Skye reaches into a backpack that hasn't left his side since we'd got here and pulls out a book the size of a telephone directory, 'was this.' Skye turns the book to face me, showing me the same pattern that had been on the stone.

'You're kidding me, right?' The calligraphy on the book suggests it's old, but the white cover with its gold edging is in pristine condition that it could quite mistakenly been removed from the Best Sellers shelf at WHSmith. There's only one word on the cover that I recognise – Elementar.

'And you've read it?'

'I wish. There are sections I can't open or won't open, and trust me, this isn't exactly the type of book you show someone.' He sounds like he's talking from experience.

'Can I have a look?'

'Thought you'd never ask,' says Skye. He drops his sleeping bag and shuffles closer before carefully handing me the book. The moment I touch it, the blue segment of the star glows so brilliantly I have to shield my eyes.

My heart starts to race.

'Great. That's what I was hoping would happen,' says Skye fidgeting with excitement. 'Happened to me too, except with the yellow one.'

'Are there any other surprises you want to tell me about before I open it?'

He grins. 'Nope, you're all good.'

I fold back the first page, revealing his identity. It doesn't matter that he hasn't answered my question about how he got onto the pontoon without getting wet, his secret is out. If he's the AirWhisperer, my guess is, he can fly.

'I can't read what it says.' The three horizontal wavy lines on the top of the page are yellow. There are references to three blue zigzagged lines, red vertical swirly lines and green vertical straight lines. 'What does it mean?'

'You can't read it? Wow! Wasn't expecting that. Maybe because it's not meant for you.'

I shrug. 'Yeah, maybe?'

'I can read it perfectly,' he continues. 'This symbol is me, I think,' he says pointing to the three yellow horizontal wavy lines. 'The blue is you. The red belongs to the FlameMaker and the green is the EarthHealer. Each section of the book is for that particular Elementar to read and them only.'

'And you know this because ...'

'I don't ... for sure. It's just a guess.'

I slide my fingers under the page and it flips over with ease. There is a blank page with three blue horizontal wavy lines on it.

'I've been waiting six years to see what's written on there,' says Skye. 'What does it say?'

I turn the page to find it's a very similar format to what was on Skye's page, except one obvious difference. I *can* read it.

'Well ... Do you understand it?'

'Give me a minute.'

The first part is a poem.

WaterLover, WaterLover, why do you feel so deep
Place your heart inside her heart and feel
before you leap
Bring with you, your love and trust, or forever
you will weep
Have the courage, take a chance or never
shall you sleep

My mouth drops open.

Seconds pass, and I've forgotten how to breathe. Time has abandoned me and if I move too quickly I might slip into an alternative universe, like my whole life has been a dream, a lie, a mistake, and that now I'm finally awake, to be *someone*, to be of *worth*.

'River,' Skye barks at me. I carry on reading.

The second part is headed, 'WaterLover - The second of the Elementars.'

Nereus, the second immortal, was fashioned as a companion for the FlameMaker, Nuria, the first of the Elementars. Nuria with her flame and destruction required balance - something to dowse her fiery nature. Nereus was the perfect choice, his watery cloak used to calm Nuria to the point she fell in love with him. She was his opposite in every way but his one true love. He lavished so much love on Nuria, finally, it destroyed her. Out of control and pining for Nuria, Nereus's emotions ran wild. He covered the entire planet with water from his tears until Amun was created to act as a brother for Nereus. Amun, an AirWhisperer, taught Nereus how to channel his emotion, how to store it and how to reign it in so he wasn't consumed by it all the time. He taught Nereus how to absorb all fluid, all moisture and liquid through his skin – to take back the emotions that had flowed erratically from his being.

When Nereus realised what he had done to the Earth, he asked Amun for help. At first, Nereus struggled to correct his mistakes, and in his haste, the land rose too quickly from under its watery prisons, causing many parched deserts to form across the Earth. As he acquired more control, more of the Earth ascended until great mountains took shape, awash with snow.

'River, for fuck sake, man. What the fuck does it say? You're killing me here.'

'Wait,' I grumble, holding a finger close to Skye's face. I hear him groan and re-adjust his position.

Without removing my eyes from the page, the next page has a heading, titled, 'Powers.' I begin to read:

Nereus has total power over the element of water. He can manipulate it into ice, cause tsunamis, floods and monsoons. He has more of an affinity to water than he does with land, never needing oxygen as he walks beneath the waves. The water is healing to him, and is where he finds his true strength from.

Being the first emotional entity on the planet, emotions such as love and hate, anger and peace, happiness and sadness, envy and goodwill and all the other hundreds of traits that had nowhere to be stored, were encased in all the individual cells of Nereus's body, knowing they would be safe and protected, surrounded by water. However, two escaped. Love and Anger. These emotions dominated him, intensifying his physical needs.

I lift my eyes from the book. Shocked. Stunned. Breathless. Wordless. There is no denying it – I am some form of Nereus … re-incarnated.

'Wow.'

'Wow, what?' says Skye, ready to burst at any moment.

Ready to unload it all, I tell Skye what it says.

He sits back and runs his hands through his hair. 'Shit yeah. That's so cool. Mine was pretty similar. A quick rundown of the Elementar and the powers and some other stuff, but I didn't get a poem.' He pouts his lips. 'And did it make any sense to you?'

'Totally, especially the part about the physical need.' Skye chokes with laughter. 'Yeah, don't know how you've put up with it so long. It must be a real downer, busting to get into bed with every chick you meet.'

I've never mentioned that to him. 'How do you know that?'

A tight smile pulls at Skye's lips. 'Ummm …' A moment of dread rips through me. He starts to tap his fingers against his trainers. 'I can, sort of, zero into your thoughts through the airwaves.' He recoils a little.

'YOU WHAT?'

165

'It's like a direct passage into your thoughts. I can't help it. It's part of the AirWhisperer's power. I can't turn it off.'

I stand up, not giving a shit about the book, which falls to the ground with a heavy thud. I step away from the fire.

'All this time, you've been able to read my mind and you haven't said anything?'

Skye picks up the book and lays it gently on top of a log before getting to his feet. 'Don't get all high and mighty with me about intruding into people's heads, Fabio. Not when you do exactly the same.'

He knows I can read emotions. 'How?'

'That night, after you left the Cage of Death, I followed you back to that sleazy motel.'

My heart stops working. '*What*?'

'I was outside and I heard your thoughts. I heard what you said to that chick about no kissing. I saw what was under her dress in your thoughts when she ripped it off.'

'I can't believe this,' I spit through my teeth. 'All this time, you've been spying on me.'

Skye squints into the distance, to where darkness looms and shadows meet. He doesn't move. Doesn't speak.

My temper surges. '*Well*?'

He snaps to, confused. 'Have you ever dreamt with your eyes open before?'

Now *I'm* confused. 'What the hell are you on about? Quit the games and answer the damn question.'

He blinks several times. Shakes his head. Breathes in slowly. 'I wasn't spying. Not really. Well, ok, yes, kind of, but not all the time. I …'

'*Enough.*'

'I had to be sure you were the one,' he says, taking a cautious step away from me. There's still a light-hearted tone to his voice.

All the feelings of brotherhood dry up and any emotional breakthrough I might've had now lays around me in torn up pieces.

166

'I can't fucking believe you. First, you play all these stupid, childish games with me, sending me off looking for clues that you already have the answers to and not having the guts to be up front with me, all the while, sneaking around my house, stealing from me and listening in on private thoughts and conversations. Who the hell do you think you are?'

A darkness grows in Skye's eyes. A shadow. A cloud of unspeakable terror. Distant thunder rolls in from the east, bringing with it a blast of icy wind that hits me in the face and chest, knocking me back a step. And then is gone.

'Don't be so naïve.' His voice has no light. No shade. No tone. The voice of another. Someone I don't know. Someone I don't think I want to know. 'You think your thoughts just disintegrate after you're done with them. Hell no, they travel on airwaves and guess what … I can pick them up. It's not pretty and I'm not apologising for it. You've got no idea what I have to deal with, day in day out. So, stop thinking of yourself for once in your miserable life, and get over it.'

Our cosy little camping trip is over. I don't give a shit that he has no way to get home. With his talents I'm sure he can come up with something.

He takes a breath, the lightness returning to his face. 'And the redhead …'

'*Don't* even go there,' I threaten, my voice close to breaking.

'I get it. You're drawn to her, like I'm drawn to you. If you've been dreaming about her non-stop, like this moment has been etched in my brain, bringing us together, it leads me to believe one thing.' I draw my fist back ready, regardless of whether he can stop me or not.

'I think she's the FlameMaker,' he blurts out.

Whether he's read my mind or come to the conclusion himself, it does ring true for me. 'She escaped from a fire that killed her parents, didn't she? We're all being brought together, for a reason. Don't let your anger drive me away. I think we were meant to meet, and I think we're meant to go and find Ember.'

'I don't want you anywhere near her.'

'Why? Are you worried she might like me more than you?'

I am burning up with rage, my fuel the worst fury I've felt in a long time. Anger, nestled in my heart, is winning this fight. And I'm letting it. It's taking over. Doing its thing. Doing what it always does – pushes people away, turns friends into strangers, girls into nobody's. But like desire, the will to stop it is too strong.

I need to leave.

'Not on your life. If that book is anything to go by and what you're saying is all true, then she's meant to be with me.'

'Can you hear yourself, champ. She's *meant* to be with me. What about free will? What if she doesn't like you? What if she sees through your emotional rat-trap? What then?'

'Just. Keep. Out. Of. My. Head.' I say the words slowly so he won't misinterpret their meaning.

'I will if you will.'

I walk over to the tent and pick up my bag. He can have the tent. I just want to leave. 'I'm outta here. Thanks for the history lesson, but I think I can handle this one on my own.'

'How am I supposed to get home?' Skye throws his arms in the air. 'You can't do this.'

'And that's my problem because ... put your cape on, Batman, and fly.'

I click the car sensor and open the door.

I don't hear Skye approach.

'Fine. Let it rule you. Let yourself be the monster. But it will never change you unless *you* want to change.'

I grab my bag and chuck it in the car.

'One more thing before you go ...' I turn, resting my hand on the roof of the car.

'If she is the FlameMaker, it is vital that she come to

that conclusion by herself, without help or persuasion.'

His face is deadly serious.

I'm curious. 'Why?'

'Because in order to gain control of who she is and why, she must come to this understanding on her own terms, and besides it says so in the book. You can't go off half-cocked and offload this on her. She'll run a mile. She won't believe you and that then puts us all at risk. Shit, dude, it's taken months for you to come around to the idea. You need to swear an oath. It says so on my page that we do.' I want to ask him how he knows all this, but not wanting to be near him another minute, I concede.

'What?'

'An oath. A bond between two brothers. I don't mean in blood or anything. You just have to swear that you will not tell Ember who she is or who we are, and in return I will do the same.'

I grind my teeth together. It could be another ploy, another of his games, but if it's not, I could be responsible for a lot more than leaving him to find his own way home. I hold out my hand in good faith. 'If she is the FlameMaker, then I have an addition to that oath. You have to promise not to pursue her, and that *I* am to make full contact with her without you leaning over me, listening in on my thoughts.'

Skye deliberates for a second and then thrusts out his hand. 'Deal. But it's not the last you'll see of me. I know we're all being called together for something.'

THIRTEEN

I finish setting the table and go back to stirring the spaghetti sauce, adding a few dried herbs just like Wally does. I hate cooking, but I need to make a real effort here. Tonight's conversation is going to be tough. Asking him to uproot his life here and move down south with me isn't going to be pretty or easy. But it has to happen, and me cooking his favourite meal might sweeten the deal.

God, I hope it will.

His early morning text said he'd be home by six.

I check the clock. I've got five minutes.

'Smells great,' comes a voice behind me a minute or two later. I didn't hear the door.

I walk towards him, offering him my hand. His shirt looks a little crumpled from the three hour drive and his eyes tired. His hair, parted, combed, is immaculate as always.

'Good to have you back,' I say over his shoulder as he pulls me in for an awkward man-hug.

'Have I got time for a shower?' he asks, frowning at something behind me.

170

I turn to see steam billowing out of the pasta pan. I rush over and remove it from the heat. He doesn't really have time. Everything is ready. But I say yes anyway.

'Be back in a jiffy.' Wally picks up his bag and heads upstairs.

I grate a chunk of parmesan, trying to ignore the nerves that are trying to rob me of my appetite. *Would he come with me? Would he move house, town and county ... for my sake?* I wish I had Skye's book with me as proof of who I am, just in case I need it, but for now, I hope Wally will trust me on blind faith.

The sound of the water shutting off upstairs spurs me into action. I plate up the pasta and take it to the table. I sit down and wait, too anxious to even steal one of the buttered French stick slices. Knowing how much Wally loves the ambience of candles, I jump up and light the three candles on the dresser and quickly return to my seat. The look on his face when he finally makes his entrance is that of surprise and humour. He joins me at the table and reaches over for a piece of bread. I sit frozen to the seat, unable to move.

'Looks like you've gone to a lot of trouble here.' He tears into the bread, dipping it into his sauce before taking more bites.

'Oh, you know,' I say casually.

'Relax, son,' says Wally, a soft giggle tickling his throat as he speaks. 'I'm coming with you.'

At first, I'm not sure I hear him right, but his exuberant smile is still there as I race around the table and hug him out of his chair. 'Take it easy, take it easy. I do want to get down there in one piece, you know.'

'Sorry, Wal.' I let go of him and return to my chair. 'What made you change your mind?' My appetite has miraculously returned.

'Actually, it was something your friend, Skye said to me the other day.'

In mid-chew, I suddenly stop and look up. 'What did he say?' A mountain of things run through my mind.

'Just that we were all children in our own right still and that sometimes we don't choose when those rights are given up.' I place my fork down, the same time he does, to listen. 'He told me his parents were killed too, and it kind of got me thinking about your parents. They certainly weren't the perfect mother and father, and there were many times I saw you go without.' I look around at the lavish furniture and expensive decor. 'I don't mean money, River. I mean their time and affection. I don't like to speak ill of the dead, but I think it's time for you to hear this.' I feel a frown bearing down on me. 'Whenever I would come over for business dinners, I saw the look in your eyes as your father pushed you away, too busy to spend even a second of his time with you. And your mother was no better, always out at one of her auxiliary meetings. I don't think the woman had an emotional bone in her body.'

My jaw clenches.

'I could see you becoming more and more withdrawn. Of course, I never said anything back then. I mean, who was I to say? I'd never had kids.' Wally lifts his fork and twists some spaghetti into his mouth before resting it back on the plate again. 'The way I see it is, you never had the chance to outgrow your parents and leave the nest on your own accord like most kids do, which is why I think you still need a parent-type around. They were taken from you, abruptly I might add, and so now, if you need me, I'm here.' Wally takes in a long, slow breath. 'I know I said you were a man with your own journey ahead of you, but for a reason even I can't explain, I know I'm supposed to come with you. Maybe it's because I don't know how to let go. I wondered about that too, let me tell you. Maybe I still need *you* around? But whatever the reason, I'm in for the long haul.'

I'm having another emotional moment, I think. My throat feels sore, kind of clogged up, I think, like I want to talk but I don't know what to say, what words to put together because I might be happy and sad at the same time, if I only knew what they truly felt like. And there's something pressing behind my eyes too, a stinging, burning feeling that begs to be released but I don't have the instructions, don't have the built-in knowledge that should trigger immediately, telling my body what to do.

To cry.

Nobody has ever spoken to me like that before.

'Wal ...' My voice breaks off.

'Now don't get blubbery with me, lad. Give me the lowdown? What am I in for?' I can tell Wally is struggling to keep it together because he is looking everywhere else but right at me. I have only seen him cry once. I came down the stairs to get a drink late one night and found him crouched near the kitchen cupboards, his head in his hands, sobbing uncontrollably. He didn't see me and I've never asked him about it. It was just after he moved in here.

A weak smile teases my lips. 'How do you feel about being my butler?'

With a mouthful of food, Wally coughs. 'I have to say, I wasn't expecting that.'

'Look, I have to pretend to be her age, right? So I can go to school with her.' The whole idea of being twenty by the time we arrive in Gloucestershire is making me a little … uncomfortable, considering she is still a minor. 'And the plan is, that after my parents died, my Uncle Terry and Aunt Annabeth took me in, exactly like they did. I want to stick as close to the truth as possible, and by telling her they're photographers, which they are anyway, and always on some shoot somewhere, which they were, you, Wally the butler, have been appointed to watch over me.'

'It sounds a little flimsy,' says Wally, taking another piece of bread and pushing his empty plate away.

'I know, and I hate that I'm lying to her, but it's the only way.' My heart is racing. 'Telling her, I'm a twenty year old who has moved all the way down here because I've been dreaming about her for ten years, isn't exactly normal either. She'll run a hundred miles, just like you said. And accidentally bumping into her and then trying to start a random conversation, to be honest, scares the shit out of me. I don't think I'm capable of that. Plus, she's a minor.' I am rambling. I slow my thoughts and inhale long and deep. 'Being at school, I can *ease* in to it and take my time. It won't matter if I come across nervous or immature because most teens are like that anyway, plus I will be on a more even playing field with her, giving us time to get to know each other. Talking to girls and dating them is a whole new ballgame for me, you said it yourself.'

Wally sighs. 'I can see where you're coming from, son, but I still think the lies will be your undoing. Why not just tell her the truth – that I am your guardian. Why the whole butler scenario?'

I've thought long and hard about this. 'Because if she asks about why it didn't work out with Terry and Annabeth, I'll still have to lie. She definitely won't want anything to do with me if I tell her the truth. The trouble I was in, and all that. You remember what happened with me, right?'

'Yes, lad. I remember. It wasn't a good time for you.'

'Right. Either way, a lie is imminent.'

Wally scratches his chin. 'But somewhere down the track, you're going to have to have that conversation with her. If things get serious.'

I drop my head. 'I know, I know. But at least she will have given me a chance. Wal, I don't know what I'll do, if she says she's not interested.'

My heart recognises the panic, the pain. Beating then not. Waiting, stalling, and then rushing to play catch up with a thousand erratic pulses, returning it back to me, used up and worthless. I've tried on so many different scenarios and they all suck, as much as the next one. Whichever way I tell the story, there will be a lie. I don't want to have to tell her about the hundreds of girls I've had sex with, or the binge drinking, the all-night parties,

174

the fact that I'm three years older than her, that I have a criminal record, for breaking and entering, theft and assault. These don't paint a very enticing picture of me.

Wally gets up. His face is grim. His hand falls to my shoulder and pats me there. His voice, thin, papery, like it might tear at any moment. 'Son, if that is what life has in store for you, there is nothing you can do to change it. All you can do is choose the road with the least amount of traffic.'

'And that's just it. I don't feel like I have a choice. Either way is a bad situation. I'll get hit by a bus or a lorry, whatever comes first.' A sigh comes out and I drop my head. I am sinking. If, and when she finds out, I hope she understands it's all coming from a place of love and nothing else.

'Alright. Let's leave it for now. Something might come up. First things first. We need to find a house,' says Wally, a little brighter.

'And preferably with an indoor pool because we still have *that* problem to deal with,' I add.

Wally nods nervously. 'Get a good night's sleep and we'll start fresh in the morning.'

Two weeks come and go. So much has happened and yet nothing has happened. Wally ended up finding the perfect house for us, complete with an indoor pool for the bargain price of a little under two million pounds, exactly the limit Mr Freeman had set for me. It's less than twenty minutes from Ember's house and only a short walk to the school. Wally reckons it had our name all over it, like it was fate or something. I don't know about that, although the paperwork and Legals are going ahead so smoothly, it's like I'm being tugged along, knowing that everything is happening as it should be.

The rest of my life has fallen into obscurity. For one, the beast is unusually quiet. A nervous tremor has lived inside me for over a week now, a numb panic clinging onto every thought that comes, every word I want to say.

It's like each day I am holding my breath, waiting, waiting for the pain to start, for the primal urges to take over. I fooled myself into believing that the extra time I'm spending in the pool is the reason for the decline in my need for sex. But that isn't so. Or that maybe the breakthrough I had at the lake with Skye is the reason that I learned to tame H!M, perhaps discovered a way to deceive H!M.

I've never been more wrong.

Only last night He hissed in my ear good times are coming and to prepare For the ultimate conquest. I realise I am merely a puppet to be taken out and played with when desired. I know that now, and I'm truly fearful for what is to come … for that first time I come face to face with Ember. The first words I say to her, because I know He will be right beside me in my pocket, manipulating and controlling like always.

I have to stay strong.

I can't let H!M in.

I won't let H!M win.

To make matters worse, I get the distinct impression Serena is up to something. She hasn't answered any of my calls, which is very unusual for her, and even avoided me at the pool with a couple of offhanded comments of being too busy. The fact that she knows how long I can hold my breath for, concerns me. She is another problem I'll have to resolve before I leave here. I've had to alternate between Siobhan and Sophie which I hate because I wanted to cut ties with both of them before the move. Now, they are more in to me than ever.

But all this pales to what I am about to face - the hardest part of my transition into my seventeen year old self again – a fake birth certificate to enable me to enrol at school. And there is only one person who can get that for me – Iris Perkins.

Standing outside her apartment, I contemplate my next

visit. Last week I paid off one more of my sessions with her, leaving me in her debt by three. It was a call, right out of the blue, 7am to be precise. The sex was nothing out of the ordinary this time, no fanfare or fireworks …just a good old-fashioned release that left me wanting, which kind of caught me off-guard. I was banking on the standard thirty hours of bliss to tie me over. The traditional glass of tomato juice, I threw up next to the wheel of my car.

I'm guessing now my sex-debt is about to increase, but to what number I can only imagine. A fake birth certificate definitely warrants double figures.

I knock three times and hear movement inside. Air rushes into my face as the door flies open. She doesn't look surprised to see me.

'So, what do I owe this *unexpected* and rather late night call?' Iris squints her eyes at me as I stand in shadow of her apartment door. 'I thought I stated quite clearly that your debt was to be repaid on my own terms.'

I have already thought of my way around her 'no business policy at home' rule. I turn on the charm, sensing the beast standing to attention in my skin. 'I'd like to increase my balance.'

Her eyes sparkle. 'Come in.'

I head into her stone-cold lounge room, to see Lawrence the doorman, slipping a t-shirt over his head.

'Sorry, I didn't know you were busy. I can come back.'

'No need. Lawrence was just leaving.' The young guy regards me for a few seconds, picks up his leather jacket and leaves without saying a word. Iris sits down, taking the red chair, again leaving me with the white. Her journal, the one she always writes in whenever there is an arrangement or transaction between us, is resting in her lap. For the first time, I wonder *who* and *what* else is in there.

I get straight down to it, hoping there will be enough time to redeem one of those dreaded half hours. 'I was

177

wondering if you knew of anyone that could get a fake birth certificate.'

Iris purses her lips and then chews at them. 'I might. What would it be worth to you ... and me?' Wearing a black, silky camisole that falls almost to her feet, the thin straps exposing her shoulders and plunging neckline are an unwelcome distraction. She gets up and stands in front of me. A perfume I still can't decipher, follows her. My control starts to waiver.

The word, 'A lot,' is all I can muster. 'Name your price.'

'Very well. It'll take me a few weeks to rustle up, but it shouldn't be a problem.' She brushes her hair back from her face and positions herself at my feet, very subserviently. 'Now to the fee.'

I hold my breath. *How many more times will I have to have sex with this woman to settle my bill? Ten? Fifty?*

'I want you to deposit ten thousand pounds into my personal account.' I must be frowning for her to ask if I have a problem with that.

'You want *money*?' I can't believe what I'm hearing.

'I have expenses, the same as you.' I doubt that. Money isn't a problem for me, no more than it is for her. I know it well and she reeks of it. I have four hundred thousand pounds in my personal account, just lying idle for me to find something to spend it on. I could transfer it over without having to notify anyone about it.

'Fine,' I say, relieved.

She frantically scribbles down more notes. 'Good.' Iris looks up and clicks off her pen. 'I'll text you my bank account details tomorrow.' At first I think she's about to kick me out because she stares at me for so long, not blinking and not saying a word. 'But, while I've got you here ...'

'No problem,' I say, pulling her into my lap, all the while thinking, four down two to go, four down two to go.

I'm nearly free.

Iris stays true to her word. Around midday, her text message comes through with her bank details. I stop off at the branch on my way home from the pool and transfer the money as though it's just another bill. Things are going to plan. The house settles in three weeks and ready to move into three days after that, giving me a full week in Gloucestershire before school starts. The removalists are booked in for the 24th of August, the day after my birthday, and I am enrolled at school, on the proviso I produce my birth certificate to the office on my first day.

Everything is set, all I have to do is wait.

With that waiting comes nervousness and worry. Skye has disappeared off the planet, which as much as I hate to admit it, I'm a little concerned about. He's been the pebble in my shoe for the last few months and all of a sudden, I'm back to walking without a limp. I haven't contacted him since that night by the lake and he hasn't stopped by or texted me either, which is totally out of character for him, even though it's what we both agreed on. I can't help wondering what he's up to or if he's ok. The WaterLover conundrum still bothers me, but with the prospect of Ember becoming a reality rather than a dream, the whole paranormal not-of-this-planet persona hanging around my neck is nothing compared to the adventure I'm about to embark upon.

Every few minutes, Wally checks his watch and looks out of the window.

'Where is he? Simon is never this late.'

He's referring to our postman.

He adjusts the curtain and steps back. 'I don't know how you're so calm about all this.'

For the tenth time, I repeat my answer. 'He'll *be* here.' I'm anxious to see the fake birth certificate too but I can't let on. Can't show him I'm falling apart with worry. That I haven't slept more than ten hours in the last week. All he needs to know; is everything is cool and that I have everything in hand. He's already grey enough.

Wally paces. Three steps one way looks out the window and three steps back, a frown picking its way across his forehead. For a quick second, my resolve falters and doubt creeps in that I've done the wrong thing getting him involved in all this. Poor Wally is too straight for his own good and certainly doesn't belong in my world.

From the study, the grandfather clock, strikes nine. Wally tuts and glances at his watch again.

'Chill out, Wal. It'll probably come tomorrow.'

He wipes his forehead with the back of his hand. 'Donna from the post office said it would arrive today because you have to sign for it …because it's a *legal* document, and I assured her you would be here.' He raises his eyebrows at the word legal.

The doorbell rings.

Wally is there in a blink. After a brief hello with Simon and a rushed signature later, he eagerly leans over my shoulder as I slide my finger slowly under the flap of the envelope.

Before the certificate is totally free of the envelope, he snatches it out of my hands and turns it over and over, eventually wafting it in front of his face. 'Looks genuine enough.'

I let out an exaggerated laugh. 'And how many fake birth certificates have you seen?'

He raises his eyebrows and gives me one of his *I'm older than you which means I know more than you* look. 'It even has the little stamp on the back,' he says, handing it back to me. I let out a huge sigh. 'Wal, I only have to fool some school secretary … not Scotland Yard.'

Wally hums under his breath.

This is the last hurdle transitioning me in to my new life.

Somehow, without me realising it, the months leading up to this have turned into weeks and the weeks into days. This has become real now, and the thought of seeing

Ember in the next few days feels like I'm about to step off a tall cliff with jagged rocks at the bottom. I am about to be torn apart.

FOURTEEN

THE day of the move arrives.

And I want to be sick.

I want to rewind the last six months.

I want to forget this whole stupid idea.

Because if I do, my heart will beat like it used to. Will be numb like it once was. Will do the one thing it's meant to do – beat - and keep me alive. Nothing more. No extras. No emotions.

This *feeling* stuff sucks ... big time. I've never known anxiety. Never understood uncertainty. Yet here I stand, my life packed into the back of a removalist lorry, my father's business associate looking more worried than I've seen in a long while, waiting by the car, ready to leave, and me ... I have no idea who I am, how I feel, or who I should be.

I *feel* changed.

But I'm not sure if I'm ready to trust it.

I know what I'm capable of, and that arsehole, could return at any moment. I find I can't keep a straight thought in my head.

I look back at the house, realising I can't put this off any longer. I lock the front door, refusing to spend one second more in a house that means nothing more than bricks and mortar to me, and say a silent *good riddance* to a life of solitude and pain.

Four hours later, with a minor pile up on the M42 and a quick stop for a bite to eat, we pull up in front of a magnificent Victorian house, or perhaps to some, it might look like a manor. The removalists are already well underway carting in my parents' furniture.

I turn into the horseshoe-shaped driveway. 'Bigger than I thought,' I mumble, wondering if this is going to be a help or a hindrance to the plan. Not a single tiny pebble out of place. No leaf has dared to drop.

'It does have to house a swimming pool, don't forget.'

Yes. I can't wait to see that.

I've never been excited about a house before, and even though it's paid for with my parents' money, it feels more mine than any gift they'd ever given me.

The house has been built from flat, grey stone and has two large pitched gables; one in the middle of the house accentuating an elaborate white porch, and the other on the far right with a double garage underneath. The white colonial styled windows, upstairs and down, vary in shape and size adding an almost *regal* look to the house.

'C'mon,' says Wally.

We cross the silvery pebbled driveway and stop at the front door. A long, golden rod hangs next to a curly bell.

I poke Wally in the ribs. 'Jeeves, there's someone at the door.'

'Oh, very funny, River,' retorts Wally, testing it out. The faint sound of chimes come from inside the house. 'I like the Weeping Willow at the front though. Nice touch.'

Wally grins, looking pleased with himself.

I take a step back and examine it. It's nice, as far as willow trees go, not that I've ever really taken the time to consider trees before, but it looks kind of poetic, kind of romantic and summery, somewhere I could imagine Ember and I laying beneath, discussing our favourite ice-cream flavours. A few taller trees hug two stone pillars at the entrance of the driveway, failing dismally to hide a large black gate.

Wally lets out a low whistle as he cranes his neck to look up at the *almost* mansion. 'How much did you get this for again?'

I look at him in surprise. Normally he never asks such things unless we're discussing the monthly budget. My family's assets and personal money are off limits in Wally's world.

'A steal, really, according to Mr Freeman. After taxes and stamp duty, it came up just short of fifty quid.'

Wally rolls his eyes and shakes his head at me.

We head into the main foyer to discover large white tiles on the floor, white panelled walls instead of your average paint or wallpaper, a massive wide staircase and a chandelier to boot. Not bad as a first impression. The house certainly casts a pure and honest reflection of its owner, and not the lying criminal that I am.

I continue to walk from room to room, stopping briefly to admire the décor. It's all very similar, with soft pastel colours, panelled walls in every room, a kitchen my mother would have killed her own family for, not that she ever cooked … it was all for show, and a study twice the size of my fathers. But it's the pool I really want to see. The last door I open steals my breath.

Inside, is a thirty-foot pool. The deep blue calls out to me, tempting me in, begging for me to join it. The walls and floor are the colour of terracotta and the full-length window at the end of the room looks out onto a field. Was it worth every penny? Hell YES!

I hold back, knowing I have other things that need to be done first, and to be honest, the urge really isn't there right now … which worries me. I never thought I'd hear myself say that. Twelve months ago, I would've cut off my left ear to have one day of zero sex drive.

I leave while I can and backtrack through the house.

'You need anything out of the car? I left my phone in there,' I call out, not knowing which room Wally is in.

'No thanks. Hey, River. You should come and see this. It has its own library.'

'I know,' I yell back, making my way to the front door. I had been amazed about that too.

I pass two guys in mauve t-shirts with REST Removal Company on the front and click the car open. I reach across the front seat and make a grab for my phone.

'Need any help moving in?' calls a voice behind me. I close the car door just as a lanky looking kid in fluro shorts and singlet walks towards me, his hand extended. 'I'm Chris Rotherham. I live two houses down.' He grins and instantly reminds me of Daniel. Same hair, same goofy innocence. Shit! Daniel! Who I hadn't even told I was leaving.

He has a firm grip for someone with such long, stringy arms. 'No, but thanks. They've got it under control,' I say, gesturing to the removalists.

'You still at school,' asks Chris.

Here's my first test. 'Sure am.'

'What year are you in?' he asks, following me into the house. Chris stops when we walk into the main foyer. 'Wow. I've always wanted to see inside this place. It's frigging huge. It's got a pool, hasn't it?'

'Yeah,' I say, heading towards the kitchen. I open the fridge. 'Wanna coke?' I had Josephine, the real estate agent, make sure the cupboards and fridge were stocked for our arrival. She didn't disappoint. It's amazing what someone will do for an extra hundred quid in their pocket.

'Thanks.' I lob him a can.

'Year eleven,' I say confidently, answering his question from before.

Chris grins again. 'Excellent, same as me.'

Wally huffs past me with an armful of cushions. 'You wanna lend a hand your royal highness?' he says around a laugh.

Chris immediately looks uncomfortable. 'Yeah, dude you look busy. I should go. Me and a couple of mates are meeting up tomorrow though, if you're interested?'

Wally raises an eyebrow in an encouraging way and I automatically feel the pressure to respond.

'Sure. Why not?'

And that's what happened the next day.

Between emptying packing boxes, I stole a few hours to socialise *teenage style* with Chris. He showed me around the area and introduced me to his friends. Marcus seemed okay, but Kaleb and Brock spent more time arguing about who had the coolest hairstyle that I headed off early. My desire to swim was back, except, when I finally got home, the need, urge, whatever name it uses now, wasn't there. I swam anyway but it was like water and I were strangers.

Four days pass and my need to swim has all but vanished.

Until now.

I knew then, I was running on borrowed time. Today, I've been in the pool over seven hours. You see, whilst I wasn't watching. Whilst my attention was elsewhere, trying to set up each room, trying to make everything look perfect, trying to make friends and ease my way into my deceptive life here, pain has slowly been seeping in through the pores of my skin, reminding me of who is in charge. I didn't totally notice it at first. A cramp here. A twinge there. I put it down to being busy.

Then last night.

The beast returned.

I woke suddenly at 2am with the most excruciating abdominal pain I've ever experienced. For an hour I couldn't do anything but rock from side to side, sweat drenching my pillow, fingers gripping my sheets. When I finally did make it down to the pool it took four hours to take the edge off. I couldn't swim, couldn't stretch out, only bobbed about in the water like a shark attack victim.

186

Exhausted, I managed to crawl back to bed to rest.

But now I need a girl.

It's the only choice I have to reset.

But most of all, I need to give myself a fighting chance with school starting up in two days. I need to be at my strongest and it's already been six days since my last session with Sophie. **He** is bursting for the chance to prove **His** power.

I towel off and walk back into the main house, texting as I go. I want to see if Chris feels like catching a movie tonight. A cinema is the second-best place to pick up a chick. I can't rely on my usual, find a bar and turn on the charm for the nearest bimbo, because I'm supposed to be seventeen and I can't run the risk of running into a teacher or worse.

Chris texts back that he can make it and the rest of the day is spent in the pool, doing what I can to keep a grip on reality.

By 8pm, I am literally a shadow in my own skin. I have all but rusted out from the inside. Feel empty. Feel useless. Feel fatigued to the point every step is an effort, every smile another slice of pain.

It all comes down to one thing … I need a girl. I had contemplated driving the three hours back home and casually dropping in on Iris or Sophie, but I'm not too confident I'd make the trip in one piece. As usual, I have left my run too late. Tonight, is all I have left, because tomorrow … I am meeting the girl I've been dreaming about my whole life.

'Don't be late, River,' calls out Wally as Chris and I head out the door. 'You do have *school* in the morning.' I hear a titter of laughter coming from the lounge room.

The one thing I hadn't thought of buying, was a less conspicuous car. The BMW and Audi, which was driven down by paid drivers, arrived a couple of days ago and sit side by side in the garage. Chris almost has a seizure when he sees the options before us.

'The Audi,' he says, tentatively reaching out to touch the boot.

'Can't. It's my dad's.'

'Or the BMW,' says Chris laughing. 'I'm not fussy. I haven't even got my provisional licence yet. And here you are, driving your own car.'

Shit, I didn't think of that either. 'I got it earlier than everyone else because my old school offered a drivers Ed course.' I swallow down the lie with ease.

I zap the car and we get in. 'Did I ever tell you, you're the coolest mate I've ever had?'

I turn to look at him running his hand over the cream leather seats. 'Haha. Buckle up.'

By the time we arrive, the cue out the front of the cinema is just what I was hoping for. Time to let the beast loose to do its work.

I decide to look for a secluded backstreet rather than park in the busy car park. If I have to drive to some dodgy motel half an hour away, I want to make sure to keep a low profile.

Chris and I head up the street, and as sickening as it is, I turn up the charm, the beast champing at the bit with every step.

A brunette, not really my type, is the first to spot me as we tack onto the end of the cue. Chris's face is nothing short of amusing as the young woman in her early twenties approaches me, slips her arm through mine and tucks a small piece of paper into my hand. She will do.

'Whoooah,' says Chris after she leaves. 'Do you know her?

'Nope.' I fake a laugh.

'Did she just give you her number?'

I unfold the paper and look at it. 'Yep.'

He chuckles. 'God, did I ever tell you, you're ...' The cue starts to move.

'Coolest friend I've ever had. Err, yeah,' I finish off

for him.

Already considering option number two, I turn to see a blonde checking me out. She is standing three feet in front of the brunette who gave me her number and who can't keep her eyes off me.

But something distracts me, turns my head, awakens my senses. It's the distinct, sharp aroma of Iris Perkins's perfume.

My body becomes a statue. A corpse. The steel lamppost next to me. I scan over the heads, inspecting every face as my heart tries to thump its way out of my chest. Palms wet. Heat prickles the back of my neck as I look left and right. The feel of her eyes on me, turns my skin into different layers of cold.

'You ready?' asks Chris. The cue has moved, and he is waiting for me to catch up.

'Yep. Sure.'

We venture inside and pay for our tickets, before heading into the darkness to find seats.

The second I sit down; my phone vibrates in my pocket. I quickly change it to silent before seeing who the message is from.

'Get fucked,' I mutter under my breath. It's none other than Iris Perkins.

I glance over my shoulder, expecting to see her leaning over the seat behind, holding her phone. The message says: *I want you here in twenty minutes.*

Without deliberately meaning to, I not only failed to tell Daniel and Serena I was leaving, but Iris too. The more I see the selfishness of my parents, the more I see it in myself. I send Daniel a text saying that I'd moved down south and I'd explain later. His message comes back less than a minute later with a thumbs up. Serena and Iris will take a little more tact.

There is no way I can be there in twenty minutes, not even in two hours and somehow, telling her this, isn't going to whip her into a frenzy of excitement like I'd done all the other times she'd summoned me. I have to think fast.

And then it comes to me.

I text her the following message: *Sorry Iris, I can't make it. I have the flu.* It's a feeble excuse and not one of my best, but it will give me a week or so to think up a solution. I wait five minutes. There is no reply.

The movie begins with a traditional 'shoot 'em up' cop scene, but my mind is back to the hunt. The **beast** squirms irritably every time I shift position, not wanting to be held down any longer. I need to release some tension.

Keeping my phone well-guarded so no one can see, I send the brunette a text asking her to meet me outside.

'Need a piss,' I whisper to Chris as I get up.

'What? It's only just started,' Chris answers.

I shrug and step over people until I reach the end of the row and then fly down the stairs and out into the foyer. I don't have to wait long for her.

'Too irresistible, huh?' she asks confidently. I agree, but it's the temptation that lures me out ... not her. 'My name's Brittany. What's yours?'

Whenever *they* ask, I always give *them* the same response. 'Rob.' It's a much easier name to forget, than River.

'Well, where are we going, Rob?' Brittany's eyes become more and more glassier by the minute. 'Do you wanna get outta here. Do you have a car?' I don't particularly want to take her anywhere and risk the chance of someone seeing me. This place isn't like Sheffield, where I could be a little more flippant about who I see and where. Here, Ember could know people.

My gaze pans around the room and stops at the door of the girl's toilets.

She catches my drift. 'Could be fun,' she says, 'I'll go and check.' She leaves and is back within seconds, rolling her eyes and blotting her lip gloss with her finger. 'Someone's already beaten us to it.' She lets out a high pitched laugh. I look to the boys' toilets. 'I'm not going

190

in there. It stinks.' I draw in a breath and bear down to keep the monster at bay. My tolerance is dropping ... rapidly.

'I know. Follow me.' She grabs my hand and leads me through a back door to the cinema and out onto the very street I'd parked on. Although it's still relatively light, the alleyway next to it is dark and fairly secluded. It will do. And from the eagerness of the devil climbing out of my skin to get to her, it will be over quickly too.

She reaches under her skirt, pulls off her knickers, rolls them up and pops them in her handbag. The bag falls to the floor as she runs her hands over my biceps and shoulders.

'Mmmmm. I'm so glad you work out. I love to do it standing up.' I can't wait another second.

Zipper down, trousers around my thighs, I can barely hold myself together as she straddles her legs either side of my hips. Her tits rub against my chest with every thrust, but this isn't foreplay, this isn't a moment to indulge. This isn't even pleasure. It's a release and nothing else.

However, not the excitement of having sex in a public place, or the impending euphoria that is only seconds away, I can't dismiss the very real presence of Iris Perkins's perfume again. It definitely isn't coming from Brittany. Her neck and throat convince me of that as she hangs off me.

She moans her pleasure into my chest as the beast takes a bow.

Ten minutes later I re-join Chris in the main theatre.

'Long piss,' he whispers as I sit down.

'Yeah.' I'm about to add that I stopped to get a drink and popcorn too, then realise I have neither with me, so I leave it at that. Feeling slightly better, I relax back into my seat and watch the remainder of the movie.

It's after eleven when I get home and I'm anxious to get in a few hours swimming before I turn in.

Everything hangs on tomorrow.

FIFTEEN

'YOU nervous?' Chris asks as we head through the school gates the next morning. He is rummaging through his backpack as we walk.

I am, but not about being at school. I'm nervous of seeing her, seeing her and praying to god I don't fuck it up.

'I'm good,' I manage to say, barely paying attention to him. My body has been on full alert ever since I woke, precariously balancing on the brink of life becoming everything I hoped it could be to deteriorating into a pile of ash at my feet.

4am, I woke. I swam for two hours. Couldn't eat the piece of toast that Wally had pushed under my nose several times. And now, find myself frantically scanning every person who walks past me, in front of me, behind me, desperate not to miss a single face. I'm on the look-out for that red hair.

'Shit,' mumbles Chris, veering off the pathway onto the grass. He drops his bag to the ground. 'I can't believe

I've forgotten my fucking wallet.' He pulls out three books and a mangy looking pencil case and dumps them on the ground.

I check my watch.

Anger sneaks up my spine and into my jaw. I feel it tighten. Teeth clench against each other, grinding. Becoming dust. Only five minutes remain before the bell goes.

I'm running out of time.

My bones have begun to ache in the most unusual of ways – not quite pain, but like a heaviness has set it, like it doesn't want me to go anywhere. Like I need to stand in this one spot forever and wait.

And that's when it happens.

In that solitary moment I'd indulged in self-reflection, in thinking about myself and how I'm feeling, a girl with the reddest hair I've ever seen has slipped beneath my radar and passed me.

And I didn't see her face.

My mouth opens and words come out. Not the words I should be saying or even want to say. Just words, because I can't believe I am here, right now, in this moment.

My heart is quiet, my blood, a tangle of heat and velocity.

I can't move. I might never be able to move again.

And yet, my mind has become a frenzy of crazy thoughts and dreams, not wanting to be still, no longer wanting to be contained.

I want to call out to her.

I want her to stop and look through her bag, just like Chris is, and then slowly, she will realise I am watching her and she will gaze up at me. Our eyes will meet, just like I've dreamt many times before.

I wish for my life to be broken down into freeze-frame moments where I can take all the time I need to find the right words, the right smile, the right me. Except, reality says, the clock is ticking. I haven't got all the time I need because she is still walking away from me.

I turn to Chris. 'Who's the redhead?' It isn't a question that needs an answer, not when she seems to have heard me say it.

She spins around and faces me, her hair fanning out in a blaze of coppery sunlight, her eyes scorching me until I can hardly see her.

It's her.

It's Ember.

The earth falls away from my feet, far away as though I'm standing way above it, no pulsing gravity holding me to it, just a feeling of lightness and air and thundering beats that tell me this is no dream. She is more beautiful than any photo, than any conjured memory.

I want to run up to her and pull her into my arms. Such profound ecstasy, for that is what it must be, because I can think of no other word to justify this feeling, is mounting inside me that I can hardly breathe. *I can hardly breathe.*

I want to tell her how long I've waited for this, how this moment has been tucked away in my thoughts, in my soul, for all of the sad and lonely years of my childhood. For a lifetime. For an eternity. And that now I can finally be next to her, see her with my own eyes, hear her voice if I was ever so lucky enough to have her speak to me. Just to tell her ... that now ... I belong in her world.

Until this point, my whole life has been put on hold, but now my life can now begin. It can really begin.

A shadow passes over me.

Disrupts my pleasure.

Disconnects my lifeline.

The beast rises up, stronger and more determined than I've ever felt. It wants her ... right here ... right now. Doesn't care who is watching or what people will say. *Or is that me that wants her?* I can't tell the difference, the emotion is so intense.

The monster consumes me, overriding my desires, replacing them with an insidious hunger born out of deception and greed. I can't speak. I can't even summon a simple greeting. This is nothing like the scenarios I had put together – me walking up to her with confidence and introducing myself as she shyly smiles and tells me her name. No, it's nothing like that.

It's fear and shock. Fear that if I move, I won't be able to hold back ten years of desire, and shock, because those desires can be real whenever I want them to. All I have to do is drop my defences. Let **HIM** conquer.

Her eyes continue to search mine, probing me with such intent, I wonder if she can see the evil that lay beyond them.

I want to reach out and touch her hair, just to see if it's as real as it looks. I want to run my finger across her lips and wait for her to whisper my name. I want so many things, and yet, I am in unfamiliar territory - I want to give so much of myself to her. I want her to know me, not the vicious creature that I can be, but the real me. I know then, I will do whatever I have to, to win, to be whatever she wants me to be.

In that moment as words fail me and the **beast** cries victory, she turns and walks away from me.

After much deliberation by Chris, as to how he'd left his wallet at home on the first day of school, he finally accepts some money from me for lunch, promising to pay it back the second he gets home. He shows me where the office is and waits outside while I take my fake birth certificate in, which the office lady barely looks at, and runs it through her photocopier before issuing me with a timetable.

'That was quick.' Chris falls into step with me. He points out where the science block is, where the maths and tech rooms are and stops when we arrive outside an enclosed area.

'This is F block. It's where we hang out, eat, study and pretty much ...'

I'm no longer listening.

Ember is sitting on a wooden table, talking to a girl – a girl who coincidently, would be just my type. The blonde pales in comparison to Ember but that doesn't stop me thinking about how much this girl resembles the S girls and how much I want to release my ever-increasing urge.

Chris follows my gaze. 'That's Rachel Winters. Cute, huh?'

'And the other one,' I mutter.

'Ember something or other. Riley, that's it. Ember Riley.' In that instance, she turns around and catches me staring at her for a second time. Like before, my mind becomes a jumble of words that mean nothing, that don't form sentences, that could be in another language for all I know.

My fists clench.

I can't believe this. And although my brain has deserted me, my movements haven't. I nod my head in her direction, and even at a distance, I swear I see her mouth pop open a little. But I can't claim responsibility or take credit for that gesture. My irritation has rallied my adversary and the beast smiles from within and licks its lips. I have to leave ... right now.

My second right royal fuck up.

I hang my head, figuring at this rate, I might get to speak to her in 2050.

Chris shows me to my home room, where my attendance is marked off, and after a little shuffling to and from rooms to get text books and familiarise myself with new teachers, a group of us hang around in the break-out area and wait further instructions.

I stand in the corner of a hexagonal shaped room, checking my phone for messages, while half listening to a group of guys talking about how they hate re-introducing themselves each new year in Miss Freebody's English class.

'What do you think 'the freak' Ember Riley will say

196

this year. I bet it's got nothing to do with her parents,' says a boy with top and bottom braces on his teeth.

I spin around, curious.

'I know what my question will be,' replies a ginger-haired boy with freckles to match.

A tall, lanky kid eating a bag of crisps laughs. 'You're going to ask her the same questions as last year, aren't you, Troy?'

'Yeah, so what. I want to know how she got out of the car that turned her parents into deep fried chicken. She should have been charcoaled.'

'Troy, is it?' I interrupt.

'Yeah, who wants to know?' The boy looks in my direction. 'Hey, you're the new kid, aren't you?'

I pull Troy to one side. 'My name's River and I have a delicate business proposition for you. Are you up for it?'

Troy frowns. 'What kind of proposition?'

'You know Ember Riley, right?'

His frown remains. 'I wouldn't say *know*. I mean, everyone knows what happened to her and how she's a witch, who killed her parents.'

'*Right*. Whatever.' His words anger me, cause my jaw to tense, my knuckles to rupture into rocks of steel, but I do what I have to, to find out what he knows.

'And so you're going to give me five quid if I find out her birth date?'

'Yes.' In good faith, I place the five-pound note into his hand. 'And an extra tenner if you find out anything really interesting,' I add.

Troy grins. 'Okay, deal.'

'Meet me behind the gymnasium after class.'

'Sure.' He jogs back to his friends who are already leaving.

I take off through the tunnel that separates the humanities block from the maths block, making no sense of the school map the lady from the office gave me, and continue down the path towards what looks like the

English classrooms.

I round a corner and see Ember standing side on to me, eating an apple. Wherever she is, I feel a natural compulsion to be there too, as though we are two ends of the same piece of rope.

Instantly, I freeze.

I'd convinced myself that the idea of coming across her again before lunch, was about zero, and was planning to mentally prepare my next move as I wished away my first maths class.

That is not to be.

This lack of self-confidence *thing* that has taken over is as unwelcome as it is inconvenient. It's like year three all over again.

Come on, River. Pluck up the courage and talk to the girl, I hear Wally saying in my head.

I take a look around. There are only a few kids loitering close enough to hear me fuck up the first words I will say to her. I can handle that.

I need a prop.

The bin is as good as any.

I pre-empt her next move, lift the lid and wait for her to turn around. When she does, the words I *hadn't* yet prepared, and any others that should have been there, but aren't, shrivel up against my tongue. At this rate, I might never say a word to her in my life.

Time ticks by so slowly.

And she is staring at me, a confused expression in her eyes, twitching her lips, trying to hold back a frown. Her eyes are so vibrant, almost searching, that every bone in my body breaks and heals in one single second. I've never known this face before.

I'm suddenly curious. What could she possibly be thinking? I want to ask her, but I haven't even said hello to her.

I become aware that more girls have arrived, and from the looks on their faces have noticed me too. The beast steps out from my shadow and shows himself.

198

This isn't the right moment. I want our first conversation to be perfect. I can't have a group of harpies hanging off me.

I have to leave.

Say something, just say something, I repeat over and over in my head. Words stacking up against my tongue, ready to be spilt. I open my mouth.

'I'm not standing here all day.' The moment the words are out, I want them back. I wish I could tell her that wasn't what I meant to say, the words weren't really for her, and that they weren't even said by me. Because I would have gladly stood there forever and waited for the perfect introduction. The perfect moment. Instead, the beast wraps its black fingers around my throat, squeezes until I see black.

Ember doesn't appear to be put off by my brusqueness and when she walks towards me, I deliberately hold my breath, wanting to keep one thing about her that would make our next meeting all the more complete.

Her perfume.

Her eyes smile at me and my heart aches in a way it has felt never before.

The beast slavers. He … no, *I* want her.

I replace the lid. 'Thanks,' she says, shyly, grazing her teeth against her lip.

I need to breathe.

I walk four lonely steps away from her and then stop.

I don't turn around.

I can't.

Because if I do, the urge to seduce her will win through, will override the little willpower I have left to not let the beast loose on her. As much as each step pains me, I walk away.

Maths is just as boring as it had been when I'd attended school the first time around. But this time, it's worse.

Ten times worse.

I'm not used to having girls in my class. My last school was an all-boys school. Their smitten faces, gazing at me from every corner of the classroom is beginning to freak me out. All they want is one smile. One very slight curl of my lips, and I'll have a riot on my hands.

I keep my head down the whole lesson, pushing the beast as far down inside as I can physically stand.

Mr O'Brien, my maths teacher, doesn't appear too worried about my lack of interest, or that I am a new face in his classroom. He is as Irish as shamrock, and rattles on regardless, his accent so thick he might as well be reciting limericks the entire hour, and nobody would notice the difference.

My mind begins to wander...

Maybe Wally was right, and that I've gone too far with this whole charade. School seems like a ridiculous idea now. I definitely hadn't thought it through properly. I know that now. But I can't just up and leave either. I didn't factor in a co-ed classroom or that I can't swim whenever I need to keep the temptations at bay. Swimming, whenever I want, has spoilt me, and when finally, Mr O'Brien releases us, I make a beeline for the gymnasium and head straight for the boys' changing rooms. There are showers there, but I don't have time or a towel with me.

Instead, I scoop up handfuls of water and splash my face, making sure my entire head is soaked. I then shake out the remaining water. I might as well have covered a gaping wound with a plaster for all the good it does.

With only minutes to spare and knowing I have to meet Troy; I grab my bag and circle around the gymnasium wall until I'm standing with my back to the cafeteria. I lean against the orangey-red bricks and wait with a hundred-and-one feelings all trying to break loose at once.

Troy appears a few minutes later, looking incredibly happy with himself.

'Here you go. Easy as pie.' He thrusts a note into my

200

hand.

I already have the £10 ready to give to him. 'Thanks.'

We both look up at the same time, to see Ember marching towards us, her face so dark, so menacing that a stone finds its way into my throat, into my chest, making it hard to breathe.

Before Troy takes off, I stuff the note into my back pocket. 'I hope it was worth it,' he mumbles. *Me too,* I think.

Ember cuts me down with her eyes. 'What did Troy give to you?'

I crumble. I become dust. She's never looked at me like that in my dreams. That spindly web, Wally warned me about, grows thicker by the second. I shake my head. 'I don't know what you're talking about. I don't have anything.'

The lies begin.

For her.

For me.

Her gaze skewers through me, inflicting pain in places I rarely spend time thinking about – my knees, my left elbow, the arch in my foot.

She reaches out to check my hand.

I pull away quicker than she anticipates, making her stumble forwards. Instinctively, my hand shoots out to steady her, not wanting her to fall. Only wanting to protect her. Except, for one micro-second, my hand resembles claw-like fingers, gnarly and grotesque, desperate to have one little touch of her. Startled, I drop my hand promptly.

She gathers herself. Stunned.

'I saw him give it to you. Show me your other hand.'

I open my palm, the note safely tucked away in my pocket.

'B-but, I saw him …' she mumbles, confused.

I try to act all adult-like and cool. 'I think you are mistaken.'

I hate myself.

What have I become?

Lying continuously to this beautiful girl I've fallen in love with is the most despicable thing I've ever done. Definition number thirty-five.

How will she ever trust me after this? How am I ever going to make it up to her? I don't want her to leave me like this. I can't let her walk away for a third time and not say something.

For God's sake, say something.

Anything to let her know I'm not an arsehole and that there is more to me than a lying, cheating man-whore who takes women for his own gain. I feel as close to the decay of society than is humanly possible as she mutters her apology and drops her head in shame.

She turns to leave, but before she does, her eyes flash with something that stills my breath. Breaks my bones. Brings warmth into my cold heart.

I can't let her go.

I throw out my hand, almost fainting at the instant delirious pleasure that soars through me as my skin comes into contact with hers. *She is real, she is real, she is real*, is the line being repeated inside my head.

I can feel her.

I can actually feel her.

Her skin is hot to the touch, and like her hair that reminds me of fire, the possibility that she could be the FlameMaker suddenly seems all the more real.

Her eyes hold me … accountable, in surrender, and at arm's length, and yet I can't withdraw my gaze. I am enslaved by them. They fill all the empty spaces inside me with that magic only she possesses, dispelling all logic. All sense.

I open my mouth. Words come out. 'Ember, has anyone ever told you before that your eyes are the colour of molten lava?'

Her lips part.

Her eyes widen.

She won't look away.

Can't seem to look away.

The **beast** has her cornered. Trapped.

And the only emotion I detect coming from her is fear.

Disgusted by everything I stand for; I can no longer stand in her presence.

I walk away. Head low. Heart lower.

I cut through the quadrangle and head to my science class. The pain hasn't even had time to wear off before I see her sitting at the back of the classroom. I feel her eyes on me as Mr Butcher, my science teacher, tries to make a humorous example out of me. I'm not in the mood for it, find my seat and for another lesson, I sit with my head buried in my arms.

That afternoon, I walk home alone.

A screw-up, a liar, a nobody.

Wally is standing in the kitchen, looking out of the window and drinking a cup of tea when I come in. His face, once excited, falls when he sees me. I throw my bag down and collapse into a dining chair.

'Didn't go as well as you hoped?' Small wrinkles crease around his eyes as his face winces.

'It was a total train wreck.' I drop my head onto the table with a dull thud.

'I'm sure it's not as bad as you think.' Wally takes the seat opposite me, his voice soothing. I shield my face with my arms so he can't see me.

'I fucked up. I should've listened to you, Wal, but no … I lied my way down here. I've lied to everyone that matters. I've totally ruined everything, and I might as well quit. ' I draw my head up. 'And now, I've lied directly to her face.'

Wally lets out a breath. It wasn't a *I told you so* breath like most parents do in a moment like this, it's a, *I don't know how to help you fix it* breath.

'It's only the first day, lad. What did you expect? For her to fall into your arms and pledge her soul to you?'

'No,' I mumble, 'but something more than this shitty

feeling. I fucked up so badly I don't think she'll even look at me, let alone talk to me.'

I want to offload. I want to scream and shout how unfair this prick of a life is. I want to open up and tell him about Skye and the Elementar book and let everything out. Let the words fall where they will. The urge to unleash this pressure presses against my lips.

I force it back, knowing it isn't the right time. I need a swim, and a chance to calm the **beast** that is pushing my threshold to overload.

I get up and slide the chair back under the table, while Wally continues to sit there with a helpless look on his face.

'I've fucked it, Wally. I'm a no-good piece of shit, who doesn't deserve her.'

The pool is located on the southern end of the house. I open the door and take a look around. I can't believe it's possible, but the room seems to have lost its appeal. Even the massive thirty foot pool, glistening back at me, doesn't even raise a pulse.

That can't be real. Can't be true. It's the one thing in my life that has held me, comforted me and made me feel whole.

I step out of my clothes, leaving my boxer's on, and dive in. It's going to take some time to swim off how I'm feeling.

Two hours later, I come up for air.

I look up to see a sandwich and a glass of milk has been left on the bench, beside my clothes. The time has flown and I only marginally feel better. I decide I need a game plan and the only thing I can come up with, is avoiding Ember like the plague until I come up with something better ... that way I won't have to lie to her anymore. Because if I can't trust myself to *say* the right thing while I'm around her, how the hell will I be able to *do* right by her. I dive back beneath the surface and continue with my laps.

Time slips into memory.

Memories slide into darkness.

Darkness finds a new place inside me.

Finally, I stop swimming in mid-stroke when I notice the lights flashing on and off. Wally is standing by the light switch.

'It's nine o'clock, lad. I think you should quit for the day.' My muscles aren't the least bit tired, but everything in between hurts way more than it should. Wally turns to the uneaten food. 'The pool will still be here tomorrow, son.'

He's right.

I hop out and dry off as he walks around the edge of the pool, inspecting the soft torch lighting slung along the walls at three metre intervals. When he gets back to the bench, he picks up the plate and glass.

'Might as well start acting my part,' he says with a chuckle. I follow him out and dump my clothes in the laundry basket.

'Give us it here,' I say, taking the plate from him. 'I'm gonna turn in for the night.' I eat the sandwich as I head upstairs.

I flick the bedside light on and lay down, praying for the first time in my life as I close my eyes, Ember's face won't be there.

In less than a blink, a message comes through on my phone.

It's Daniel. Guess who else didn't know you were moving?

The room starts to spin.

Life starts to unravel.

I don't get a chance to ask who. His next message reveals all.

Serena. And she wasn't happy you didn't tell her.

Fuck! She's not about to just get over this any time soon. The phone beeps again.

She told me to pass this on to you. *Get your arse back to Sheffield or else.*

I need to go back and sort this out.

And soon.

The next thing I know, *Born in the USA* is blaring through my alarm. I hate Bruce Springsteen and swat the clock with my pillow. It crashes to the floor, but the muffled tune continues to play. I groan as I lean over and yank the cord from the wall.

And then I remember …

I didn't dream about Ember last night. The first time in forever. I can't begin to understand why or what it means.

I roll over, not wanting to go to school today and although legally, I don't *have* to, I know I *have* to. Maybe Wally is right, and I *am* reading too much in to it. Regardless, I'm still going to stick with my plan and steer clear of her.

A swim should help that.

Just like I thought, the day dawdles at its own pace. I catch glimpses of her walking in corridors and standing in doorways with the blonde-haired girl I'd seen her sitting with on that first day. It goes against the grain, passing her, pretending not to know her and not saying a word to her.

I'm desperate to know her thoughts, her dreams, her wishes, her secrets. This tongue-tied shit is almost as bad as worrying about saying the wrong thing, but when Chris comes to me at the end of school, towing Marcus behind him, to see if I'd heard the rumours about Ember Riley and the shower incident, my words suddenly flow freely.

'But she's alright?' I ask for the second time as he tells me about the two other girls who were *apparently* burnt beyond recognition in the showers.

'Well, that's just it. According to Trent Brown's sister, who was there, she didn't have a scratch on her. That's why she had to go and see old Fish-head.' I frown and realise he's talking about Mr Fisher, the headmaster.

'They think *she* burnt them?' I ask.

'Dunno. Sounds suspicious though, doesn't it?

Especially after what happened to her parents.'

I half shrug as the word FlameMaker flashes across my vision. 'But there wasn't a fire, was there?'

'No, but it looks like the changing rooms are going to be out of action for a few weeks.'

'What? Even the boys'?'

'No hot water. The pipes have to be changed or something …' This is bad news for me. I was relying on those showers as a last resort, in case the urge became too unbearable during school hours and I needed to cool off. 'And I heard from my sister that we might have some kind of country dancing instead of sport.'

Chris was right.

The country dancing rumour *was* true, but the gossip about the girls being burnt beyond recognition, *weren't*. It was serious, but not in the grave manner in which he delivered it. So, now I find myself the next day, sitting in the cold sports hall, waiting for some stupid DVD to start about Scottish country dancing.

I settle into my seat. The lights go out and I close my eyes, wishing I was anywhere else but here.

Ember is sitting in the chair two rows in front of me and three spaces to my left, except I can't open my eyes and look at her long red hair, curling down her back in fiery waves, a second longer. I saw her enter, as we filed in, and something painfully delicious pulled at my heart when she noticed me.

The DVD isn't on for as long as I hoped and when the lights come back on and the chairs are cleared away, I conclude the worst is yet to come.

I chance a glimpse at her to find her staring at me. The beast is silently at work, tapping into her from under my radar. I avert my eyes, angry that she catches in a moment of weakness.

We are told to form two groups, and I deliberately move as far away from her as possible. Two girls, normally my type and who look similar, come to stand beside me.

'My name's Eliza,' says the first girl, 'and this is Cherie.' Cherie giggles like a hyena. The sound rattles my bones into irritation.

I take a step away from them.

Eliza mimics me and closes the gap so that there *is* no gap. Her cheap perfume switches the beast attention. An aching throb in my groin pulls me back into the moment.

Deliberately, she presses her tits into my arm, and it takes everything that I have to not rip her shirt off and stuff her D cup breasts into my mouth.

I'm thoroughly disgusted in myself - by how I can turn from monster to meek in the space of thirty seconds.

Now there seems to be a debate going on.

Mr Martin is discussing why there are too many students in one group and not enough in the other. He asks volunteers to join the other group … Ember's group, and without thinking, I step forward. 'I'll go.' It's riskier here than there.

I look over at Ember. Her eyes wide. Completely terrified by the idea.

I intentionally keep my distance from her, and stand on the opposite side of a circle, only to realise, the safest place would've been directly behind her as we begin to weave, hand over hand, boy, girl, boy, girl, in figure of eight patterns.

I see her coming closer, and there isn't a damn thing I can do to stop it, save drop to my knees and fake an injury.

'Stop, stop, stop,' yells out Mr Martin.

Saved!

Ember and I stand in front of each other, hands stretched out at the ready.

I hold my breath.

My heart twists.

She finally releases me from that look. That pleading, scorching look - hotter than a branding iron, imprinting something into my skin, something to make sure I will never forget her.

I steal a moment to think.

I wish Cherie hadn't roused the monster because it is making it all the more difficult to look at Ember with the love that I feel. Her eyes are becoming more glassier by the second.

'Everybody return to your positions,' calls out Miss Lindsay, the girl's PE teacher.

The music begins again, and this time Mr Martin pulls the pin before Ember and I can get close. A girl with wiry brown hair stands between us.

Miss Lindsay is strutting back and forward, nursing an injured hand. She keeps checking her watch and tutting as Mr Martin gives a one-on-one lesson to some kid. 'I think we have time for one more go,' she shouts. 'Take your places, everyone.'

It isn't a look into the future that I have, or a flash of déjà vu, or an image from my dreams, but something familiar to me. Something so transparent in structure, so warming and memorable, my body screams out *at last*. In that moment, something clicks into place for me. No matter how much I try to put this off, coming face to face with Ember and holding her hand, inevitably has to happen.

Hands begin to link and release, link and release and the more people I pass, the more she passes. Her left hand stretches out to the wiry-haired girl between us, and then her right hand, as though it's made for my hand alone, slips snugly into my palm.

My whole body shudders.

Comes alive.

Wakes from the worst nightmare I've ever had.

I suddenly feel brave enough to tell her exactly how I feel and yet shy, embarrassed, confused, in awe.

So many feelings.

Some I don't know the names of.

Everything is muddled and rushing up to me that I don't know where happiness begins and passion ends. Where my true feelings lie or how much is being engineered by the beast. It's exhilarating and euphoric and a hundred different thrilling words all rolled into one.

I let a breath in. Really breathe her in. Letting myself enjoy the wonderous aroma of her that has been kept secret from me for all this time.

My head swims in euphoria.

I'm surprised to discover there is no overwhelming perfume, which I love. It's subtle, like Pears soap and honey. Like jellybeans and lilacs. An elusive array of uniqueness, just like her skin is.

My thumbs seem to. have a mind of their own, caressing the back of her hand, unable to stop, not wanting to be anywhere else, and when she looks up at me, my world spins out of focus.

I need to blink.

I need to remove this film from my eyes because I'm afraid a tear might escape, the emotion that intense. That powerful I might just cry.

A thunderous crack from above us brings the dance to a standstill.

Brings me back into the room.

A monsoon drums on the metal roof outside and yet I cannot draw my gaze from her. The images of tempestuous seas rising up and engulfing the burnt orange lands, lands of fire and lava and volcanic eruptions convince me more and more that Skye was right. She is the FlameMaker. And it's all too easy to read her emotions.

She is curious about me.

And she doesn't know why.

She finds me infuriating. Interesting. Is drawn to me.

But her mind is full of confusion.

I swallow hard, pushing down the beast so I can see her, and evaluate her, with my own eyes. Her top lip is a little plumper than her bottom lip. Her cheekbones are high, though not overly pronounced and there isn't a hint of makeup anywhere on them. Her eyebrows, a brownish-red in colour and shape themselves over the most perfect pair of eyes I've ever seen. Eyes, I will never tire of looking into. Eyes that look beyond the monster to see the real me – a boy who has loved her since he could ride a bike.

The second the connection between us breaks, and my hand dangles by my side, alone, I know I won't be able to stand another day of not talking to her. And although today is not over, and she is right in front of me, saying everything I want to say, has its restrictions.

I turn, hesitating for a moment.

Not here, not now.

It will have to wait.

SIXTEEN

MY step feels lighter as I walk home that afternoon with Chris, so much so, I don't feel the need to swim the second I walk in the door. I find Wally in the library, staring at the top corner of one of the huge floor to ceiling bookcases.

'I reckon the reason the house costs so much is because of this room,' he says, not averting his eyes. 'Do you know how many books are in here?'

'No,' I answer with a laugh.

A broad smile finds its way to his face. 'You sound in a better mood. Did *we* make progress today?'

'Kinda. How many?'

Wally shifts his position but not his gaze. 'How many *what*?'

'Books?' You're not counting them, are you?' I hold back a laugh.

'So what if I am. Aren't you curious to know?'

'Not particularly.' I knew the house came with a fully stocked library, its previous owner, a scholar and philanthropist, had gone into a nursing home, leaving them here.

A minute or so later, Wally turns to face me. 'Glad to see you back to normal again. I was getting a bit cheesed off with the broody *I'm a loser* thing you had going on there a while.'

I raise my eyebrows still waiting for his answer, waiting.

'See, I knew you were thinking about it. At a rough count, give or take a few that I might have skipped over, there are 96,784 books. How's that for impressive?'

This time, I can't help but let out a laugh. 'How long have you been in here for?'

Wally frowns. It's the kind of frown that says he's been here a lot longer than he'd like to say. 'A few hours, maybe four.'

'Well, I'm gonna leave you to it. I'm going to a party tonight, and with any luck, a special someone might be there.'

'What? When did this happen?'

'Today at lunch,' I tell him, brimming with excitement.

Chris let slip at lunch that Marcus's older brother, Cole is having his eighteenth birthday tonight at some place called The Garages. 'Who's going?' I'd asked him. He'd listed a dozen or so names I'd never heard of before. And that is when my mind had sprung into action. What if I could somehow get Ember there too, and be able to talk to her, out of school, away from gossipers and eavesdroppers, and not be bound by rushing through a conversation in fear of the school bell about to ring. 'Any chance you could extend that invitation, to say, a couple of year eleven girls?' He'd said, no problem.

As I take the elegant sweeping staircase, two steps at a time, I wonder if life could get any sweeter.

I take longer in the shower than I normally would, first trying to remove the smell of chlorine from my skin, and

213

second, to make sure that even though it has been four full days since I last had sex, my record being seven, that I am as calm and composed as I possibly can be. Tonight will be a real test of my strength ... and hers, I hope.

Chris arrives in a pair of smart trousers and shirt and I wonder if my faded jeans and white t-shirt, straight out of the tumble dryer, are a little ratty. I decide to dress it up a bit as we head out and slip on my blue suit jacket hanging in the cloakroom.

Chris straightens his back and tightens his lips. 'Will we be taking the Beemer tonight, Jenkins?'

Grabbing the keys off the hall table as I pass, I nod and then holler a cheerio to Wally. Chris's face breaks out in a satisfied grin. 'Excellent,' he declares. 'That's what I like - arriving in style.'

The Garages don't look like the kind of garages I'm used to ... you know, the underground kind, dingy, sleazy and dark. The result of a poor renovation job that had run out of money. This place is pretty high class. It has that posh wine bar look, all glass fronted, wooden tables and chairs outside and an impressive string of outdoor lights around the roofline.

'Not bad, huh?' says Chris as we pull up. 'They've hired the room at the back for more privacy.'

I park, aware of thumping music from the other side of the car park. Marcus is already standing out the front, waiting, and nods to the 'Meat Tank' minding the door, checking off names. He then waves us in.

The first person I see is Cherie.

This could be complicated.

She flies across the room in a skirt, so short, it could be mistaken for a belt and flings her arms around me. She's obviously had too much to drink and it's not even eight o'clock.

'Marcus said you were coming, but I thumped him one for telling lies,' says Cherie, running her hand around the curve of my arse. She then stands back to take a look at

214

me. 'And don't you look good enough to eat.' I feel instantly nauseous, regardless of how horny I am. 'Will you dance with me later, you know, when the slow ones come on?'

'Cherie, come on,' yells Eliza over the music, frantically beckoning her to leave.

'I'm not going anywhere until River saves a dance for me.'

In that moment, I would've done anything to get rid of her. 'Sure,' I say through gritted teeth. She squeezes my arm and wobbles back to Eliza, who grins at me with the whitest teeth I've ever seen. I was planning on leaving *long* before the slow dances begin and if by chance I'm still here, there will be only one girl I'll be saving myself for.

Chris nudges me and laughs. 'You won't be lonely tonight.' He has that right and it doesn't seem to matter whether I'm alone or in a crowd, Cherie is there, patting me like her favourite toy.

Until I see her.

I freeze.

My body becomes ice.

My mind, a desert.

She doesn't have to do anything amazing. Just standing there … the way she fiddles nervously with the plastic cup she's holding and timidly looking up every so often, has me falling down.

Helpless.

Powerless.

Vulnerable.

I find I can't prise my eyes away for her.

Someone bumps my arm and I turn to apologise to find it's only Cherie again.

'Oops,' she squeaks after blowing me a kiss. I turn back to where Ember is standing, only she's gone.

I shrug Cherie's arm off me and head for the door. I see Ember's hair before anything else and cut through two tight groups of arm-waving, tit-bouncing dancing girls, to finally stand in front of her. With her head down, she doesn't see me until I reach out and touch her arm. The empty cup flies out of her hand and disappears from sight. A squeal, not girlie, like I've heard girls do before, but a stifled, practiced squeal that says more about doing it quietly rather than doing it at all, comes from the back of her throat.

My brain melts and my words liquefy as she stares up at me with those gorgeous coppery eyes. *"For fuck sake, River, say something"* comes the only line my mind is able to muster.

'You're not leaving, are you?' *Break-through*, yells my brain. *Houston, we have lift off.*

'Pardon,' she asks shyly. Now here's the test. Can I make it two lines in a row? *Stick with what you know*, repeats the voice in my head.

'I said, you're not leaving, are you?'

Her eyes smoulder at me. 'I need some air. Why?'

Why indeed? I don't get chance to answer before Cherie appears at my side, her long arms and wandering hands touching me. Claiming me.

Whether I imagine it or not, I can't say for sure, but for a brief second, less than that even, I swear I see a hint of sadness touch Ember's face before she drops her eyes to the floor and heads for the door.

'I'm not interested,' I growl to Cherie. She giggles, loudly, and I grab her hands and remove it from my jacket. I follow Ember outside.

Ember is standing with her back to me as I walk up behind her, her arms wrapped around her body. She looks cold, dressed in a thin shirt and skirt. 'Are you cold?' Instinctively, I remove my jacket, not waiting for her reply, and without thinking, place it over her shoulders.

Her cheeks look redder than normal as she mutters her thanks but that could very well be the cold, still air that makes the silence between us all the more noticeable. Our eyes keep meeting as if we are two skilled fencers drawing our foils at the same time. I try to imagine the wonders in her life, her troubles, if she has any, and whether I can be the kind of person she could talk to about them and maybe one day, depend upon.

Her gaze draws me in, and I can't stop myself from taking a step closer to her. The cold breeze around us becomes warm and welcoming and as much as I really want to be near her, I don't push my luck. She is still wearing my jacket so I must have done something right. I stand there and let her presence consume me.

'How do you do that?'

'Do what?' she whispers back.

I have no idea where I'm going with this or that I'd spoken until she answers, and so I urge my brain to fire up and give me a reason. 'Hold me in the palm of your hand like that? Like you ...' I pause. I have nothing. I'm wading through thick mud with concrete boots, not making any ground. I take a breath. If I'm about to fuck up, it will be right now. 'L-Like you can make me do anything you want.'

'Me,' she gasps.

I feel myself falling ... falling into a pit that has no bottom. I have upset her. I've said the wrong thing ... again. This getting to know someone bullshit, when you're in love with them and they don't even know you exist, is total bollocks. I want to leave, give up, go home, go back to Sheffield where I can pretend to have some kind of a life, instead of facing a reality that's more trouble than it's worth.

I lower my eyes, defeated, ready to hear her *get away from me creep* speech. With nothing to lose, I add the final nail to my coffin. 'Your eyes are ... mesmerizing.'

I look up to see tiny lines crimping her forehead. Bronzy orbs of fire stare back at me with wonder and confusion. '*My* eyes. *Your* eyes.' she says determinedly.

This isn't the reaction or the lecture I'm expecting.

My brow grows heavier.

This isn't about me.

This is about her and how she makes my body come

alive without uttering a single word. 'What do you mean, *my* eyes?'

She stops moving. Stops blinking …the same way my heart has slowed down, refusing to beat. My brain frantically tries to put together the pieces of a puzzle I've never seen a picture for.

An argument breaks out a short distance away.

Ember turns her head, the same time I turn mine - as though we are puppetted by the same strings. Cherie is marching towards them, but then promptly changes direction as soon as she sees me.

'Oh, River. I didn't know you were out here ...' she glances over at Ember, '... with *her*. I wondered where you'd got to. I thought we were going to have that dance you *promised* me.'

How I feel about Cherie, goes way beyond mere agitation. I have no time for her games.

'So, River ...' begins Cherie.

That's all I'm giving her.

'Can you give us a moment, Cherie. I'm just in the middle of asking Ember something.'

Her eyes bulge.

First glaring at Ember and then back at me. She storms off, leaving me with a sense of relief

I return my attention back to Ember, who is staring up at me with curiosity. Her 'my eyes, your eyes' comment is seared into my brain.

'You mean to say, you really don't see the flashes of burnt oranges and red when you look in the mirror?'

At first, I think she is about to burst into fits of laughter as her face begins to soften slightly, although there are still remnants of confusion there.

'No, and neither can anyone else, it seems.' She pauses and wraps her arms around her waist, pulling the edges of my jacket further around her. 'Anyway, who tells someone their eyes are the colour of molten lava?'

I can't hold back a smirk. I'm not laughing *at* her, or at the once dire situation I'd found myself in ten minutes ago, which is now moving into a halfway decent conversation, but that of all the dumb things I've said, it's *that* which she remembered. And that she's obviously spoken to someone else about *me*.

My world is brimming with a new kind of happiness.

'You *actually* asked someone after I *said* that?' I really don't mean it to sound so patronising and I can only blame it on the hope that has sprung up inside me that we are actually talking.

'Yes, I mean no ... I mean.' She's flustered. It's so easy to tell. The redness in her cheeks is exquisite.

Confidence rises within me and the **beast**, who I'd almost forgotten about, senses it too. 'What exactly *do* you mean?'

'I don't know. Just forget I said anything. Most people do.'

The response I was hoping to come out of my mouth, went something along the lines of, 'I'm sure that's not the case', or 'I could talk to you all day', but neither come out.

'That's not what I've heard,' are the words to my undoing.

In that second, she slips off my jacket and hands it back to me. 'Thanks, but I don't need this anymore.'

My head falls forwards as though the weight of it is just too unbearable to hold any longer and before I can think, I reach out for her. My hand falls against her arm, her skin surprisingly hot for how cold she looks. The words, 'please don't go,' tremble out of my mouth before I can stop them.

Just like before, the visions of fiery volcanoes and gushing seas flank me, flashing across my blank gaze. This time I have to ask. 'Tell me you saw that?'

Her gaze fades until she can look at me no more and her head lowers. 'I saw nothing.'

And yet something inside me says she's lying.

I hang around outside for a few minutes after she leaves,

reeling from sheer stupidity, before heading back inside to find Chris. He is still standing in the same place I left him, trying to chat up the same year twelve girl.

Ember is nowhere to be found and neither is her friend. Once again, I've blown it, and her absence gives me ample time to remove my rather large foot out of my equally gaping mouth. It was a breakthrough though, for a few brief minutes, and I'd managed to talk to her, regardless of it going down in history as one of the most disastrous conversations of all time.

Now that I'm alone, I am hyper-aware of the other females in the room. Their gawking faces hadn't registered too much with me before, probably because of how much I was concentrating on Ember. But now their closeness radiates towards me like the rippling heatwave on a road to nowhere. With no desire to drive the delectable honey that I am, my body judders impulsively as the bees begin to swarm.

One vivacious, girl wearing a thin strappy top and tight jeans is the first to make her move.

'Haven't seen you around here before. Are you one of Cole's friends?'

Cole? I have to think for a second who Cole is. *Oh yeah, the guy whose party it is.*

'Kind of.' She flicks her dyed burgundy hair one way, and then the other as she steps closer, shamelessly slipping her hand around my waist. I want to move, but the beast digs in deep. It isn't going to give this one up without a fight.

'How do you know, Cole?' I ask her, taking a quick scan of the area to see who is watching. Plenty are, mostly girls with faces of fury who wished they had made their move sooner.

'Oh, I don't. I don't even live here. I'm staying with my cousin.' She points to a solid girl who wouldn't look out of place competing at a Russian shot-put event. 'Why? Do you wanna get out of here?'

I do want to leave, but I don't want to be seen leaving

with a girl – new boy, smaller town and all that rumour bullshit. 'Meet me outside. I've just gotta say goodbye to a few people first.' My resolve and promise of purity for Ember is nothing more than a cheap memory.

She shrugs and then winks. 'The mysterious type. Just what I'm up for tonight.'

The beast grins sadistically. It has won … yet again.

The next morning, the guilt doesn't *quite* wash off the way it usually does, and for seven hours straight, I swim.

'You're like one of those monks from the twelfth century who whip themselves for penance,' says Wally as we sit at the table that night. 'Do you feel the slightest bit better?'

'Not really,' I mutter, playing with my food. I push my chair out. My appetite has vanished, along with my self-respect, not that there was much there to begin with.

'So instead of doing something about it, you're just going to let her slip through your fingers for a second time?'

'No,' I bark, instantly forgetting who I'm talking to. 'No,' I repeat, remorsefully. 'I'm pacing myself.'

'Oh. Is that what you call it?' Wally smothers a laugh.

'I don't want to scare her off.' I grind my teeth at such a pathetic line.

Wally shrugs. 'Of course. I mean, what would a forty-five-year-old know about dating these days? You obviously know what you're doing.'

I rise from the table the same time my phone beeps. Two messages are waiting. The first is from Skye. It says, *Dude, where are you? Your house is deserted.* The second, stops me dead in my tracks. It's from Iris Perkins. It reads; I knew you liked redheads but didn't figure you for the dyed burgundy type. Have you replaced me? We still have an arrangement.

The sound of my heart thumping away in my chest is almost deafening. She's here. She's seen me.

'River?'

What was she doing here? Spying on me? Why?
'River.'

I look up, stunned to find Wally staring at me. 'What's wrong, lad?'

'What? Oh, urr, nothing. It's okay.' I drop my phone into my pocket. 'I'm going to bed,' I mumble and leave without giving him a reason.

For the next hour, I lay looking at the ceiling, trying to figure out what made Iris Perkins different from the bimbo's who had stalked me before. She has money, of course, and isn't after mine, but it's more than that. There is a determination to her, and as much as I hate to admit it, I think it's her sole purpose to take ownership of me.

I let out a sigh. I know what I have to do.

When the alarm goes off at six, I pack an overnight bag and jot down a quick note telling Wally I'll be back in a day or so and could he phone the school and let them know I have the flu or something. I leave the note on his bedside cabinet, watch him sleep soundly for a few minutes and then get in my car and drive straight to Sheffield.

It's almost lunch by the time I arrive outside the Iceberg Rose Investigation Services. I stare across the street at the sign realising for the first time that each capital letter spells out the name IRIS. A shiver finds its way down my spine.

I head up the stairs to her office, surprised I'm not greeted by a familiar perfume. In fact, I wonder if anyone is here at all and that perhaps the door had accidently been left unlocked. Tania isn't sitting behind the desk, painting her nails or trying to look busy. And the door to Iris's office is wide open.

I knock anyway, just in case she's under the desk or behind the door, but when no answer comes, I walk in to find the room as clean as ever, minus one seriously control-freaked woman. On her desk, my eyes fall to her elusive red diary with the gold metal edges on the corners.

Next to it, is her briefcase. A file with my name on it protrudes from the opening. Curiosity launches into overdrive.

I swing around to double check I'm not going to be sprung and reach for the file. The first few pages are general information, my name, address, interest/enquiry that brought me here, that kind of thing. The next page is the contract I'd signed in her presence and the following pages are all blank. I flick back to the contract page and written in green pen beneath the title, *Conditions of Contract* are the words, "See Avery".

I stuff the file back into the briefcase and go straight for the diary. I open to the last page. I am disappointed to find that each entry is written in French. There are a few words I do understand, like my name and Ember's, and a few verbs I manage to recall from the handful of French lessons I'd opted out of, but as I flick back through to the beginning of the book, I am surprised to find not only is Ember Riley's name in capitals, repeated over and over, but the words *La limace dégoûtante* quite a number of times in the same entries. The weirdest part is, the page is dated well over a year ago.

The sound of a door closing has me rushing to replace the journal in the exact same position I'd found it. I then step away from the door just as Iris enters. She looks up at me, clearly flustered.

'River. How long have you been here?'

I shrug, trying my best to look naive. 'I only just arrived.' Iris's gaze skims across the desk to her journal before returning to me, more settled. 'We don't have an appointment, do we?'

She knows we don't. She's too astute to forget a detail like that.

'No,' I say calmly as she walks around her desk. She picks up her diary and slips it into the side pocket of her briefcase, tucking the file, my file, down further when she's done.

'Then what do I owe the pleasure?' Playing it very

coy, prompts me to play her at her own game.

'You tell me? Wasn't it *you* who text *me*?' This is her chance to tell me what she wants and why she is stalking me, but something tells me from the way the corner of her lip turns up ever so slightly, she has no intention of divulging that information.

For a moment, she looks confused. 'Oh, I was just wondering what you were up to.' Like an infectious rash, I watch as the lie spreads across her face.

'Right. And I'm supposed to believe that?' In one quick moment, her expression changes from an alluring seductress into calculating bitch. The hairs on the back of my neck stand up.

'Believe what you want. It's the only answer you're getting.'

This spacious room suddenly feels smaller than a pine box, and I know right then, I am dealing with someone who, not only is exceptionally experienced in what she is doing, but how dumb I am for thinking I could possibly go up against her. Ember's name, written in her journal from over a year ago, still presses inside my head, urging me to ask more. It's my duty to find out why, but broaching the subject, I am convinced, will produce absolutely zero. I need to get that book away from her, without her knowing, and there is only one person I know foolish enough to break into an apartment. I only hope Skye knows how to speak French.

I recoil back into my shell, staring at her with cautious eyes as she smooths the back of her skirt down before sitting. The high-backed leather chair doesn't make a sound as she reclines backwards a little. She undoes the first three buttons of her shirt, exposing a ribbon of lace from her bra. It isn't hard at all to force the beast down this time, as if it knows, she will never taste as sweet as she once had. Never knowing what it feels like to shy away from a guilt-free fuck, instinctively, I take a step forward.

'So, you *are* interested?' She smiles and her tongue
224

flicks out to the corner of her lip.

'I never said I wasn't.' The lie dries hard against my tongue.

Iris finishes un-buttoning her shirt, slips it over her arms and throws it at my chest. 'Prove it.'

All I can think of as I lift her body onto the desk, carelessly pushing papers and files onto the floor, is I only have one more session with Iris … and then I'm done.

Yes, one more session to be free of our contract, but never out of her little red book which I'm sure, will haunt me forever.

SEVENTEEN

I pull up outside Skye's place and send him a text, hoping to hell he's home. Ten seconds later, a message pops up saying, sorry he's sick and that he isn't up for visitors. If Skye is anything like me, as an Elementar, that means he probably hasn't had a sick day in his life.

He's lying.

And I need to find out why.

I tackle the fifty billion stairs to his flat, thankfully no vomit this time, and knock loudly on his door. I'm about to knock again, when I hear footsteps on the other side. The door is wrenched open and a tall, blonde guy towers over me.

'Who the fuck are you?'

I want to ask this stranger, with a neck thicker than a petite woman's waist, the very same question. There is a familiarity in his eyes and then I remember. 'You must be

Skye's brother ...?' A mental blank replaces his name. 'I'm River.' His body blocks the entire doorway so I can't see in.

'And.'

'I was wondering if Skye was home.' He continues to stare at me as though I'm a bug squashed beneath his shoe that he'll have to go to the trouble of scraping off later on. He flexes his neck sideways, the cracking sound saying more about his brute strength than the way the tight cotton of his deep purple shirt pulls away from the buttons.

'He is, but anyone who wears their hair like a try-hard fag, isn't someone of any importance. Plus, you have the kind of face I wanna rearrange with my fists. So, no. He isn't in. Now fuck off.' He then slams the door in my face.

I blink once, trying to work out if anything I'd said had set him off, and when I come to the same conclusion time and time again, that he is a massive dickhead, with an ego to match, I leave.

Back in my car, I pull down the visor and look into the mirror. I have no idea what passes for a try-hard fag's haircut anyway? Mine is fairly short, not that dissimilar from his.

With phone in hand, I deliberate texting Skye again, although I don't want to risk his brother intercepting my message. I decide to wait awhile because returning to Gloucester, with a bag full of unanswered questions will not only keep me up at night, it could possibly entice Skye to come and find me. And that is something I can't let happen ... not just yet.

After scrolling through my playlist several times, not particularly wanting to listen to music, but desperate to drown out the deliberation of whether I'm wasting my time sitting here, I see Skye's brother exit the tatty block of flats.

I recline the seat a little, stealing glimpses out of the corner of the window as he swings his leg over a canary yellow Ducati.

I check my watch.

It's almost four.

I still have no idea where I'm staying tonight. My original plan had been to crash at Skye's, but after meeting his brother, my car looks a much safer option.

Waiting another fifteen minutes to be sure Skye's brother hasn't just ducked down the shops for a bag of sugar, not that he looks like the kind of guy who would duck anywhere or even eat sugar, I then type the hardest text message to Skye I've ever written – *I need your help.* I quickly press send before I chicken out.

The reply is almost instantaneous – *I'm your man. Give me ten and I'll meet you out front.* I wonder whether he is looking down from his window as he texts, watching me sitting in the sleek, expensive, sweet ride of my father's Audi.

Dressed in his normal attire, jeans and a hoodie, Skye taps on the window my head is leaning against, even though when I'd checked a few seconds ago he was nowhere in sight.

He makes his way around the car, an impressed look on his face, His fingers trail behind him, along the side door and over the bonnet. He pauses by the passenger door, before opening it.

'You want a formal invitation?' I call out. 'Get in.'

The door opens and Skye slides into the seat next to me, nodding. 'This is the coolest car ever. What does this button do?' He presses a button on the dash and a cup holder appears. 'Sweet.' His index finger is still erect and ready to go again.

Frustration ignites.

In three seconds flat, he's become a rash against my skin. Itchy. Irritating. That must be an all-time record even for him. I hear a low chuckle at the back of his throat as he steals my thoughts for his own kicks. I try not to think, try to calm myself without the need for thinking. I need a way to divert his attention.

228

I come right out and say it. 'How do you feel about breaking and entering?'

My words have the desired effect, and his hand drops into his lap. He turns to face me, a frown forming across his forehead. That's when I notice two thin white scars criss-crossing at the edge of his cheekbone, I'm sure, hadn't been there before I'd left.

'Are you serious?' he asks, swishing his hair sideways, partially hiding one eye.

'Totally.'

'Where? Who? When?' They were the first questions I was expecting him to ask. I grimace as he asks the second. 'Does this have anything to do with that girl, Ember?' I'd been particularly careful to keep her out of my thoughts.

I sigh, letting out the breath I'm holding onto. 'And it involves me too.'

Skye's tone and expression are as serious as I've ever seen them. 'Like I said. I'm your man.'

I explain to Skye about the diary and its owner and although he isn't surprised about the lengths Iris has gone to, to meticulously record every detail of her business, he does appear exceptionally curious when I inform him about how Ember's name has been entered in the book eighteen months ago. I leave out my deal with Iris, for now.

'What do you think it means?'

I roll my eyes at him. 'That's why I want the book, *Genius* – to find out.' I rest my hands on the steering wheel. 'But there's a problem ...' Skye looks up. 'The entire book has been written in French.'

'Great!'

'But before that, we need to visit someone else.'

Serena's house is half an hour away from Skye's place, a much nicer area of town, plus the sun has made a brief appearance after a mostly dull and cloudy day. Giving me hope.

'So, she knows you're a WaterLover?' Skye asks after I fill him in on a few details.

'No. Not as such. But she knows I'm not *normal*.'

Skye laughs. 'We all know that.'

'Ha-ha. Very funny.' I glare at him. 'She saw me underwater.'

'And?'

'For like … an hour.'

'Oh.' The smile disappears from his face.

'And even though she hasn't threatened to tell anyone, I can't be sure she won't. *I*, I mean *we*, don't need that kind of attention.'

'You really know how to get yourself in some shit, don't you?'

I shrug. 'Can you help me or not?'

Skye smirks. 'So, let me get this straight. You want me to bail you out … *twice*?'

My fists tighten.

My jaw like stone.

I say nothing.

My actions are all the answers he needs.

'As it happens, I can. But can I add just one more thing to this conversation before you try and punch me in the face again…'

I roll my eyes.

'I told you, you'd need me, didn't I?'

He's not wrong.

It feels kind of strange to need someone … for anything. Wally pretty much lets me play my own fiddle and nobody else comes close to being reliable or even mean that much to me that I would ask a favour. Skye has filled a space I didn't think was possible.

I see Serena twenty yards away from the front door of her parent's place, dressed in her work t-shirt and trousers. Her hair is loose, which is unusual as she normally wears it up. She must've just finished her shift at the pool.

There's a strut to her step, and her face says, she's not

230

happy to see me. No sexy smile. No wink. The closer she gets, the more I am freaked out about the colour of her eyes. They're much darker than I remember. Almost black.

The temptation to let the beast out, to do my dirty work, is appealing, except I'm not here to win her over. I'm here to put an end to this, and if Skye can really do what he says he can do, then this should be done and dusted in minutes.

We get out of the car and Serena tilts her head at Skye. Squints at him even.

'Who's this?'

'A mate,' I reply.

I ignore his soft awww and subtle nudge.

'And?' Her lips are tight.

'And …*nothing*. He's just a mate.'

'So, he doesn't have anything to do with the high-class hooker that keeps calling me, wanting to meet up?'

'Hooker?'

'Iris. Your fucking slut girlfriend you're shacking up with now.'

The world becomes unfocused. Out of rhythm with me. Brain racing to come up with an explanation.

'But what I can't understand is that you made it clear you didn't want a relationship. What you should've said, was that you didn't want a relationship with *me*.'

'I … I,' I begin to say.

'I, what, River? You can't back-pedal now. And to think I was going to keep your little WaterLover secret to myself.'

I open my mouth to say something.

'Iris said you wouldn't know what to say if I mentioned that word. And she was right. What the fuck is going on here …'

I look to Skye for help.

He's already on it.

His eyes have glazed over. Almost catatonic.

The air is still, deathly still, as though the grim reaper

231

himself is here to take us all. Then out of nowhere, a sudden gush of wind chases the leaves up the gutter beside me, tangles Serena's blonde hair into a nest of straw, surrounds her. But doesn't touch me in the slightest. Or Skye.

A mini tornado begins to spin around her and yet she seems totally unaware anything unusual is happening.

A cloud descends from the sky.

It surrounds Serena and for a moment she is lost in a vacuum of fog. The wind suddenly stops.

'Here goes,' mumbles Skye.

All trace of expression is lost on Serena's face. Her lips have parted slightly, her eyes heavy like she is trying to stay awake. A low hum, almost a chanted mumble whispers from Skye's lips.

The fog lifts in seconds, the whole episode taking less than thirty seconds.

'My name is Skye,' says Skye, holding out his hand to Serena.

Her eyes blink twice before she seems to come around. She smiles, the way she always does.

'I'm Serena,' she says, punching me gently in the arm with her fist. 'If only River was well-mannered enough to introduce us.'

She laughs. The light blue colour has returned to her eyes.

There's no trace of *neurotic* Serena. 'So, do you guys wanna grab a coffee or what?'

'Love to, Serena. Unfortunately, River and I have to be somewhere.' Skye looks at his watch and then at me.

I nod, no words forming in my head.

'Shame,' says Serena. 'See ya, River. Good luck with living down south.' She leans in and kisses my cheek. In that moment, I pick up that she has no memory of how long I can stay underwater for or that we've ever been intimate. She actually looks happy. No longer tormented.

I wave as Serena turns and heads for home.

Skye has that smart-arse grin on his face again. 'See,

told you, you can't get by without me.'

I'm impressed. 'That's a cool super-power you have there. How does it work?'

'Hmmm. I'm not sure you'll understand. It's kind of complicated.'

'Try me.'

Skye sniffs. 'Well, you remember how I told you that I can pick up your thoughts through airwaves?' I nod. 'It's kind of like that - only instead of simply listening, I can somehow drop a blanket of air over those thoughts, kind of dissolve them once they hit the air. You've heard of brain fog, right?' I nod again.' 'Then just think of it like that. She was already thinking about seeing you in the pool and confronting you about it as she was walking towards us. It was easy to pick up those thoughts and erase them. As if she'd never ever had them.'

'And what about the *other* bit?'

'That was extra,' he says with a smirk. 'She seems like a nice kid and I wanted to put her out of her misery.'

I place a hand on his shoulder. 'And for that, I offer you my sincerest thanks. She is a nice girl, and if just one girl can be saved from the damage I've done, then ...'

I pause.

Some kind of emotion, I'm not sure which, is bubbling up inside me.

'You're welcome,' steps in Skye. 'Like I said, I'm here for you, bro.'

'Pity you wasn't around earlier; I could've done with that little trick. When the hell did you realise you could do that?'

Skye lets out a laugh. 'Long story. I'll tell you about it someday.'

We've been sitting outside Iris's apartment block for the last hour.

I'm cramped.

Bored.

And needing a shower.

Six hours have passed since we were at Serena's place. Our plan of action was discussed over a greasy meal of fish and chips a few hours back and which now isn't sitting well.

'How much longer do we have to wait?' asks Skye for the millionth time.

I glare at him from across the seat, refusing to answer.

'I'm bored,' he moans, stretching out his legs and cracking every finger.

'So, are you going to tell me how you're going to get in?' I ask him.

'Don't stress. I've got it covered.'

'But how?'

Skye swivels in his seat. 'If I gave away all my trade secrets, what use would I be?' A glint of a smile passes over his lips.

I look at the digital clock on the dashboard. It's almost midnight.

'*When*?' he hisses out.

'She's not exactly the be-in-bed-by-nine-o'clock chick, tucked up with her favourite book and a mug of hot cocoa, you know.' Images of Iris, padding around in a red basque, all tied up with ribbons and secrets to whoever she's summoned is more likely. 'Another half an hour. Just to be on the safe side.'

Skye blows out his frustration.

'Well, it's not like you had any other plans,' I say. 'Weren't you supposed to be sick?' One corner of his mouth twitches. 'Because from where I'm sitting you *seemed* to have made a remarkable recovery?'

'Yeah, about that. What can I say … my brother is the biggest cocksucker around.' The gloomy haze that falls over Skye's face steals what little enthusiasm he has left. For the first time since I met him, I feel sorry for him.

'At least you have a brother. I have to envy your piece of shit.' An abrupt snigger from Skye eases the tension. My thoughts drift back to the task at hand. 'So, how are you going to get passed the security door, the lobby desk

234

and into her *locked* apartment?'

'You don't have very much faith in me, do you?' I raise my eyebrows. 'Don't worry, I'll be as quiet as a potoroo.'

'A what?'

'A potoroo. It's an Australian animal about the size of a rabbit, but a cross between a rat and a kangaroo.'

'Whatever.'

'I could have said numbat or bilby, but I thought you were an educated man. Everyone knows what a potoroo is ...'

I slowly inhale. 'Go. Before I rethink this whole stupid idea.'

Skye is out of the car and blending into the shadows so well, I lose track of him twice as he races across the main road, through an almost vacant car park before reaching the elegant entrance of Iris's building.

Then I lose sight of him.

Now, the real worrying begins.

The minutes steadily tick by. The dashboard clock blurs from staring at it so much leaving me more and more on edge.

Half an hour passes, and I can't stay put any longer. I get out of the car and start to pace. There's a nip in the air, not quite winter but definitely heading that way and with no moon and only a sprinkling of stars, the night is as black as my soul.

My head spins with the possibilities of what I should do.

First, I contemplate sending Iris a text to see if she wants some company, then wonder whether I should go in after him, or perhaps stick to the original plan and wait for him to come out. Maybe I could cause a water pipe to burst, evacuating the whole building or boldly knock on her door and demand she tell me everything.

And I can't even begin to allow myself to unravel the reasons why Iris would contact Serena or how she even knows about the word WaterLover.

I decide to give him five more minutes, but he only needs two of those as he suddenly creeps up behind me, poking me in the ribs with his phone.

'For fuck's sake, what took so long?'

Skye simply grins.

'Did you get it?'

He shakes his head. 'No.'

I can't believe it. '*What*? Some frigging burglar, you are.'

'I didn't think stealing it would be very smart.'

'And you're the expert, I suppose. Why the fuck not?' There is sourness in my tone. I can taste it.

'Because first of all, if she found out that somebody had stolen it, she would find out who, and probably string them up by their balls, from what you've told me about her. And second, we wouldn't be able to see anything else she's planning or subsequent updates because she'd have stashed it away so well, we'd need a friggin' bloodhound on steroids to find it.'

I let out an irritated sigh. 'So, what *exactly* did you do?'

'I took some photos of random pages with my phone.'

Relief breaks in my chest and I concede to his rationalisation. 'Well, that's something. How many pages?'

'Around ten. By the way, you didn't tell me she barks like a chipmunk when she's having sex. And who the hell is Lawrence?'

So many things fall into place, and yet I still have no idea how Skye sneaked passed the main foyer, how he acquired the book, but more to the point, how the hell he got into her apartment.

'Did she leave the door unlocked for you?' I say sarcastically.

'Doors have never been a problem for me,' he says, smirking. 'I'm your run-of-the-mill Houdini.'

I glare at him.

'Ok, ok – I used my cloak of invisibility if you must

236

know, Harry Potter!'

'You can turn invisible? Whenever you want?'

Skye shrugs matter-of-factly. 'Yeah. No big deal.'

A new found respect for him surfaces and I slap his back as a gesture of good work. At least, I know he can get into Iris's place and copy more pages of her journal, if needed.

Skye rounds the car and opens the door. He leans against it for a moment, twitching his lips left and right. 'We just need someone who can read French.'

'Don't need to,' I say, opening my own door. 'I have that under control.'

The sound of a police siren, miles away, has me staring into the darkness, my heart pounding.

'And about before ... with my brother ...' Skye begins to say.

'Forget it. There's one in every family.' But it does get me thinking about where I will be sleeping tonight.

'I would invite you to stay over, but ...' He twitches his lips to one side. 'I don't know whether *he'll* be back tonight or not.'

'S'okay. I'll sleep in the car. AND ... keep out of my frigging head.'

'You can't sleep in your car. Let me make a call. And for the record, I can't turn the hearing-thoughts-rubbish off, so quit getting on my case about it.'

I ignore his last statement.

I'm tired.

I need to rest, but more than that, I need a girl or water. Whichever comes first. I'm fine with either.

'It's almost two,' I say. He ignores me and punches a number into his phone.

'Grant, it's Skye, mate. Can we crash at yours tonight?' I wait for his response. 'Sweet, man. See you in a few.'

I press the button for the ignition and listen to the purr of the engine. 'Where are we off to?' I ask, turning to Skye. He is messaging someone.

'What? Oh, turn left at the end of the street and then take the next right.'

I follow Skye's directions, eventually arriving in front of an old brick semi-detached house with a white fence and gate. A light glows from behind a poorly hung curtain.

'This is me mate, Grant's place,' says Skye as we walk up the path to the front door, weeds brushing across our shins. 'He's an Aussie too, but he's been here longer than I have.'

He rings the bell and an indigenous Australian with hair and eyes as dark as chocolate, and skin as deep and as rich as ground coffee, stands there with a smile on his face that eliminates any explanation for a drop-in visit at this time of the morning.

'Come in, come in,' he says, still smiling. 'Too hot for yer at home again?' Grant gives Skye a questioningly look but somehow doesn't seem surprised to see him. He does glance back at me several times though. 'Who's this fella?'

'This is me mate, River. He's had a silver spoon shoved up his arse most of his life, but he's fairly harmless.'

'Hey,' I chip in. 'I can't help being born into wealth no more than you could help being born a smart-arse wanker.'

Grant lets out a whoop of a laugh. 'Touché, man,' he says, punching me on the shoulder. 'I like him. You're welcome anytime.' Skye's frown lasts all of a second before he breaks into a smile.

After introductions, Grant leads us into his lounge room, which looks more like a computer repair shop. There are terminals and monitors everywhere. Coloured leads snake across the floor, entwine together, to where an old green and white striped couch sits flush against the wall.

Grant sits down. 'Maker yourself comfy. Sorry there's not much room. Computers are a bit of a … hobby for me.'

'A problem, don't you mean,' injects Skye. 'I thought it was chockers in here the last time I stayed over.' The smirk on Grant's face tells me that the two of them have a history that goes well beyond the realms of an open-all-hours bedsit.

'Do you fix them?'

Skye let out a laugh.

'No, I just take 'em apart ...'

'And then forget how to put them back together again,' Skye adds.

Grant laughs. 'Yeah, and like you know any more about them than I do.'

'But at least I don't try and pass myself off as an *Intercontinental Software Technician.*'

The white fireplace has a mantlepiece full of keepsakes and collectable junk from seaside trips and I find my mind starting to wander as Skye and Grant squabble amongst themselves. I need to know what are on those pages. It's eating me up, not knowing. 'You hooked up to the net?'

Grant gestures with his head to a laptop sitting on the edge of a red fold-out table. 'That one works. Why?'

Skye seems to have cottoned on to what I was thinking. 'Can we borrow it?'

'Sure. As long as you're not downloading porn or some shit like that.'

Skye is already reaching for his phone as I get up. I switch on the laptop and wait for it to power up.

'Fuck,' says Skye.

There is silence. 'Fuck! I don't believe this,' he groans, looking intently at his phone.

I glance up at him. A bad feeling in my stomach ... like a wrecking ball on steroids.

'There's only *two* pictures on here, and one of those is totally rooted.'

'*What*?' I'm furious.

Still scrolling through his photos, finally he looks up.

The chime from the laptop alerts me that we're ready to go. I avert my attention back to the screen instead of Skye's bewildered face, seething. 'And you didn't think to check them, to make sure they'd turned out okay?'

'I was pushed for time,' says Skye, grimacing.

'You were gone for nearly an hour,' I gasp, astounded.

'I got side-tracked.'

'With *what*?'

'How many times in your life do you get an invitation to live porn? And free, too.'

Grant jerks his head in our direction and Skye waves him down.

'But you weren't invited,' I say. It's a dumb thing to say but if I don't reign it in, I think I might want to break every bone in his face.

A sulky, almost anger-like look crosses Skye's face as he hears my thoughts. 'Well, next time you want someone to go breaking into a horny woman's apartment whilst she's in the throes of it, choose a eunuch.'

'Girls, girls,' chips in Grant. 'You wanna scratch each other's eyes out, at least put a couple of skirts on and grow your nails.' Grant is still grinning, although he has turned his attention back to his screen.

I snatch the phone off him and plug it into the cord hanging out of the side of the laptop. A small hand-written diary page appears.

'Enlarge it,' says Skye.

'I know,' I growl. 'Give me half a chance.'

The page is a little fuzzy after I expand it, but legible.

'You're gonna have to type it out.'

I clench my teeth so hard, I accidently bite the inside of my cheek. It adds to my irritation. 'I know, Einstein. I did actually *go* to school.'

I hear Grant chuckle again.

This is looking to be a long night. It's two-thirty already and I'm knackered. If this was to do with anyone other than Ember, I would have put it to one side and translated it tomorrow.

As I begin to translate it, I become more and more convinced, Skye had found the wrong diary. It talks about how she doesn't feel herself these days and seems to be missing periods of time she can't account for, putting it down to the extra hours she's been working and her troubled past finally catching up with her. I scan through, wondering why he had chosen this page.

'It's there at the bottom,' he says, pointing at the screen. Sure enough, Ember's name is there.

4th April 2017

Stalking the slug. I will personally lace my fingers around his throat, before I let this innocent be harmed. The girl he watches, with hair that looks too red to be real, doesn't know the half of it.

Looking back at him, through the rear vision mirror of my car, she is unaware of the evil that I see behind his eyes. I know that evil. I have seen it before. I have to find out who she is.

6th April 2017

Breakthrough! She goes by the name of Ember Riley.

'Is that it?' asks Skye, letting out an exaggerated sigh. 'I risked going to jail ... for *that*.'

'Calm down. There's more to it than that. This diary entry shows someone was stalking Ember before her parents were killed, which means whoever was stalking her, could be the reason her parents ended up dead, so they could get to her.'

'And you came up with this all by yourself, sleuth?' I narrow my eyes at him but hold back the 'fuck you' comment that screams on the tip of my tongue. 'What *exactly* are you going to do with the information? *Tell her*?'

I shrug.

'Awesome plan. Love where your heads at. So, you're just gonna go and tell this sheila that *you*, a person who hasn't said more than a half a dozen words to her, and

241

without any evidence ... that her parents *might* have been murdered. Nice one. Let me know when you're gonna do it because I would love to see the look on your face after she kicks the shit out of you for defiling a very painful memory.'

I have no intention of telling Ember anything until I know for sure what's going on. I turn to him. 'Do you have to be a complete wanker every second of your life?'

Skye huffs.

'I'm not that fucking retarded,' I say, letting the anger slip from my body. 'But I do need some more of those pages.'

Skye snatches his phone away and stuffs it into his pocket. 'Not even if you got down on your knees and begged.'

I've discovered Skye isn't the kind of guy who stands by his convictions, and I know exactly what buttons to press. 'I'll make it worth your while.'

His head spins around to look at me. 'You think you can *buy* me?'

I raise my eyebrows at him, waiting. 'Okay. But I'm not doing it for cents ... I mean pence.'

I hold back an urge to laugh. 'How about £100 a page?'

'Get fucked.' Skye looks genuinely put out. 'How about five?'

'Five hundred pounds? Are you frigging serious?' His lopsided grin reminds me of a sulky twelve-year-old. 'Two hundred, and that's my final offer.'

'Done,' says Skye, rubbing his hands together before zipping up his hoodie.

'But not now.' Iris's guest will be long gone by now and pushing our luck to go back for seconds doesn't sit right with me. 'In a couple of days. Okay?'

'You're the boss,' says Skye brightly.

I power down the machine, get up and push the chair under the desk. 'I need to crash.'

'Second door at the top of the stairs,' mutters Grant

between a string of profanities as he twists the Xbox controller this way and that.

Skye joins Grant on the sofa and I hear them laughing as I traipse up the worn carpeted stairs. There's a distinct smell of mould and dirty linen in the air. Pushing open the second door, I find two mattresses, without sheets, and a couple of sleeping bags unrolled on top. It's a far cry from what I'm used to, but in the state I'm in, I could curl up on a rocky outcrop and still sleep like a baby.

But first things first. I need to shower.

An unfulfilled twenty minutes later, I flop down on top of one of the mattresses, not bothering to climb into the sleeping bag as unconsciousness folds its arms around me.

EIGHTEEN

THE next morning, I try to tune out the slurping noises coming out of Skye's mouth as he shovels down spoonsful of cornflakes. The dream I'd had in the early hours of this morning is still haunting me.

The spoon clanks against Skye's teeth for a third time. 'Has anyone ever told you, you eat like a pig,' I growl.

Skye looks up. He catches Grant's attention and grins. 'Like I said before, silver spoon problem.' I grit my teeth and stare into my coffee.

Ignoring him, I set about trying to figure out, *what* from my dream is urging me to return to Gloucester. Ember's cries for help could have something to do with it or is it the driving urge to see her in the flesh again. I can't decide which emotion has more pull. I do know, however, that leaving Skye with the important job of finding more information from Iris's journal is stupid on my part. I might as well be leaving a toddler in charge of a flamethrower – who knows where it will lead or what devastation it could cause. But I have no choice. Trust

244

isn't something that comes naturally to me, and trusting Skye is something I'll have to do in order to return to Ember.

'I'm leaving tomorrow, so I suggest whatever you had planned for today, you cancel. We have stuff to do,' I say, my voice cold and flat.

'But you've only just got here. I thought we were going to hang out and maybe hit the Cage of Death again?'

Grant sniggers. 'Tell me he didn't con you in to that?'

I half-shrug one shoulder.

'Don't knock it until you've tried it,' says Skye around a mouthful of cornflakes.

'I'm not that stupid,' says Grant, staring at me with a comical look on his face. 'And I'm surprised you fell for it.'

Knowing what I *now* know about Skye, I'm surprised too. The chair squeaks as I push it out and I head for the door. I turn to see Skye sitting back in his chair, spoon dangling out of his mouth, waggling it, grinning at Grant. I know it's a dig at me.

'Move your arse and let's get going.'

Skye has done nothing but whinge since we left Grant's place.

'My gut says you should stay another night. I can sneak back into Iris's apartment tonight and find out more, now I know what we're in for. And you could leave first thing in the morning.'

'It's too risky going in tonight,' I say, 'it wouldn't surprise me if she already suspects something.' I pull onto the motorway. 'Besides, I need to practice. This whole Elementar thing can't just be random. This is gearing up to *something*, I can feel it, and if I don't know how to wield this power ...' My voice drops away. Plus, I need to be near water. I need to curb my gnawing appetite. I glance in the rear vision mirror to where Skye's backpack is. 'And I need to check out that book again, to see if I missed anything.'

Skye sighs. 'You know, you don't have to study for this. There's not a test, you know?'

I consciously press my foot harder on the accelerator. 'Of course it's a test, you wanker. Do you think this is a game?' I grit my teeth at his casual approach to this.

Skye is silent … for all of five seconds.

'I'm hungry,' he mumbles. I throw him a Mars bar that I picked up when we stopped for petrol.

'So, where are we going?' I keep my eyes on the road.

'Near water,' I answer sharply. 'I can't very well practice in the desert now, can I?'

Skye turns to face me. 'Then why are you heading for a nature reserve then, Einstein.' I notice him glance back at the sign we just passed.

I shake my head, astounded that someone from the area would not know about the dam, when I realise he isn't from this area. 'There's a dam there,' I say in a much cooler tone.

'Awesome.'

We drive for another twenty minutes or so, finally turning onto Snake Pass.

'I could tell you a thing or two about snakes,' pipes up Skye. He had been silent up until this point. 'Especially brown snakes. You know, they grow to …'

'I don't care,' I snap.

He lets out a low whistle as we pull over. 'Wow. We don't have anything like that in Australia.'

Skye is referring to the seven arched viaduct branching from one side of the dam to the other. It's pretty impressive and together with the rolling green hills that run right down to the water's edge, it makes me feel right at home. Pine trees, dark green in colour and densely packed in, cover the western side of the reservoir known as Ladybower and the eastern side is a patchwork of rich grassy squares and what looks like fields of yellow flowers or rapeseed.

246

I open the door to get out.

'Wait,' say Skye.

I rest my fingertips on the door handle.

'What *is* your problem?' he moans. 'Every single second you're a total dick to me. Please tell me because I'm curious. What the fuck have I done to you? All I do is help you and am here for you, and you seem to hate me more for it. Be straight with me.'

I pause for a few seconds. There isn't one thing, it's a mixture of everything. The smirk on his face like he knows everything, and the childish spin he puts on every topic just for starters. How he is so upbeat and happy all the time, and the fact that he's just picked my brain for the millionth time today and has heard exactly what I think might be a good place to start. But I realise these are all superficial. Truth be told, I'm just not that good at making friends, I guess.

Skye laughs. 'Come on, princess. We can have an Oprah moment when we're done.'

Ten minutes later, jeans rolled to the knees, I'm looking back at Skye sitting on the bank, my feet immersed in the coolest, purest water I've ever felt.

'My Aunt Joan, who's some kind of spiritual healer, reckons we absorb energy from the earth through our feet,' he calls out to me, 'so I figure, the experiments we tried to do at the lake might work *this* time if your feet are absorbing power straight from the source.'

Makes sense, I suppose. 'What do you have in mind?' I ask, aware of the smooth pebbles against my toes.

Skye brushes the hair from his eyes, a sheepish grin spreading over his face. He searches around on the ground and picks up a long stick and holds his arms up high. 'How do you feel about performing the parting of the Red Sea trick, in good old Moses style.'

'Are you serious? I'm not sure I'm up for anything that big.'

Skye looks about himself. 'Who's going to see you out

here … the squirrels?'

It's true. There isn't a soul insight.

Reluctantly, I concede. I'm kind of curious what I can do.

'Ok,' he instructs, 'stand up, both feet in the water.' They're in the water already and I give him the kind of look he deserves.

'Right.' He brushes off the embarrassment. 'Now comes to the tricky part.'

I wait.

'Close your eyes. It helps to concentrate more.' I let out an irritated breath and close my eyes. 'And put your hands out like this.' I have to open them to see what he's doing. 'Close them, keep them closed.'

'Do you know what the fuck you're doing?'

'No,' I hear his voice. 'I have no idea. Will you shut the hell up and concentrate?' Again, I do as I am told. 'Focus on the water. Find that companionship you have when you swim, when you shower, when you drink water as though you're old friends and that you are calling on it to ask a favour.' I smirk. I think I know where he is going with this.

Like before and all the other times, I let all the crazy, unnecessary random thoughts drift out of my head. I acknowledge the water tenderly caressing my calves and the light breeze that brushes over my skin, but pay it no mind. I channel my thoughts to coincide with the calmness of the water. I accept the beauty it holds, the gentleness it possesses and the potential of great power that lies silently within.

From somewhere deep inside, and for the first time in my life, I suddenly don't feel alone.

And it's not the **beast** I'm feeling either.

I sense a *companion* inside me, hiding.

Nereus, are you there?

Everything in my body says I'm right on the money, but no voice permeates the stillness.

I know you can hear me, I continue to say, *show me*

how to use this power.

Right on cue, the litres of liquid circulating inside me respond; blood, water, lymph, plasma. There's an urgency in filling and saturating every cell I possess. Although calm in mind, my heartbeat begins to pick up the pace in preparation for something big. Emotions of every kind, ranging from frustration and disappointment, anger and irritation, hatred and disgust intermingling with happiness, kindness, love, honesty and slight whispers of humility, bombard me from every angle, trying to squeeze out of the tiny pores in my skin. There's a strong sensation of fight and flight circling beneath my skin, of adrenaline, of fleeing a lion, my blood pumping so hard, forcing every muscle to respond to help me escape, and yet, consciously, I know I am still knee-deep in the dam, my toes gently scrunching the stony pebbles on the lake's floor.

From somewhere close by, I hear the sound of water.

Lots of it.

Gushing down in torrents as though I'm taking shelter under a magnificent waterfall. Even the air around me seems moist as I focus hard on dividing the dam in half. I can't even begin to know what's happening.

My senses are on high alert, daring me to look, and yet Skye is quiet. I'm not sure if I want to open my eyes, too afraid of what I might or might not see.

'Open them,' says Skye, infiltrating my thoughts.

Head down, slowly, painstakingly slowly, I lift my eyelids.

My first reaction is of shock ...

I want to ask what happened to the level of the water, that should be around my calves but is now barely covering my ankles, but I can't form the words in my brain.

I raise my head and stare at the phenomenon before me.

'Knew you could do it,' says Skye. I detect a decent amount of admiration in his tone.

I still can't believe it myself.

It's nowhere in the vicinity of parting the Red Sea, but conjuring a wall of water, fifty feet in height, cutting the dam in half from one side of the bank to the other, three hundred feet away, with me standing in nothing more than a puddle, is pretty impressive for my first attempt.

'Holy shit. Did I really do that?'

Skye rolls his eyes at me. 'Yes, Neptune, you did. Now take the frigging thing down before someone sees it.'

He is awe. I can tell from the look on his face. I feel that familiar whisper of him sneaking inside my head.

'Easy there, Poseidon, I'm not *that* impressed, so don't let it go to your head.' He takes a fleeting look at my creation again. 'But do me a favour and let it down *carefully* and try not to create a tsunami.'

I have no idea how I conjured it, so pulling it down could be more difficult than its worth.

'Any ideas?' I call out to him as he walks over to a rock and tries to make himself comfy. It seems he wants to have the best seats in the house. There's a grin on his face. 'Nope. But it's gonna be fun watching.'

If he wants the best seat in the house, I'll give him the one!

I sneer at him and try waving my arms at the wall of water.

Nothing happens.

I slip back into my semi-meditative state and respectfully request the water to return to normal.

Still nothing.

'Fuck! Skye! This is serious.'

He gets up and comes to the edge of the water.

'Help me. We can't leave it like this. People will freak out.'

He shrugs. 'I dunno. I kinda like it. It blends into the scenery quite nicely.'

'SKYE!'

'Alright,' groans Skye, 'keep ya hair on.'

'Fly over there and try and blow it down with your wind, or whatever it is that you do.'

Skye does as he's told.

The hardest part of a prank, whenever Skye's around, is to keep your thoughts neutral, and excitement in check. I wait until he is right at the base of the wall and when he's in position, I bring down the wall of water.

'You prick,' he yells out as he flies towards me, sopping wet. The dam has been reduced to more chop than the North Sea, white foam painted on the tops of each swell.

I roar with laughter. 'Quit your whining. You'll dry out,' I shout, 'Just put your superman cape on for ten minutes and do a few laps.'

I'm waiting for his uncouth reply when I spy a person on the far side of the bank watching me. His figure is somewhat blurry, which is odd, as my vision is usually 20/20. It's almost as though the outside of his shape has been painted into the scenery to help camouflage him. And then the weirdest thing.

Laughing.

Not from Skye or myself.

Laughing that seems to come from the clouds and mountains, from the ground and trees and that echoes around me from every direction. I can't tell if its female or male. It isn't spooky, scary laughter or high pitched I'm-gonna-pee-my-pants laughter either. The only thing I can compare it to is someone laughing at me. A laugh without humour. A laugh that belongs to no-one with a soul.

The second Skye's feet touch the ground, the laughter stops. Did you hear that?' I say, turning to him.

I glance over my shoulder, staring at where the person was standing, but would you know it, he's gone.

'Hear what? More of your bullshit suggestions. Oh, help me, Skye. I've fucked up again, Skye,' he sings in a girlie voice.'

'Get your hand off it,' I say, the joke over. 'You have

251

one job to do when I go, and that is to get more pictures of those pages. And for Christ's sake, don't steal that goddam book. Got it?'

'Keep your hair on, loverboy. I'm not going to trash the little thing you have going with her.'

A deep groan ripples out of my throat. 'Just don't screw it up or it could be bad for all of us.'

The light catches Skye's eyes, telling me he knows exactly what I'm talking about. 'I'll text you when I have some news.'

I nod, but the confidence I'd had, vanishes.

Returning home and being questioned by Wally was pretty much what I'd expected the second I walked in the door. As usual I lie my way around it, saying it was a legal thing to do with my parents' estate.

Before I turned eighteen, Wally had sole control over my parents' assets, but after my eighteenth birthday, everything had been transferred to me, leaving Wally out of the loop, not that he minded too much. In fact, he'd said it was a relief not to have those figures going around in his head.

'S'pose you're off to the pool?' asks Wally as I come downstairs after unpacking my bag.

I stop at the door that takes me down those five tiled steps and into a cool corridor where the pool awaits. 'Geez you're sharp today, Wal. Not many people wear shorts and carry a towel over their shoulder if they're going shopping.'

Wally says nothing, only rolls his eyes at me and shakes his head.

Right now, I need to swim.

More than I need to breathe.

Less than twenty-four hours have passed since I was with Iris, and I'm no better for it. This solo 'pact' bullshit of self-restraint I'd set up for myself, which in my opinion at this moment is fucked, is barely worth the effort, because no matter what, I won't be any purer at the end of it, even if I promised to bathe in holy water for the rest of my life.

'Back to school tomorrow?' I hear Wally call out. I shout back 'yes' and pick up my pace.

It's almost midnight before I finish.

I fall into bed, mentally exhausted, not even bothering to set the alarm, which in turn, has me racing around first thing in the morning dragging school trousers out from under my bed, and hastily smoothing out an excessively creased shirt with a semi-warm iron. The idea of driving my father's BMW to school is a temptation, but in the end, I have Wally drop me off at the end of the street and eventually make it into registration with one minute to spare.

By the time lunch arrives, I'm wrecked, emotionally, physically and sexually. *I don't want to do this anymore.*

Twice, I see Ember and twice she deliberately turns away from me. The rest of the day follows suit, so does the next day *and* the day after that. I'm beginning to feel like the invisible man.

I push my food around my plate at the dinner table, three evenings later, with a face that Wally says looks like the world's about to end. I can't understand what I've said that has caused her to have such a hatred for me. The way she looks right through me …

Crushes me …

Rips me open …

Exposes me as the fraud I am. Surely, it can't *still* be from the party. That was well over a week ago.

I need to talk to her alone.

And my big, brave plan is … find out where she lives, so we can walk to school together. It's piss-weak, I know, but twenty minutes every morning and afternoon should give me sufficient time to conjure more than the few measly words I'm currently battling with.

So, I have three options.

Go through Iris, which I definitely don't want to do. Break into the school office, which is highly illegal and stupid, and check their records, or the easier, more do-able choice, is to follow her home. Sure, I could go ask her or maybe invite myself to walk her home, but after our last conversation, I'm probably the last person she wants to be near. So, I'm going for option number three, the surprise, chance meeting, however, locating Ember at the end of each has been challenging.

It takes me a week to discover her routine.

On the days she stays back to study, she departs through the main gates which exits onto the high street and then on the other days, she leaves via the school's back gates.

Then yesterday, to drive the rusty old nail further into my coffin, just when I was about to make my move, my final class for the day was held back for unruly behaviour. It's as if fate is deliberately trying to keep us apart or more to the point, keep me away from her.

A dark thought visits me.

Clings to my shoulders.

Wraps its black tentacles around me and whispers that *maybe* I'm not supposed to be with her.

My mind shuts down. Goes blank at the thought.

Now, sitting at my desk the next day, knees bouncing, jaw tense, I know I can't wait any longer. The guy in front of me keeps looking back at my continuous tapping pen,

I stare him down, before putting my hand up. Mrs Gregory, my art teacher, who is 'fabulous at forty' and doesn't mind telling everyone, comes over.

'Yes, River.'

'I'm not feeling well. Can I leave early?' This woman is already so intrinsically woven into my web of power that I only have to smile at her and she turns into a wobbly mess. She has developed an insufferable urge to squirt exotic perfume all over herself whenever she's near her handbag.

'Of course, just make sure you sign out at the office, okay, dear?'

I nod and throw in a grimace for good measure.

I grab my bag, swing by the office and then head for the back gates, with plenty of time to spare. I don't have to wait long to hear the pips echo through the school grounds.

The clear view of kids spilling out of classrooms, crossing the faculty carpark, heading straight for me, doubles my anxiety. Triples my heartrate. I send up a silent plea to the dreary, rain-filled clouds above me, to cut me some slack, and that if this is meant to happen, now would be the perfect time.

I lean into the old, un-used telegraph pole, just inside the school grounds, pretending to scroll through my phone and wait. Out of nowhere, a surge of confidence fills me from head to toe. To hell with this sneaking around bullshit. I'm just going to tag on next to her, and ask her if she wants some company.

Easy as that.

Her hair is the first thing I see as she makes her way down the narrow concrete path towards me. Her cheeks are flushed from the cold. So is her nose.

My heart pulls in a thousand different directions.

Mouth turns to dust.

And the beast rises, frothing with excitement.

And it's then I look deep into her eyes. They have lost their lustre. There is no laughter there. No life. I see and feel sadness all around her.

Something says, this is not the right moment.

Without thinking, I drag my hood up and turn my back.

In the same second she walks past me, a message comes through on my phone. Thankfully, three nerdy guys from my science class cut in front of me, blocking her view as she swings around inquisitively.

The message is from Skye.

Sorry, but she's had the book with her every second. Don't fret. I'm going in tonight.

Keeping at a safe distance, I tack on behind the nerds who are heading in Ember's direction.

Her house looks as ordinary as any other, a little on the neglected side but never enough to change how I feel about her. Thankfully, she'd only turned around once to check behind her, but I think I got away with throwing myself into a rosebush before she saw me.

Task one accomplished.

Pleased with my progress, I contemplate my next move. As much as I want to boldly march up to her front door, knock twice and ask if she wants to take a slow walk down to the shops with me for a bag of chips and an ice cream, everything inside my body says I should wait. I have the beginnings of a headache coming on, my first in months, and the beast has begun to salivate madly.

I need to swim.

I need to be at my strongest for tomorrow.

Without giving it another thought, I get up, turn the music up high on my iPhone and power-walk home, drowning out the lewd suggestions of the beast.

Quarter to five the next morning, I don't feel any better, or stronger, even after six hours in the pool last night. I head to the bathroom and stare at myself in the mirror.

Abstinence is beginning to show.

My cheeks look a little gaunt, skin colour more grey than pink. Dark crescent moons have fallen from the sky and crept under my eyes and yet the colour of my eyes is more vibrant that ever.

I swim for another three hours, skip breakfast and hightail it back to Ember's neck of the woods. I loiter nervously at the end of her road and wait for her to appear, stamping some warmth into my feet whilst ignoring the repeated curtain lifting from someone who really needs to repaint their disgusting green door. It's a foggy, cold, morning, not quite artic cold, but frosty enough to steal the warmth from your mouth.

My heart thumps twice when I see her close her front

gate.

It's now or never.

I jog to catch up.

She turns to face me before I reach her, her face not yet bitten with cold. A light touches her eyes and I see the resemblance of a smile in them. This is a good start.

'Can I walk with you?' I fall into step with her without waiting for her answer.

Like it's the most natural thing to do.

Like we've been friends forever.

'Sure.'

River, don't fuck it up. The speech I'd rehearsed about asking her out sticks like glue in the back of my throat. Anyway, who does that? Ask out a complete stranger? Not me.

I wait for her to speak.

She says nothing.

I wait for my mouth to roll out a few words. One, even.

Again, nothing.

The silence is torturous and each step closer we get to school, the more it digs in deeper, the more my body twists with agony. I need to say something, anything. Just something simple, something normal, something she can find an easy answer to.

We enter the school gates and before I can think about it anymore, my mouth opens. 'Do you have a study period this afternoon?'

She nods but doesn't give me the pleasure of her voice. I need to hear her.

'And you'll be in the common room for that then?' A location is a necessity.

'Actually, I'll be on the roof.'

Her humour makes me smile, makes everything in my world that little bit brighter, that little bit more glorious. But with her friend fast approaching, I don't have time to indulge. 'Good. We need to get a few things straightened out. I'll meet you there after lunch.'

Ember's friend passes me, giving me a second glance

as I fast pace away from her. Yes it's cowardly, and yes it's not the way I foresaw this whole morning going with her.

But it's done.

I heave a sigh of relief as my stomach makes those last clenches of anxiety.

The next few hours of waiting and wondering will be unbearable, especially knowing I have science with her in second period.

I only hope she turns up.

Deliberately prolonging the moment, I hang back waiting for Ember to enter Mr Butcher's classroom. I couldn't handle her driving the stake in hard telling me she had no intention of meeting me, not in front of everyone. *Coward* whispers a voice up from my soul.

I take my seat, conscious of the eyes searing through my shirt and into my flesh. Slouching into my chair, not really giving two shits about which Element group I'm going to be placed in, I switch off, until I hear Mr Butcher call out Ember's name. Instinctively, I turn to face her only to find her eyes are already on me. Reluctantly and with a puckered brow, she picks up her chair and goes to sit in Cherie's group. Her face brings lightness to my soul - even when she's cross, she still looks cute.

'River Fulton.' I look up. 'You are in water and Josh McTavish is in fire.'

I tune out again, and apart from hearing someone let out a high-pitched laugh from the back of the class, which causes me to turn and catch Ember's gaze once again, the lesson finishes on time.

I slide my books into my bag the same time Mr Butcher pushes a piece of paper onto my desk. It says, "stay behind after class".

Fuck. That's all I need.

Mr Butcher hovers over my desk, waiting for everyone to leave. I need to get to the showers, which were re-opened a couple of days ago so I'll be as prepared for this 'alone time' with Ember as I can.

The door closes behind the last person. Mr Butcher paces back and forth, his eyebrow twitching.

'Mr Fulton?' I crane my head back to look at him. 'There's something different about you.'

I swallow but recover to give him my best line. 'Oh, you've noticed it too.' Mr Butcher narrows his eyes at me. 'You're not the first one to say that. And you probably won't be the last.' I can see the questions rolling over in his mind, but he says nothing. 'Is that all then, sir, because it's lunch and I get kind of lightheaded if I don't eat regularly.'

'Yes, yes, but before you go, I wanted to apologise about putting you in the water group. I completely forgot about what happened to your parents.'

'S'ok.' I pick up my things and head for the door.

'So,' I'm swapping you around. You'll be in the fire group.'

I reach for the handle and then realise, I never put on my school application form that my parents were deceased. Or that they'd drowned.

How the hell did he know that?

I turn to see him busily scribbling notes. I don't have the time or inclination to ask him right now, but I will.

Hurrying across the quadrangle and past the queues of unfamiliar faces, lining up for lunch, I go to the one place I feel normal. Water, and lots of it. My last school had an Olympic size swimming pool, and being captain of the swim team, meant I had more access and more excuses to get in there than I needed.

The next forty minutes go by in a blink and I make sure I give myself enough time to change and get back to the common room before she arrives.

The meagre furnishing of the public school system astounds me as I wait in a room that has less personality than a rock. Drab colour schemes, cracks in walls, dirty windows, *curtain-less* windows, and no carpet. Certainly not like my last school.

My attention is diverted the second I see Ember coming up the stairs.

I don't know why, but I didn't think she would come.

My eyes begin to water from not blinking.

My brain wants to go into its crazy-shut-down mode, but I pull up just in time. Before it has chance to silence me.

'I'm glad you came.'

Stupidly, I push my books to one side, somehow thinking they're taking up too much room. I gesture to the chair opposite me.

'Please, will you sit down.'

She gets out her books and her eyes tell me she still doesn't quite know what she's doing here. 'It sounded important.'

Important probably wasn't the right word to use this morning. I was flustered, grasping for any words.

'I don't know about important, but I do think that maybe we got off to a shaky start. I thought, maybe, we could rewind and start over.'

Ember's lips part and her eyes become dreamy.

I quickly check in.

The **beast** is still chained. Still suppressed. Still silent. *Yes. Touchdown.*

I haven't said the wrong thing, yet, and this conversation looks like it's finally going somewhere.

And I think it's all me.

'So, this isn't about the colour of my eyes then?' she asks. I freeze in my seat for a full three seconds before looking away.

Fuck. Don't clam up now. I say the first thing that comes into my head. 'You're very astute and my answer is both yes and no.' *Keep going, keep going, you can still salvage this train wreck.* 'I figured because we have something in common, we could be, well, friends.'

I seem to tweak a nerve and her body not only matches

260

mine for stiffness but also I see a fire in her eyes.

'And that is?' She is feisty. Not what I expected at all. I like it. By the sounds of it, she wouldn't back down from anything. But I need to be subtle.

'Your parents were killed in a car crash, weren't they?' Her face turns from pale pink to chalky white in one blink.

It is the beginning of a downward spiral for me.

Now the lies begin from my own lips ...

Except now, it's time to tell the truth.

PRESENT DAY

NINETEEN

I turn to look at her.

Ember is still wedged up against the pillows, her knees drawn up and away from me. Any life I could've had with her is about to end. Her eyes are cold, lonely and her smile is nowhere to be found.

'Say something.' I can't imagine what she is going through. Part of me shies away from her, knowing I didn't have the courage to tell her the truth about everything, but that's the kind of coward I am.

'Honestly, River, I don't know what to say. Did you ever consider that I might *want* to have sex with you? Were you ever thinking of my feelings, or was it all about *you*?'

She sounds just like my father and she's right. It has been all about me and what I want. But how can I ever explain that the spell she has over me was written down before time began.

Before life existed.

She needs time to process, time to decide if she can

still be in the same room as me without hating every word that comes out of my mouth because that's all she'll let me see in her eyes at the moment.

Her teeth nibble the corner of her lip and she swallows. 'How many? How many girls?'

I squeeze my eyes shut, her questions causing more pain than she'll ever truly know. How can I answer that? How can I tell her I lost count at five hundred? How can I tell her that? I don't want to lie anymore, but I don't want to drive the dagger in any further.

'Does it matter?'

'*You* seem to think it does, otherwise, why bring it up in the first place.'

My recollections over the last twelve months are easy enough to remember, but actually saying them aloud, to Ember of all people and inviting her into my world, is something I don't know if I'm ready for. And the worst of it is, she doesn't know about Iris – Iris who is still very much in the picture and who could ruin everything between us.

'River.' I hear my name, but I can't bring myself to look at her. 'I think I deserve an answer.'

I lift my chin, my eyes the last to follow. 'Yes, you do deserve an answer and I'll understand if you never want to see me again ...'

She cuts me off. 'Where *else* do you expect me to go?' Her voice is pitchy. 'I have nothing.' There are tears waiting. She's so strong, much stronger than I am. 'I have nobody.'

'You have *me*.'

'Do I, River? Do I have you? Because right here, right now, I'm not sure. You are in a place I can't reach. You want to tell me something, but can't. You want to touch me but refuse to, you want ...' She drops her head and the gut-wrenching sound of her crying has me on my knees.

She's not strong.

She's just like me.

Vulnerable, afraid, alone.

And I don't know how to fix it. I'm not even sure it *is* fixable.

'Em, oh god, I never wanted to hurt you. All I ever wanted was to be with you and I've screwed that up beyond …' I pause, quietening my mind, my voice. 'It's always been you, Em. Everything. My whole life.'

Sadness adorns her face in a way I can't possibly explain. Hurt, betrayal, abandonment, they're all there, so many emotions pulling her deeper into the chasm of pain I've created. Tears leave trails of agony behind, agony I will never be able to erase or soothe. She doesn't deserve this. Any of this. Not after what she's already had to do to survive.

A knife twists inside me. The truth reveals itself.

I don't deserve her.

I should walk away. I should give her up, to someone more worthy. It's the right thing to do.

There's a light tap on the door. Wally appears. 'Master River, you have a visitor.'

'Can't you tell them I'm busy?'

'I've already tried that, sir, but *he* won't leave. Not until *he's* seen you. He said it's important.'

I nod. 'I'll be right there.' Wally closes the door behind him.

I turn in time to see Ember wiping her face with her hands. Her eyes, red, her cheeks blotchy.

'I'll be back in a minute. There's still so much more to say.' I reach over for her hand, but like before, she recoils from me. I leave without a backward glance.

I find Skye sitting in Wally's favourite armchair, hugging something tightly to his chest. I had a feeling the visitor might be him, even though he's three months late! I smile my thanks to Wally for not letting the cat out of the bag with Ember. She still doesn't know that Skye and I have a history. *He* is another secret I have to explain.

'Where the fuck have you been?' I growl through my teeth. 'I've tried phoning, texting. Have you any idea how

267

I'm going insane down here without a scrap of news.'

Skye looks straight through me. 'And as per usual, Mr Sensitive, you're the first to think of yourself. Have you even considered the idea I might've had a lot on my plate over the last few months? It hasn't been easy, you know. I've had my own stuff to take care of. This superhero shit takes its toll ...' He doesn't elaborate on the *stuff*, and I'd be lying if I said, I wasn't the tiniest bit curious.

'Yeah, I get it, but the last thing you said to me, was that you were going in that night. What was I supposed to think? No news. No phone calls.'

A gentle smile pulls at Skye's lips. 'Aaahhhh sounds like you were worried about me. Sounds like someone missed me? Did I finally get underneath that thick armour of yours and find a soft, snuggly place in your heart?'

'No,' I snap.

'Not even a little.'

'Ok, I was worried,' I say, 'but only because I know who you're going up against.' And obviously more worried recently after being exposed to Ra-Mon, plus everything we found out from Mr Butcher in the last two months.

My thoughts return to Ember. She's probably still crying into her hands. I need to wrap this up. There will be time to fill Skye in on all the details of the last few months, but for now, Ember comes first.

'By the way, how the fuck did you find me?'

Skye taps the side of his temple. 'Built-in antenna, remember?'

I blow out an irritated sigh. 'Well? It better be important.'

'Didn't disturb you, did I?' Skye glances upwards as though he can see Ember sitting on her bed. He then launches himself out of the chair. 'It can wait, you know, if you're ... busy?'

I pause for a moment, digging deeper inside my soul for some kind of composure. I feel my teeth grate together. 'It's fine,' I say, trying to keep my irritation under control. Skye resumes his position, a smile creeping over his lips. 'What did you find out?'

I take the chair across from him. Wally, as usual, has made himself scarce.

'That woman is a real piece of work.'

I huff out a breath of acknowledgement. 'You have *no* idea.' I wait for the rest, growing more impatient by the minute. 'And?'

'I managed to get another four pages of her diary, photographed and translated.' He jiggles the book, Peri Phuseôs tôn Ontôn, which he holds close to his chest. 'You are *not* going to believe what I found out.'

Slowly, he peels the book away, opens it and removes a few loose papers. 'Here.'

I take them without hesitation, switch on the standard lamp and fall back into the chair. I get through the first paragraph and look up.

'What does Iris not having a good relationship with her own father have to do with anything?' I ask.

'Keep reading,' says Skye. He gestures with his head for me to go on.

I begin from where I left off.

'She goes on to talk about still not feeling *herself*. Saying she has changed and has moments when her memory is fading. What does this have to do with Ember?'

Skye says nothing.

Line after line has me leaning further and further forward until I'm as far on the edge of the seat cushion, I might as well be squatting.

I can't take any more in.

I now wish I hadn't felt the need to delve into Iris's sordid world.

Information, I didn't want, now rests with me and I have to decide what to do with it. Skye is back in my brain again, reading my thoughts. 'Are you going to tell her? She has a right to know.'

'I know.'

'She needs answers, River.'

'I know.'

'She deserves the truth.'

'For fuck sake, Skye. I know.' I fold the papers and put them into my pocket. 'Is this the only copy?'

'Yeah. What would I want one for?' I frown at his childish response.

'What about on your phone?'

He says nothing.

'Did you keep a copy on your phone?'

His lips twist this way and that.

'If you've still got it ...'

'Alright,' he barks. 'I'll get rid of it.' Skye pulls out his phone and I watch over his shoulder as he deletes it.

'It's for your own good. Because, if *Iris* finds out you've got evidence of her plotting a murder, you might very well be her next victim.'

Skye clicks off his phone and returns it to his jacket pocket. 'By the way, have you told Ember about me? Does she know I'm here?'

'No, and no, and that's the way I want it, for the time being.'

'What's the big deal? You gonna need my help more than ever now. Come clean. Stop being a pussy about this and front up to the girl. What's the worst that's gonna happen? She'll be shitty with you a few days and possibly leave to get her head together, but she'll get over it. All chicks do.'

'You don't know what she's been through already. I can't do that to her.'

'Can't or won't.

'It's not that easy.'

'You can't keep her in the dark anymore. She's the FlameMaker.'

'I feel the heaviness of the last forty-eight hours pressing down on me – the excursion to the fire brigade ... Ember going up against Ra-Mon ... 'Was.'

I have Skye's full attention. 'What do you mean,

was?'

I fill him in on a few of the details, telling him that she knows I'm the WaterLover, but that I didn't mention about him or the other Elementar, and give him the watered-down version right up to Ra-Mon ripping Nuria out of her body.

'So, now she knows more than *us*?'

'This isn't a competition, Skye. There are lives at stake here.'

'I know, I just mean ...'

'No, I didn't tell her about the book you dug up, or what we spoke about at the lake. All she knows, is that Nuria, the very first FlameMaker is, as we speak, under-going some kind of binding ritual and that I'm next on this *spectre's* hit list. Then he's coming after you.'

Skye hums out a breath. 'That explains a lot.' Confusion has found its way into his forehead and eyes. There are more questions I want to ask him, but there isn't time right now.

I pull the papers out of my pocket and wave them at him before stuffing them into the safety of my jeans pocket again. 'So, you can see why offloading all this new shit on her might be a *tad* too much.'

'Yeah, I can ... but.'

'Enough. It's my call. If she chooses to hate me, then that's something I'll have to live with.' The thought of her hating me sends a shudder over my body.

'Who are you talking to?' Ember's voice startles me. 'And what will you have to live with?' I spin around to see her standing in the doorway, her long hair tumbling across her face. She brushes it back with her fingers as she comes to stand beside me.

I look across to Skye, who is casually sitting there with his arms folded across his chest, his legs outstretched and crossed at the ankles and wearing the biggest grin.

'Who was your visitor?'

Skye silently sniggers and that's when I understand. Ember can't see him.

271

'Oh, nobody.' Skye glares at me. 'Nobody worth mentioning anyway.' His eyes grow wider. 'C'mon, let's finish our conversation upstairs.'

'Okay.'

'Go ahead, I'll just lock up.' I watch as she heads up the stairs, checking back on me every few steps. 'It's okay, I'll be there in a minute.'

I wait until she's out of sight before turning back to Skye, who is now up and out of the chair, and now leaning against the doorframe.

'Your invisibility thing is *subjective* then?' I mumble.

'Mmmm, looks that way, doesn't it?' For a reason I can't explain, his answer would've normally raised my pulse in aggravation, but all I can think of is how this power will benefit us.

I raise my eyebrows, fairly impressed. 'Handy.'

'I suppose that's us done then?' says Skye, shrugging his shoulders.

'I guess so,' I reply, nudging him out the way so I can open the front door.

'And kicking me out on the street, in the cold, with nowhere to go, sits okay with you?' There's a shadow of hurt on his face, for just a fraction of a second, but his smile soon hides it.

'Yep, and I'll sleep like a baby too.' Yes, it's harsh, but I need to get rid of him. I need this time to repair some of the damage with Ember and I don't want him close enough to earwig on my thoughts.

'Well, just for the record, man, this is the last time. If she still doesn't know the next time I see you, I'm gonna tell her myself. Consider yourself warned.' I don't want to get into a heated discussion here. I wait until he steps out and onto the doormat.

'See ya, and thanks for the info.' He nods once as I close the door.

If there is one thing I've learnt about Skye Buchannan, his word is his bond. Next time, he will unleash hell and I'll have no way of mopping up my lying shit any longer.

TWENTY

I find Ember sitting on her bed, her hair hanging over one shoulder, aimlessly plaiting a few strands. She looks up as I enter, her gaze not leaving me even as I prop myself on the bed, a safe distance away from her.

'Sorry about that.'

She still watches me, intently, too intently. 'What are you sorry for?'

I don't realise I've shrugged until I see the weariness on her face. She sighs very lethargically. 'More secrets? I should be used to that by now, but they sting all the same.'

'I don't want there to be secrets between us ...' My words are severed as she reaches out to me. I want to take her hand but I am too far away to grab it before she withdraws it.

'Then talk to me. Tell me, so I can understand.' I haven't heard this tone in her voice before, a confused begging accompanied by an unknown fear.

I bite back my guilt and let the first words to my

ultimate demise unravel. 'I've been dreaming about you for ten years, Em. Ten years. Every night you were there when I closed my eyes, smiling, crying, running, waiting for me, and every morning when I woke, you were gone. It became a way of life for me, needing to see you, wondering if you were real. Some part of me knew you had to be, but that's crazy right?'

Ember says nothing as I gather myself. The warmth that had disappeared from her face slowly begins to shine through. 'For a long time, I thought there was something terribly wrong with me or I was going crazy. I couldn't get you out of my mind. Then puberty hit, and I became a different person. There was this deep, dark urge that started to take over. Whispering to me that sex was what I needed. I read everything I could about the sexual urges a young boy has, but what I had was *different* to everyone else. More intense, somehow. More powerful. I tried to push it away, so many times, but the more I did, the harder it was to control. To the point where ...'

I look into my hands. *Please help me find a way to say this gently.*

'Go on,'

'I had to find a release.' I cringe when I say it. 'I was thirteen.' That's not the hardest part over with. 'She was seventeen, which at the time, I thought was ancient. I thought it would cure these incessant cravings ...'

My lips become glue.

My mind, a minefield.

'Only, it didn't. It made them ten times worse.'

I look up to see Ember frowning.

'I know this sounds like an excuse and I'm not sure if I'm even right in what I'm saying, especially after all the weird shit we've faced over the last few months. But ... this seems ... kind of ... *tame* compared to ...'

'Compared to what?'

Torment buckles in my elbows. Twists in my shoulders, robbing me of strength and stature. I can't believe I'm about to open up to her and tell her about the

274

beast. 'Compared to what's really going on inside me. It's like someone else is living in my skin, making these urges more than they should be, reeling in all these unsuspecting women for its own pleasure, not mine, which I can tell you, dissolves like ash in my mouth the second it's over. There is this dark voice that taunts me, haunts me, tells me it's ok to do what I'm doing.'

I swallow, waiting for the verdict.

She says nothing.

But I'm positive she is experiencing a hundred different emotions at once, if only I could hold her hand and hear them for myself.

When the silence continues, I finally say, 'It's a curse, Em. It's something I can't control.'

'You seem to be able to control yourself around me,' says Ember so quietly I almost miss it.

'Barely. You've got no idea how hard it is for me to not give in. I work harder at it because I...' I pause for a second. I can't tell her yet. It's not the right time.

Her hands fall into her lap.

She looks at them.

Looks back at me.

I begin again. 'You know how vampires lust for blood, well, that's me. I crave for something I know I shouldn't have, because it hurts people, and yet, most of the time I don't care. Or didn't care, up until recently.'

She frowns.

'What I mean to say is, I'm selfish, Em, and I want sex all the time. Every girl and woman believe they're in love with me, but they aren't. It's part of this wretched curse. I become an addiction for them, and they don't know why. They can't stop it any more than I can, and I can't turn it off either. I don't know how to.'

'How do you know that's what's happened to me? I'm different than your average *human*, or *was*, as of yesterday.' Her eyes glaze over. 'How do you know I haven't genuinely fallen in love with you?'

'I don't ... but,' I begin to add.

275

'Then why don't we just see how it goes. If you're honest with me, and you tell me how you feel, then at least we'll have something to build on. Lies tear it down. Secrets tear it down.' She nibbles her lip. 'One thing I know, because I feel it right down to my core, is that I'm in love with you, River. I know it. I feel it so strongly, Stronger than I've felt anything in my life. I know what deception feels like. I've experienced pain. I've lived with torment. Love is similar, but with happier feelings. Intense. Confusing and painful.'

A lump forms in my throat. Words I have longed to hear blow across my face, make a home amongst my bones. Words I never thought would be spoken to me, let alone from her.

She carries on. 'I'm free from all of that now. Free to make a fresh start, as are you. There are times I don't understand you. Sometimes you leave me with more questions than answers and I don't want to pry into your life or make it difficult for you because I don't invite that into my own life. We all have a past, but you have to promise to be honest with me.'

I nod.

'Can we try?' she asks. She has hope, which is more than I have. 'For example, tell me how you're feeling right now.'

'I wanna rip your clothes off and not leave this bedroom for a week.'

The first parts of a smile pull at Ember's mouth. 'Just so you know, I want that too.' My heart pumps so hard in my chest, I might die. Breath ragged. Pulse racing. Racing so fast that I can barely see her, hear her. 'But until you can remove this entity, or become a hundred per cent *you*, whatever that looks like, then maybe think about it this way. Remember, as far as I'm concerned, I am a virgin. I haven't *willingly* given myself to anyone, and although I want you to be the first, I need you to understand it's something that is very important to me. You take that from me, deceptively, like … ' She bites her lip harder.

Tears bubble in her eyes. 'Like someone else did, and you'll never see me again.'

Wow, that really put everything in perspective for me. I'm no raper, and regardless if all my victims are willing, I would never dupe Ember into losing the last fragment of purity she has.

'I understand. I swear on my life, for what it's worth, I will never let that happen.'

'That's why you swim, isn't it?' she says. 'To control it. I suppose it makes perfect sense, what with you being the WaterLover.'

We laugh, and the tension dissolves.

Ember moves closer and places her palm against my cheek. 'I don't want to make this hard for you, that's not my intention, but ...' her cheeks tint a beautiful shade of pink, 'will you kiss me?'

She checks in with me before crawling into my lap. There's something so innocent, so utterly naive about her actions. Her fingertips trace over my lips, my chin. 'When you kiss me, I know everything is ok between us.'

She presses her soft lips to mine and I am transported back to the moment when she first leaned in and kissed me at the bonfire night.

It was the most magical moment of my life.

A moment when dreams became real, where the past became the present and all the ugliness inside me was washed clean and forgiven.

I often get lost in thought, thinking about that kiss. The way my body became fire and ice, became a thousand smiles all at once. Felt whole for the first time in forever. A kiss that will never have an equal, will never diminish in my mind.

And then that special kiss under the mistletoe and how sweet, how perfect, how absolutely desirable she was and how I let myself go, just that little bit more, speeding out of control on a road with no end. No conclusion. No limits. And I was free to kiss her with every ounce of love I felt for her.

But a moment, not that dissimilar from this, only a few short weeks ago, on this very bed, the beast nearly claimed her. The chains that kept him down, broke. The glory of her filled me everything I'd hoped it would. All my wishes realised. My desires satiated. My hunger for her, gorged. It would've been all too easy to seduce her and savour every taste of her, every delectable inch of her body as I discovered it intimately. But I managed to find something inside me. I still have no idea how I did it, or where I found that scrap of decency from. But it was there in that final minute when I needed it – self-control.

Those precious minutes are beyond any pleasure I've experienced. The memory never turning to ash, like every other girl, but is as fresh, as raw and as blissful, as the day it happened.

My hands find their way either side of her neck, her bronzy curls streaming through my fingers.

It's the perfect time.

I pull back a little.

Her eyes are glassy, her breath racing but so sweet.

'Em,' Her eyes focus. Look to my lips and back to my eyes. 'I am so in love with you that it hurts to smile, to simply look at you.' A lost, dreamy smile, almost as though she's just woken from the most wonderous dream finds its way to her lips. I double check to make sure the beast is tethered and it's me she's seeing. 'My life has always been about you. I never thought I could be this happy. Never once believed that I *deserved* to be this happy. I have loved you since I was a boy, when you didn't know me, when I never knew you. I've loved you when no one loved me back. You've been a candle in the darkness to me when I was alone, and lost, and in despair with who I was. You kept me sane in the midst of madness.' My words are whispers. Promises. Declarations.

I sweep my hands over her cheeks, my thumbs smoothing out the corners of her eyebrows. I drop a small kiss on her nose, and then on her lips. 'I don't ever want to think about my life without you. Every morning when I wake, I smile because it's another day with you. I will do whatever it takes …'

'I know,' she says tenderly. 'I know you will. But I won't lie in admitting that all I want right now is to snuggle under the sheets with you.'

'Soon,' I say.

I kiss her once more, losing another little piece of myself to her, committing to memory the softness of her lips and the eagerness pouring out of her body for me. Maybe this won't be as hard as I think.

I get up and head for the door.

I look back at her, her smile growing as mine loses its lustre just a tiny bit because … I realise I'm deluding myself.

I still have to tell Ember that I hired a private investigator, slept with the woman to gain more information about her, lied countless times in order to get closer to her, am in cahoots with the next Elementar, and right now, the piece of paper in my pocket, burning a hole in my thigh is just waiting for me to spill my guts about her past.

The time has to be right, and I'd rather leak it out little by little rather than ripping the plaster off in one reckless tug. I will be honest. There will be no more lies. But I have to be cautious. I will not risk losing her, not when I've almost sold my soul to the devil to get where I am.

I lay awake, fighting sleep every inch of the way. So much has happened and so much is yet to happen. I don't know whether to tackle the past or the present first, and to top it all, I've still got to figure out how to master this so-called water power, the same way Ember learnt about fire. Maybe channelling my energies into this, will divert my urge to unwillingly seduce her. I say the word, unwillingly, in my mind, with bitterness because I am conscious of every advance I make towards her, though I have little control over it when the **beast** chooses to rise.

It is no lie, I want to feel her bare skin against mine, feel her hot breath on my neck as she whispers my name. But I want it to be me she sees in her eyes and not the monster that has done this a thousand times before.

A two-hour swim was the first thing to cross off my list this morning and now sitting across from Ember, watching her nibbling at the corner of a piece of toast that looks as though it tastes like dirt, I can tell something is on her mind. She manages a smile but I can tell it's an effort.

'I think you should go and see Mr Butcher today,' she says, brushing her hair away from her face. 'You need to be more prepared than I was. Ra-Mon is strong and it's not going to be long before he comes looking for you.'

He is next on my list today.

I rest my knife against my plate and tilt my head. 'I know.' But I don't want to be without her today. 'Do you want to *chaperone* me?' I don't fancy spending the whole day alone with some over-the-hill immortal whose sense of humour dried up with the 'big flood'.

Her lips turn down. 'Actually, do you mind if I stay here. I'm not feeling very social today.'

My heart sinks. 'I've blown it, haven't I?'

'Noooo.' She reaches for my hand and traces her fingers over my knuckles. Then rests it on top. 'I just think you need to concentrate on *you* rather than *me* at the moment. Anyway, I'll be a distraction ...'

'A welcome one,' I add.

'But not the kind you need right now. Besides, Wally asked me to help him in the library and I've already told him I will.'

I feel my head falling forwards but jerk upright when I hear Ember's chair scraping on the floorboards. She crouches by my side, still in her PJ's. Her hand rests against my thigh and I draw up inside myself and beg my body to behave. 'I will be here when you get back.' Her words offer little comfort.

She presses down into my leg as she gets up, forcing more lust into my veins, and leans in. Her hand cups my cheek. Kisses me on the temple. She looks through my eyes and into my soul for one full second before leaving me alone.

Mr Butcher, or Empedocles as he originally was known, is already waiting at the front door of his tiny terrace house when I arrive.

'What's up with you? You look like the end of the world has already happened.'

'It might as well have,' I murmur as I squeeze past him and enter his shabby, sparsely clad living room.

'Just as well then,' says Mr Butcher cryptically. I glance back at him still standing in the open doorway. My brow feels heavy with confusion. 'That's why I sent for reinforcements.' On cue, Skye sails through the door and shakes Mr Butcher's hand.

'Christ. Are you trying to kill me slowly or what?'

Skye grins cheekily. 'Chill out, bro. I'm here to help.'

'Yeah, well I don't need your kind of help. It comes with too many strings.'

Mr Butcher chuckles. 'Boys. Boys. Just how I remember you.' Nostalgia creeps across his face. He closes the door and ushers Skye to sit down. 'Did you bring it with you?' he asks. Skye nods and produces the book he vowed never to show anyone.

'What the hell are you doing?' I hear my words ringing in my ears.

'Calm down, stud. Mr B is one of us.'

'I know he's one of us, you fucking moron. I knew about him before you.'

Skye sniggers and flicks back his hair. 'Yeah, sure you did. I've got a ruler here if you need one.'

'*Boys*. We're not going to get anywhere if you don't find some common ground here,' injects Mr Butcher.

I ball up my irritation and sit in the chair furthest away

from Skye. I don't give a fuck about common ground, not when he is sitting there so smugly, like he owns the place.

'Skye, show River your hands.' Skye gets up and comes over to me, his hands out in front.

At first, I don't notice anything different, but then Skye breathes on the back of his hands, in the fleshy part between his thumb and forefingers and two small yellow triangles appear. I look up at Mr Butcher first, then at Skye. They are both smiling. I'm curious.

'So … what does this mean? And why don't I have one?'

'It means we have to go to Paris. And you *do* have one. Show him, Mr B.'

Mr Butcher gets up and I can hear the sound of running water from the kitchen. He returns with a small jug of water.

'Don't even think about throwing that on me?' I warn, leaping out of the chair.

Mr Butcher's eyebrows knit together. He looks to Skye who smirks and shrugs his shoulders. 'It's okay, River. Turn around.'

Reluctantly, I turn.

A wet finger swipes the back of my neck, and then I hear the snap of a photo being taken. 'It will only appear when the skin is wet,' says Skye, producing his hands for me to inspect. There are no yellow triangles on his hands now but the second he breathes on them again, they appear. I snatch the phone off him. Three slightly faded wavy blue lines, almost similar to a vein, can be seen just under my hairline. 'As soon as the skin dries, they disappear. Neat trick, huh.'

I hate that he knows stuff about me I don't. Plus, how would I ever have seen it back there.

'I still don't know why we need to go to Paris. I hate France. It's full of foreigners. Besides, I have to stay with Ember. She needs me.'

Skye laughs. 'She doesn't need you, you egotistical prick, and anyway Mr B says your girlfriend has to come too.'

'*What?*'

'That's right. The three of you need to go,' says Mr Butcher.

'How come I'm the last one to find this out?'

'You're not, Romeo. You have to go home and convince Ember to come.'

'Yeah, that's going to be an awesome conversation. Would you like to come to Paris with me because …'

'Because you won't be able to defeat Ra-Mon if you don't,' finishes Mr Butcher.

'But why Paris?'

Skye runs his hands through his hair. 'River, I've been dreaming of triangles my whole life, not to the same extent you dreamt of Ember, but seeing them in my waking life. Seeing them everywhere. Mr B said recurring thoughts or dreams for an Elementar are clues - that he set them up *specifically* to bring us together. I mean, you wouldn't have gone looking for Ember without those dreams, would you?'

I shrug. 'Suppose not.'

'I was the first to receive the dreams because dreams are transmitted through electrical air waves in the brain, which I can pick up on. That's how Mr B found me. And then through me, he found you two.'

'But …'

'We can get into all that another time, but we do need to go to Paris – I need to visit Le Louvre. I don't know what we'll find there, or what we're looking for, but I'm sure I'll recognise it when I see it.'

I sigh.

Reality strikes.

All this time I've been thinking about Ember, but if we don't find a way to kill Ra-Mon, Ember won't matter. Because we'll all be dead.

It's the only plan we have.

'Okay. I'll go and ask her.'

'Oh, and by the way, I'm a bit short on cash this

month. Could you spring us for the fare?'

'Surprise, surprise.'

'And perhaps first class might be nice,' says Skye in a pathetic voice. 'Never travelled like royalty before.'

'FINE.'

'And soon, River. No looking for special deals. He's after you next, in case you forgot.'

'For fuck sake, Skye. How can I forget that?'

'And you'll need to tell Ember about me too.'

I throw him a look that says so much more than I want to.

'Easy, Hercules, I'm just saying. It's time everything was out in the open.'

I know he's right.

There are a few seconds of nervous silence. 'Is that it for today? Aren't we going to start my training?' I look to Mr Butcher.

He scruffs his beard. 'There's nothing more I can teach you, that you don't know or can't learn on the job.'

'So, you're throwing me in the deep end then? Literally.'

Skye laughs. 'Looks that way, doesn't it?'

I ignore him. 'River, you have everything you need, to go up against Ra-Mon. There's no skill I can teach you that builds self-belief. That comes from courage and experience.'

'Fantastic,' I say dryly.

'It will all unfold exactly how it should,' says Mr Butcher, showing me to the door, 'and just so you know, it is forbidden for either of us to take a human life.'

TWENTY-ONE

'**Em**, are you here?' I close the front door behind me. 'Em?'

'She left about half an hour ago, son.' Wally pokes his head around the library door. 'Said she had to go somewhere but would be back for tea.'

'Did she say where she went?'

'Nope. But I did hear a text message come through on her phone a few minutes before she left.'

I can't help groaning out my disappointment. Summoning up the courage on my way home to come clean about Skye, has all been for nothing.

The Grandfather clock strikes three.

Could be three hours, maybe four until she's home. I need to swim to get my thoughts in check.

'Ask her to come to the pool when she gets back please, Wal.'

'Righto.'

For the first time ever, I find no relief from water. It

prickles my skin instead of caressing it and for some bizarre reason the temperature keeps adjusting from warm to cold. My mind is not relaxed, and I find I'm wasting too much time thinking about how to make things right with Ember rather than focussing on the more fundamental issue at hand – how I'm going to battle Ra-Mon.

I pull out of my last stroke and reach for the side of the pool, ready to get out. What is left of the afternoon sun disappears in a blink, transforming the room into night.

The air turns cold.

The ambience, not that there was much, is now sour.

Sudden pressure pins my hand to the tiles. A decrepit, white foot with disgustingly long toenails presses down into my hand, trying to grind it into dust.

I cry out in pain, feeling the bones crackle. Agony rips up my arm to my shoulder.

As though my thoughts had just summoned him, Ra-Mon appears.

'I was wondering when you were going to show your ugly mug around here.' My words are curt as he applies more force to my hand.

'Brave boy … for a walking corpse.'

The water around me turns to ice, freezing me in time, pressing against me, holding me prisoner.

I manage to glance upwards. 'I don't understand your sick fascination with drawing this whole thing out. Why not just kill us and be done with it.'

Ra-Mon laughs, a long haunting laugh. 'Killing you is the easy part. You must know that by now. I have my reasons.'

'You mean your sick reasons. Yes, your brother might have mentioned them.'

'Then, let's not waste time. This was a simple courtesy call, to introduce myself to you, and let you know, I'm coming for you soon. I need you to be more prepared than the girl-child.

'Ha!' is the only sound out of my mouth.

'What a disappointment she was.' He steeples his hands in front of his chest. 'I had high hopes for her. Nevertheless.' I sense in my own body the volume of energy he expended in binding Nuria. How much strength it drained from his decrepit frame.

'Which is why I need you to be at your strongest. Nereus is no push-over. He will fight to the death, and I would hate ...' the way he says the word hate, it's more like a laugh ... 'for you not to survive this.'

'Your brother said it's forbidden to take a human life, so how's that going to work out for you then?'

Ra-Mon's cold, lifeless eyes bore into me, like a maggot tunnelling into an apple - searching inside me, for weakness, for a way in. I sense the sharp tendrils of his power probing inside my head, inside my heart, engulfing my body with fear. The kind of fear that is silent, calculated, transparent. His touch sends a jolt to my brain, injecting images and memories into my mind, snapshots of his plans – world domination ... and if not, reduce it to fire and brimstone.

Fury erupts in my blood. 'Fuck you. And the horse you rode in on,' I manage to say, pulling out of his control with my last remaining strength.

Pain implodes within me, crushing my bones, arching my back. I let out a mighty scream. My eyes close once and re-open.

A sinister smile crinkles the skin around his mouth as the bones of my hand shatter beneath his foot, snapping like twigs, bringing about a new wave of agony.

This time, there is no scream. No cry of pain. I don't want to give the prick the satisfaction.

'I see my brother has abandoned me yet again, to fight for some righteous cause. You tell him ...'

He releases the pressure a little from my hand and I feel a surge of boldness. 'Tell him yourself. I'm not your damn delivery boy.'

In the time it takes me to blink, his hand is around my throat, lifting me clear out of the water.

I grasp at the scrawny claw that holds me captive, struggling for air, legs kicking several feet off the ground.

His face becomes distorted.

I can't speak.

I can't breathe.

'Tell *him*, keeping himself out of your decision making won't protect you or him. Tell *him* if he thinks distancing himself from *you two* will prevent me from discovering your little plan, he will have to try harder.'

The second my body hits the wet tiles, Ra-Mon is gone. I still feel the iciness of his breath against my face, his talons around my neck. My throat burns as I suck down mouthfuls of air.

As I start to regain my senses, feel the blood rushing back into my body instead of throbbing inside my head, something Ra-Mon said has me confused and a little excited. He said, 'if he thinks distancing himself from you two.' You *two*. He doesn't know about Skye, which means we have the advantage … for now.

Night draws nearer and Ember still isn't home. Another hour in the pool fixes the break in my hand, heals the pain in my body but nothing can eradicate how on edge I am.

I clench and re-clench my fist, testing it out. 'It's not like her to be out this late, and without a car,' I say, more to myself than Wally.

'Don't worry, son. She'll be here soon.' Wally's voice of reason is beginning to irritate me.

'You should've asked her where she was going, or at least given her a lift.' I sigh. 'It's past eight o'clock already.'

The sound of the front door has me up and out of my seat. 'Em?'

Standing in the main foyer, her hair tangled, her eyes bloodshot and glassy, and a coldness on her face that far outranks my icy visitor from earlier, Ember clutches her arms around her, staring off into space.

I advance, cautiously. 'Are you okay? Has something

happened?'

She is a statue.

'Em?'

'I'm tired. I just wanna go to bed.' She makes for the stairs, stops, puts her hand on the bannister and waits a few seconds. Slowly and deliberately, she takes step after step upwards and away from me.

Fuck.

I retrace my steps back into the library and flick on the computer. Those tickets to Paris aren't going to buy themselves, regardless of how totally shit I feel about myself. There was no mention of how long we need to be there for, but I assume three days should be enough.

I text Skye straight away, telling him to make sure his passport is in order and to be here at 6am so that Wally can drive us to the airport. He is prompt with his response, adding "First class, s'il vous plait".

I don't reply.

I lay awake that night, listening to Ember stirring in the room next to me. Her cries in the night bother me more than they've ever done, and the silent treatment between us means my usual presence at her bedside when she wakes is unwanted. I still haven't told her about why we're going to Paris. She simply accepted the invitation and said she'd be ready in the morning.

A high-pitched scream pierces the air.

I race into Ember's room to see her sitting up in bed with her hands around her throat, panting. Without thinking … without waiting for permission, I rush to her bedside and pull her into my arms. She falls into me, and for a few seconds, everything feels the way it used to. Slowly, her body peels away from me.

'Bad dream?'

'Always,' she mutters. She looks a little embarrassed.

Soft lilac shadows are just visible beneath her eyes and her face has that 'help me' look that she just can't, or won't, vocalise. It reminds me of the time I had to smash her bedroom window and rescue her. Seeing her lying on the floor after being locked up by her molesting foster father, bleeding profusely, wearing nothing but a dirty t-shirt and a pair of knickers.

I feel as helpless now as I did then.

My heart is breaking all over again.

'Do you want me to leave?'

At first, she doesn't answer.

I get up.

'No. Don't go.'

My relief gives me away.

A tear escapes. Runs down her cheek. She lets it fall. 'Why do you say these things if you don't want to *leave*?'

I feel her confusion as it dissects with my own. 'Because I don't want to cause you any more pain.' I glance across at her and catch her eyes.

'Is that why you keep things from me? ... because you think it will cause me less pain?'

Ouch.

Her bottom lip trembles and she bites at it.

I can hardly look at her.

'Because you're wrong. You're so wrong. Lies are pain, River.' Her voice breaks. 'Lies are pain and being kept in the dark is a lonely and scary place to be, in case you didn't know.'

I turn my gaze to the carpet, walls, ceiling, window, anywhere but her. I don't have anything I can say that will paint me as the good guy, the one who loves her, would die for her, that would trade everything to be with her so she would never have to live through another horrific memory. She is slipping away from me, and I can't stop it.

'I *do* have more to tell you. I know that. But, every time I try and find the right time, something happens.'

Ember makes a sound halfway between a moan and a grumble. 'Don't you understand *anything*?' She pauses, straightens her back, her face grim. 'There is never going to be a *right time*. Not when Ra-Mon is out there, not when I know you're next on his list. There is *never* going to be a right time.'

She's right.

She's always right.

My chin hits my chest.

I haven't even the courage to speak directly to her.

'I have to tell you something important, Em, and I've deliberately kept it from you because ...' I trail off. How can I tell her it was because of my own insecurities with Skye?

There is silence for such a long time.

I'm forced to look up.

Her eyebrows are raised, but she no longer has that look of surprise on her face. She's already expecting me to backdown. It's another knife wound in my flesh.

She waits for me to continue.

'Because I can't stand the thought of you being with someone else.' I swallow and wait for her reaction.

'You mean Skye Buchannan?'

The earth shifts a few degrees.

My head no longer feels as though it belongs to me.

Heart rate spikes.

Cloudiness falling around me.

My senses dull and my brain unresponsive.

I open my mouth but I have no idea what to ask ... where to start or how she has come up with this name. The only two times I know of her being in the same vicinity as Skye Buchannan is at the tobogganing place and the restaurant in London.

I still haven't responded, but I don't need to.

'I know everything, River.'

More head spinning, more gravity slopes away from me.

I urge myself to get a grip and stay in the moment.

'Skye told me everything. How you met. How the two of you spent time together before moving here. How you ignored him when I first stupidly introduced you. How you insisted that he wasn't allowed to tell me you and he

291

had a history.'

I find my voice. 'Because I wanted to be the one to tell you.'

'When? River? When? When I'm *dead* and won't feel any more pain? When you have nothing left to lose.' Her tone is sharp and angry and real.

'NO.' I collect myself. 'No, Em. Don't say that. The thought of you dead has no place in my mind. I can't even …'

'You can't wrap me up in cotton wool, River, and expect me not to live my life. There is some serious supernatural shit going on in this world and we are caught slap bang in the middle of it. I have a job to do, as do you, and so does Skye. We have to support each other and let go of these childish grudges.' I know that last part is directed solely at me. She wouldn't know how to hold a grudge if she tried.

'What else did he tell you?' I am praying that Skye has some small amount of compassion and hasn't told her about Iris and the diary.

'That we need to go to Paris to look for something and that all three of us have to go.'

'And that's it?'

The suspicious look on her face tells me I should've kept my mouth shut.

'Why? Is there *more* I should know?'

I could say yes, I could say no. Ember's "lie equals pain" line repeats inside my head. But I do not want to discuss Iris Perkins or how she was responsible for hiring the person who killed Ember's parents.

'Yes, there is more, but the disgusting part of me – the liar in me –wants to reassure you and say no – there is nothing more you need to know.' I feel a shake in my bones.

The truth sucks.

'I'm pathetic, Em. I can't help it. It's part of who I am and how I've survived. It's not pretty, but I *am* trying.' I re-state my vow to her. 'And I promise, I will tell you the truth, no matter the consequences.'

Ember nods, trying to look brave, but the quiver on her chewed lips is a dead giveaway. 'Is it *that* bad then?'

No lies.

No more lies.

'Yes, it's bad, yes, but please believe me when I say, it *can* wait until we return. I want the three of us to focus on Paris. Like you said, we need to be there for each other.'

She nods submissively and leans into me until my arms find their natural place around her.

She whispers into my neck. 'And for the record, and I don't know how many times I have to say it – I'm in love with you. Not Skye Buchannan. Not anyone else. You, River. I just wish you believed me when I say it.'

I do believe her, to a certain extent, but I can't be a hundred per cent sure, it isn't the beast's influence at work.

TWENTY-TWO

NO sleep.

Brain with a thousand thoughts.

Feet fidgeting at the bottom of the bed.

Knuckles taut and white.

Heart on a wild journey of its own.

My body is already reacting to a conversation I haven't even had yet.

I watch the clock tick down from four to four thirty.

I decide to get up, knowing sleep is further from me than happiness is.

Even more surprisingly, I have no urge for sex. Mornings are usually the worst and it is a welcome distraction not to have a raging boner first thing

Breakfast is also quiet, and there is a slight awkwardness as Ember and I wait for Wally to bring the car around.

I check my watch.

Skye will arrive any minute and as much as I hate to say it, his childish behaviour is more than welcome this

294

morning. Anything is better than this.

No sooner as the thought is out of my head, he struts up the driveway in jeans and a coat - bag slung over one shoulder, a grin from ear to ear. 'Ember, hey. Just as gorgeous as ever. How did everything go yesterday with Mr Sulky over there?' He boldly kisses her on the cheek but not before dishing me a questioning glance and a nod of his head.

He opens the rear door of the car. 'Let's shotgun the back seat and whisper about River.' Suddenly, I want to eat my words.

Ember's face breaks into a huge smile. The kind of smiles she used to give me. 'You just don't know when to stop, do you?' She likes him, I can tell, and leans in and gives him a hug. The second kiss on her cheek he steals has me seeing red, especially as he winks at me afterwards, but Ember doesn't seem to mind it. She pushes him playfully into the car and follows in behind.

Faced with two options – sit in the back like a father on prom night or be the mature one and take the seat next to Wally.

I take the front, knowing the next hour, I will be subjected to Skye's deliberate taunts and him reading every one of my thoughts I have in response to it.

After saying goodbye to Wally and checking our luggage, I am laughing on the insides as we find our seats on the aircraft. Yes, we are in First Class, but I have positioned Skye two seats away from Ember and I. He winks and nods to me, like he somehow knows it's deliberate, but a congratulatory smile finds its way to his lips.

'Everything satisfactory, sir?' asks a flight attendant. Skye nods. He is brimming with excitement.

'Awesome, thanks.' He sips his drink.

'I'll be back with the menu, sir.' Skye grins and leans over his seat to me. 'This is totally, freaking, awesome. And she called me sir.'

I want to smile but don't. 'Didn't take you for the type

who likes all this pomp and ceremony. Not when you could fly there yourself and be done with it.'

'And where's the fun in that? It's things like this ...' Skye holds up his glass. '... chilled orange juice as we wait on the runway while all the plebs are being herded into cattle class.' A rather large woman passes us and throws a vicious glare in his direction.

Skye shamelessly toasts his glass to her as she pushes sideways between seats, deliberately bumping her bag over the top of his head. It nearly upsets his juice all over him.

He smirks and flicks his hair out of his eyes. 'And having a proper napkin and eating with a real knife and fork instead of that plastic crap that breaks as soon as you stab a potato is just perfect,' he says in an extra loud voice so she can hear.

I catch Ember smiling.

He does make me laugh, however, I'm still irritated from the drive. 'What's the difference, you hardly use cutlery at home anyway.'

'Let's just say, this is the coolest thing you have done for me since we met.'

There is a smile on his face that looks, well, genuine.

Like the countless overseas first class trips I'd taken with my parents, the journey is over as fast as it begins. Apart from Ember holding onto my hand for dear life during take-off and landing, admitting to her fear of flying that I never knew about, our flight was quiet and uneventful.

I spot my name on a white placard as we make our way towards the baggage claim. The man resembles so many of the chauffeurs I've seen before – bored expression, olive complexion, bald and smelling of cigarettes or too much aftershave. Except one thing is different – this guy is wearing a patch over one eye.

I reach out to shake his hand.

'Mr Fulton, may I confirm your identity?' He has a Mediterranean look but no hint of a French accent.

I get out my driver's license. He checks it over and hands it back to me. 'My name is Salvatore, and I will be your driver for the next few days. Where are we off to first?'

'Hotel du Louvre.'

'Ahh, Hotel du Louvre. Very nice, very nice. Please follow me and I will see to your luggage.'

'Sok, mate, I'll get my own bag, thanks,' chirps in Skye. 'I'll get yours too, Em.' He walks off in the direction of the baggage carousel leaving Ember and I staring at each other.

'He's Australian,' I say when Salvatore looks back at me, frowning.

Ember and I follow Salvatore to the car and a few minutes later, he returns with my bag and Skye in tow. Skye squashes into the back, making me shift over seats so Ember is in the middle, and we drive in silence listening to some swanky Latin Swing music.

The hotel is everything I remember it to be. I overlook the grand entrance with its majestic, black marble pillars and head straight to reception, leaving Skye and Ember to take in the view. I hear Skye say something about 'how the other half lives' and I smother a smile before greeting Gervais, the concierge.

I booked three rooms, all adjoining, and after a quick freshen up, we are soon heading down the Rue de Rivoli to Le Louvre. The sun has graced us with its presence but only just, and certainly not enough to leave our coats behind. It must be less than ten degrees. I'm also glad to see Ember wearing the hat and scarf I bought her for Christmas. Her nose and cheeks are bitten with cold as the wind whips her red hair into a frenzy of fiery tendrils.

Just as I suspected, there is a queue to get in and not just a queue, but a couple of hundred people waiting. The glass pyramid with some six hundred and seventy-two panels of glass looks amiss against the buttery yellow of the Louvre Palace.

297

'You look at home here,' says Ember as we wait in line.

'I've been here a few times before.' Her eyebrows rise and Skye lets out a half a laugh. 'School excursions,' I explain.

'School excursions?' squawks Skye. 'That must have been some fancy prep school your parents shipped you off to. In my dreams and only in …'

I'm no longer interested in what Skye has to say. A man is staring at me from across a sea of heads. He is at least a foot taller than the people waiting in line.

But to me, he stands out.

Like I know him.

Like some unnatural force is drawing me to seek him out.

His face could be tanned although with the hood of his thick, dark coat up, I can't be sure. It could be shadows. I can't see his hair either, but one thing I do know, his gaze remains on me.

I take a quick look behind me, in case I'm acting more paranoid than usual, and that *he* isn't actually looking at me but someone else, and by the time I turn back, he's completely vanished.

I scour the heads and stretch to see if I can see him, but he seems to have dissolved into thin air.

Ember must see something in my face to ask if everything is ok. I tell her I'm fine, but she continues to watch me.

She takes my hand.

Squeezes it.

'Have you noticed all the missing people posters?' She points out random pictures taped to lamp posts and the windows of buildings. 'I spotted at least twelve when we walked here.'

I'm shocked. 'I've never seen so many,' I say. Now that I'm acutely aware of them, there seems to be way more than *normal*.

'There were loads at the airport too,' she says,

298

stepping closer to me. 'I don't feel safe here.'

I place a protective arm around her, and she doesn't step away from me. She smiles briefly and lean in closer resting her head against my shoulder. It feels good to be so close to her again. I've missed the honey smell of her hair, and the soft strands that brush against my cheek. 'It's ok. I won't let anything happen to you.'

The queue moves fairly quickly and after twenty minutes of waiting, we take the escalator down to the first level and then further down to reception to purchase our tickets.

Skye has lagged behind, busy exchanging phone numbers with some Swedish girls.

'Oi, so, where do we start, Einstein?'

He cautions me with his finger to wait. I let out an irritated breath and hold fast. Ember is jittery too, her fingers keep fidgeting in my hand.

Skye saunters over a few seconds later, pleased with himself, flicking his hair annoyingly as he walks. 'Now, where were we?'

'*We* are trying to save the world,' I reply, 'except we can't because you're trying to get in their knickers.' A few people turn around and I smile politely back at them. I reduce my volume. 'Ready?'

'You're such a joker,' says Skye, completely oblivious to my sarcasm. 'I reckon we should start on the lower ground level and work our way up.' Skye pulls out a map from his back pocket and points to where we are. 'We're standing here at Napoleon Hall. I figure we go around each level and hope something jumps out at us.'

'And *that's* your plan? *Hope* we find something. Do you have any idea what we're looking for?'

'Nope.'

I roll my eyes at him. My jaw locks. Feels like stone. 'No ideas, *at all*?'

'No,' he says quite innocently. 'But, I think I'll know it when I see it.'

'Great.'

Skye regards me. 'Come on Em, stick with me. Mr Negative over there is about as much fun as this fella.' He points to an old guy in a painting with a sour look on his face.

Skye takes Ember's hand and drags her off in the direction of the Islamic art exhibition. She doesn't let go, but does glance back at me with a helpless look on her face and the hint of a smile, just for me.

I follow behind them, listening to them talk. The more I listen to him, the more I realise he is everything I'm not. Light-hearted, witty, endearing, feisty, attentive, and I can see how girls are taken in by it.

I hate this whole comparison thing I've got going with Skye. I suppose it's because I've never competed for the attention of a girl before, and this time especially, for a girl I have true feelings for. My one consolation is Ember's words. That she is in love with me and not Skye.

I pray it's enough … enough so that the over-protective boyfriend I've become, which let me say I hate myself for, can learn to deal with it and find some peace.

We scour the whole lower ground level, spanning the globe from Greece and the Roman Empire all the way to Egypt without the hint of familiarity for Skye.

We weave our way through majestic white halls, half-naked white marble sculptures mounted on podiums, just lounging around as though they're waiting for something interesting to happen. Men with spears, fighting lions and other beasts, don't raise even an eyebrow for Skye as we pass them. We head through rooms as long as hallways, with hand-painted ceilings similar to the Sistine Chapel, edged in thick golden filigree framework.

'What about this,' I find myself saying in every few yards.'

Skye looks and then shakes his head.

More rooms come and go with elaborate arches and black and white chequered flooring, adorned with an array of mounted marble heads, and still he says no.

'What's supposed to happen, Skye?' asks Ember as we stand in front of the Gilded Parade Helmet of Charles VI. I am interested in his answer and take a step towards them.

'Honestly.' Skye shrugs. 'I don't know. I've been dreaming of triangles and seeing them in everything I do since I was a child. Then one night I dreamt a triangle turned into Le Louvre and I knew I had to come here.'

Ember smiles. 'Don't worry. We'll find it.' He seems to take strength from her words.

'What I didn't say before was, as soon as I stepped out of the elevator, I felt something. A kind of energy telling me I'm on the right track. The answer is here. I can sense it. The same way I knew who River was before I found out he was the WaterLover. Le Louvre is somewhere I've wanted to visit for a long time and yet never understood the reason, until now. All I knew was, I had to come. That's all I've got, I suppose you'll just have to trust me on this.'

'I do trust you,' says Ember and links her arm in his. She looks back at me. 'And so does River, don't you Riv?'

As much as he grates on every nerve in my body, I do trust him. With my life. 'Yes, I trust you, brother. Just switch on that damn antenna and find this thing.'

Skye frowns.

'Don't look at me like that. You know the one I mean. The one that can pry so intently into my thoughts and emotions and read my mind.'

Ember looks confused. 'What antenna? What mind reading ability?'

An embarrassed smile slides off Skye's face. 'Secrets, Em. What can I say ...we all have them.'

Ember is quiet for a moment. She looks at me and back at Skye and then down to the floor. When she looks up, her eyes have softened and there is a flush of warmth to her cheeks.

'You're right. We do all have them ... me included.'

301

She turns to me and takes my hand.

Her fingertips are so soft as she traces faint lines into my skin, they could easily dissolve right through me. I'd almost forgotten what it felt like.

The **beast** awakens immediately, but he's easy enough to subdue.

'I'm sorry for being so hard on you, River, especially when I'm equally as guilty.' Her eyes cloud over. 'I refused to let you in when we first met, all because of secrets, because I was worried how you'd treat me or how you'd see me.' I smile back at her in an attempt to ward off her pending tears. 'Especially, when all of us ...' She pulls Skye into our cute little healing triangle, '...have lived such dysfunctional lives the last few years. None of us have had it easy, have we?'

I look at Skye, remembering what he's had to endure from his brother, Dean, and Ember with the abuse from her foster father.

Yes, we *are* all dysfunctional.

We all share a common bond that goes well beyond the realms of mystical powers. And I don't believe it's coincidental that we've had these hardships on top of everything.

I put my free hand into the middle as a gesture of unity. Ember places her hand on mine and Skye on top of hers. 'Together in pain. Bound by a destiny,' I say.

'Or we could've just said friends forever,' says Skye.

That sentiment doesn't fit, not for me. Never has. I want to be more than Ember's friend, and some days I want Skye to be more like a brother than a friend, but being caught up in the moment, I mutter a 'sure, why not?'

Ember glances over my shoulder.

Her eyes narrow.

'Don't turn around.'

Her voice is a little louder than a whisper.

Skye, of course, does exactly the opposite and makes a point of looking. She grabs his hand and pulls on it. 'I said, don't look.'

'*What*? Who are you looking at?'

She groans and jolts his arm again. 'We need to work on our communication skills if we're going to be working so closely together. And you just did the total opposite of what I said.'

I let out a short laugh. 'I thought it was only me that he did that to.'

Skye is still looking bewildered. 'What's going on?'

Ember speaks through the corner of her mouth. 'That guy over there is staring at us.' She grabs hold of Skye's chin and turns it to face her. 'Don't move. Got it?'

'Okaay. Got it.' He stands firm.

'Is he tall and wearing a long overcoat?' I ask.

Ember's eyes widen. 'Yes. How did you …'

'I saw him earlier, outside.'

Ember lets go of Skye's face and grabs for my hand. She is shaking. 'What should we do?'

Skye presses his hand into my back and I notice him do the same to Ember. 'Let's walk up to the next level and see if he follows us. We have to go that way anyway to get out of here.'

Without acting too inconspicuous, we casually walk up the ramp to the next level and begin our search again. Artefacts from Africa and Asia, plus more Greek and Islamic sculptures, fashioned in brown marble take their positions around the room. The sounds of chatter from French teenagers on a school trip hang in the air around us and the group of Swedish girls' Skye was chatting to before are now gathered around the Venus de Milo.

'He's still there,' says Skye, scratching his wrist before waving to the girls. He scratches again.

I thought he might be.

'I think we should split up,' says Skye.

'I think that's the dumbest idea you've ever had,' I reply abruptly. 'What if he doesn't go after you or I and goes for Ember. She doesn't have the powers we do.'

'I can take care of myself, River,' says Ember, conjuring a small flame in the palm of her hand before dowsing it with one quick flick of her wrist.

'I still think it's a bad idea.'

'What do you suggest, Hercules? Go right up to him and demand to know why he's following us. He's as big as a house.' Skye is still scratching.

'I think we should get out of here and come back later. And stop scratching. You're like a dog with fleas.'

Skye shakes his head. 'I can't help it.' He looks down at his wrist and scratches again. 'I think I'm allergic to something. Unless …'

'Unless what?' I ask.

He brings his wrist up to his face and drags his short nails over his skin. The yellow triangles beneath his thumbs are raised up and inflamed. 'Do you think this is a warning sign, that maybe we're on the right track. That maybe this fella is here because we're supposed to meet him.'

Ember and I stare at each other.

'Maybe,' she stutters. She grips my hand tighter. 'But he doesn't exactly look the friendly type, does he? Otherwise, he would've come up and said hello, don't you think?'

I have to agree with her. 'I think we should make haste while the sun shines.' I turn slowly to take a look at him to find him casually leaning against a mighty stone pillar. Again, he doesn't avert his eyes. 'We need to leave now.'

Skye bites the inside of his cheek. 'I'm not sure if we can. I mean, he gained ground on us pretty quickly. I'm not sure we'd get out of here without him collaring us. I don't have a good feeling about this.'

Ember trembles against me. 'He's not going to make a move whilst there are loads of people here,' I add, trying to offer some words of comfort to her.

'But there are enough twists and turns in this place, he could easily thump us and run.'

Ember bites her lip. 'Do you really think …'

'No, I *don't* think that's what he'll do. I refuse to believe you've been dreaming of this place for this long, only for us to get here and have Andre the Giant here make a meal out of us.' I grimace, feeling the impact of my words as Ember cringes beside me.

A wide grin spreads across Skye's face. 'I have an idea. Howabout I make us all invisible.'

'Invisible? I thought that was just something you could do. You never told me you could do that to anyone else?'

Ember's face shines. 'You could make me *invisible*?'

Skye smiles and winks at her. 'I did it with my dog once, back in Oz, but I might not have enough juice for the big fella too.' He nods in my direction.

All I care about is getting Ember as far away from here as possible. She doesn't fool me with that vain attempt of producing a flame. I saw in her eyes how much it cost her. She is not as strong as she used to be before Ra-Mon stripped Nuria from her body.

'Yes, do that, and then I want the two of you to get out of here as quick as you can while I'll try and lose Goliath over there. Make your way back to the hotel and we can come back tomorrow.' I can see Skye doesn't like my plan, but he reluctantly agrees.

'So, how are you going to do this?' I ask him, looking around at the crowds of people moseying about near us.

'I'm subtle.' He winks at Ember.

'I find that hard to believe.'

Skye gives me a reproachful look. 'Believe me, stud. This is one area where my skills outrank yours. Give me a break, okay?'

I can't help smirk. 'Show me what you've got then.'

Ember looks back at me with a fake grimace as Skye takes her by the hand and leads her towards the group of Swedish girls. Off to one side is an arched culvert and just when I think he's chosen that for his Houdini trick, they slip behind the two metre marble statue of Aphrodite and completely disappear.

I have to admit, it's a smooth move. Nobody noticed a thing and I can't wipe the smile off my face.

I walk off in the same direction and stop in front of the statue, noticing in my peripheral vision, the guy in the long coat has closed his gap on me, just like Skye predicted.

I speed walk, as fast as I can, around corners, down sandstone stairs, changing levels, trying to lose him. He's persistent and from his skills, I can tell he's done this kind of thing before, but I have a few tricks up my sleeve.

Ahead of me, is a child holding a water bottle.

The liquid inside is my weapon.

I summon Nereus asking for help.

I focus on the bottle, instructing the water to do what I ask. A funny feeling in the pit of my stomach sends calmness over me, as though we have already come to an agreement. The closer I get to the water, the stronger the feeling gets. The child regards his water bottle with confusion as water bubbles and fizzes over the top.

I look back to see the stalker less than a few feet away. He must have ran, although I don't recall hearing his footsteps. And from the size of him, those footsteps would be loud on this tiled floor.

As I pass the stunned child, I summon the water from the bottle, waiting for that precise moment to unleash an explosion. The stalker doesn't know what's hit him as the entire contents are discharged at him with more force than a high-pressure hose. I look back just in time to see him knocked off those massive feet and onto his arse.

The satisfaction is like a cigarette after sex, not that I actually know what that feels like, considering I've never smoked. All I know is, using my power is better than sex.

In fact, it's mind-blowing.

And the bonus is, the beast, who lay in wait as Ember stroked and drew circles into my hand has recoiled almost to the point I no longer hear it's whisper. It isn't the long-lasting cure I'm looking for. But it works.

The downside is, it's made me thirstier than I've ever

known. I could drink the Seine dry at this rate.

I cut across the middle of the room, pass the stairs and duck into the men's toilet. I throw my head under the tap and guzzle down gallon after gallon of water, barely coming up for air. I hear the door open, but pay it no mind.

I need more water.

Lots more.

I do, however, feel the sharp pain on the back of my neck and my nose hitting the porcelain of the sink. The deeply scarred face of my attacker is the last thing I see before I fall into a dark slumber.

TWENTY-THREE

WHEN I wake, a man in a brown sportscoat is standing over me. 'Êtes-vous d'accord?'

My vision is fuzzy and what at first looks like a black marble pillar, I deduce is actually a man's frame. 'What?'

'Are you okay?' he says in a strong French accent.

I'm not sure.

I reach for the back of my head and the lights above me dim.

'Be gentle with yourself. I think you may have fallen.'

I want to say, no, I was hit over the back of the head by a tall guy with a scarred face, but don't.

I stumble to my feet, my head imitating a jackhammer. The image looking back at me in the mirror doesn't look like me. My nose is broken, and blood is plastered over my lips and chin.

'You seem to have dropped this.' The man bends down and picks something up. He places a rough, silver disc in my hand. I stare at it, trying to figure out what it is or whether it belongs to me.

Nothing comes.

'Thanks, I think.'

The man hums, nods once and leaves.

I hang my head over the sink, willing myself into consciousness.

I splash my face until the ache in my nose disappears. I can't apply water to the back of my neck without getting my t-shirt wet, and I don't much feel like getting sprung stripping off in a public toilet. I'll take care of it when I get back to the hotel. I take one last look in the mirror before leaving. Apart from the dried blood on my coat, which thankfully is black, I don't look any different other than a slightly crooked nose.

I stagger to the door.

Head thumping.

Vision failing me.

The tiled floor slopes away from me.

I straighten up, grab for the door handle and head out into a room full of people.

I stop in mid step.

Ember?

Skye?

Fuck. I wonder if they made it out.

I fast pace it to the exit, the best I can, half-hoping they're there, half-hoping they aren't standing out front, exposed, waiting for me. *Skye wouldn't be that stupid, would he?*

Clutching my ribcage, gasping for air as I hurry outside the main doors, I discover there are less people out here than before. The cold air does nothing to bring my senses back and it takes me less than five minutes to work out they are not outside.

For a brief moment, I feel relief.

Then the worry sets in.

I can't decide whether to go back to the hotel to look for them or wait around here hoping they'll show up.

I need a minute to think. Get myself together.

I spot a seat next to a man and his wife.

I need to sit.

I need to work out my next move.

With my back to the triangular shaped pools flanking Le Louvre, I drop my head into my hands, the light spray from the fountains offering very little comfort.

What I really need is ... water.

Water to clear my head. Clear this fogginess.

A headache is starting to work its way into a migraine every time I look up to scan the horizon.

Fuck, Skye, where are you?

'I'm here, Fabio. Why don't you have a little more faith in me?'

Skye stands over me with a sheepish grin on his face.

'How did you know where I'd be?'

'Triangles and water, Dude. Triangles and water.'

I chance a look at him. He's alone.

'And Ember?'

'I thought she was with you.'

'*What*? *No*. She's not with me.' I get to my feet quickly, and then wished I hadn't. I feel like I'm going to throw up. Everything from my knees upwards is swaying. 'I knew leaving her in your hands ...'

'Chill, brother. She's fine. Learn to lighten up a little, will ya? She's in the toilets.'

'And you didn't think to wait for her.'

'She told me not to.' He has an indignant look on his face. 'She's not a child, River.'

'I know she's not a fucking child, you moron. Do you think I'm incapacitated because I like the helpless look?'

From the reaction on Skye's face, he hadn't noticed. 'Shit. What happened?'

'That frigging prick hit me over the back of the head and left me in a bathroom.'

'Emberrrr,' drawls out Skye.

'Ember.'

Skye takes off before me, and I limp behind the best I can. I hear him asking a lady in the foyer where the toilets are. She points him in the direction, and he takes off again without waiting for me.

By the time I catch up to him, he is pacing outside the Ladies restroom. 'She hasn't come out yet. I'll give her a few more seconds and then I'm going in.'

It isn't a few more seconds, it's one.

He sneaks behind a plant and turns invisible, not as subtle as before, only under the eyes of two toddlers in a pram. I see the door open, all on its own, and then close. In the time it takes me to catch my breath, Skye returns.

'She's not in there. She must be in 'another ladies', somewhere.' He draws quote marks in the air.

I pull out my phone to ring her.

'Don't bother. She already told me she left her phone on the hotel bed.'

'Fuck!'

I've had enough of his bullshit for one day. I muster all my strength and last ounce of energy and slam my fist into his face.

He doesn't even know what's hit him.

We make our way back to the hotel.

Empty handed.

Skye continuously rubs his jaw as we hightail it down the Place du Carrousel. 'I can't believe you did that. What about all that comradery and pact stuff the three of us made. Did that *actually* mean anything to you, or was it just words?'

'Yes it *meant* something to me. But you've had that coming for a while.'

He rubs his jaw again and drops his lip.

A new feeling, one I can only assume is guilt, finds its way under my skin. 'Ok, I'm sorry. I lost my shit. I'm worried. Really worried. Now if you can stop thinking about yourself for one minute, lets figure out where Ember is.'

I'm not completely going off just yet, because some part of me is praying that Ember is safe and waiting for us in the lobby.

Skye sniffs. 'As long as you're *really* sure you're sorry.'

I throw him a sideways glance. 'If you don't shut up, you'll get another one.' From the corner of my eye, I see him smirk.

We hurry into the lobby.

Ember is not waiting for us.

'I'll check down here. You go and check her room.'

Skye heads for the elevators as I make my way to reception to ask if anyone had seen her return.

Another dead end.

My heart becomes numb. Breaks into a million pieces. Turns to dust when Skye returns without her.

My body is falling out of rhythm.

Missing her smile.

Her smell.

I'm in that dark space all over again.

Empty.

Lost.

My world, collapsing.

Becoming shadow and sorrow.

Becoming the old me.

'Stop looking at me like that. I told you, I'm sorry.'

Muscles tighten.

This emotion stuff is bullshit.

It's as though I'm jumping on and off the same insane merry-go-round. 'You had one job. One simple job. And now she's gone.'

Skye's face is pale.

It's not hard to see he's just as worried. 'I didn't think it was, I mean, I thought she'd be ... Fuck! I never should've left her alone.' His hands rake over his hair, his knuckles white, his teeth clenched so tight I know what kind of pain he's feeling. I place a hand on his shoulder.

A failure.

A disappointment.

Totally incompetent.

Is how he truly sees himself.

My rage simmers. 'We'll find her.' My words have no effect on him. He won't look me in the eye.

'I can't sit here and do nothing. I'm going to retrace our steps to Le Lourve, just to be sure.'

I grimace. 'I'm not sure that's wise.'

'Don't stress. No-one will see me.'

I nod. 'Ok. I need water. I can't function like this.'

He nods. 'I've got my phone on me,' he says, and heads out the revolving door.

I go to my room and quickly strip off. It takes less than a minute for the water to totally heal me, eliminating the heavy lethargy inside, giving me back my ability to think and reason.

My reflection in the mirror says hopelessness. The numbness shrinks back, just in time for the real pain and heartache of losing her all over again, hits me.

I've failed her.

I put the same jeans back on, a clean t-shirt and jumper, and head back down to the bar opposite the reception area.

I choose a spot near the window, giving me a clear view of the front entrance. I want to be the first person she sees when she returns.

I order myself a drink.

Seconds … become minutes … become hours.

I'm not sure the reason Skye took his phone. He hasn't answered the four calls and three messages I've made. I'm about to head out when he saunters through the door, head hanging low.

'Hey,' I call out.

He looks up, his face tired, his body begging him to rest. He pulls up a chair and flops into it. No words are necessary. I wait for him to talk … for once.

He picks at a thread on his jeans. 'For God sake don't feel sorry for me.' He glances up at me, scrutinising my face, listening in on my thoughts. 'The last thing I need is a pity party.'

I clear my throat. Words stuck. Not sure what to say.

'I screwed up. Just like I always do,' he says. 'Like *you* always *expect* me to.'

'Like *you* always do? Have you seen my track record? I'm not exactly citizen of the year either, you know.'

Skye blows out a long breath and I realise that he has his own demons, just like I do.

I reset. 'Have you tried to tune into her, like you did with me.'

He slams his hands down on the arms of the chair, prompting the barman to look over at us. 'You don't think I've tried that,' he growls through his teeth. 'I'm getting nothing. It's like she's vanished off the face of the earth.'

I throw him a questioning glare.

'And no, it's not my power fucking up. It's something else. Someone else, I don't know.' His lips purse together. 'I've never mentioned it before, but when a power has been used, like yours for example, it leaves behind an unusual *taste* in the air.' I lean forward, a flash of hope catching in my chest. 'And there was nothing. I thought maybe Ra-Mon had kidnapped her, using her as bait to bring you in and that I could then follow it, but there was nothing.'

I slump back into my seat.

'I don't know where to start looking. We have nothing to go on with.'

'Maybe not.' I flip Skye the tarnished disc that had been left on the bathroom floor after my assault. 'What do you make of this?' I sip my drink, deliberately ignoring the olive-skinned waitress who can't keep her eyes off me.

Skye catches the disc. He turns it over in his hands. 'Looks like a coin.'

'I figured that out for myself, Sherlock.'

On one side of the coin, is the head of a man with accentuated curls, and the other is that of a thin man with a spear in his hand. 'I wonder how old it is.' He reaches over and places it next to my drink.

'*How old it is*? Are you tripping on something? This

314

might be the only clue we have of finding Ember and you're worried about how old it is?'

Skye shrugs and drops his head to his chest. 'What's the big deal with it? It's just a coin. What do you want to do, take it back to Le Louvre and ask them about it? How do you know it wasn't stolen from the museum in the first place and then dropped during the heist?'

In all honesty, I hadn't thought of that. My plan was to take it in there tomorrow. But what if it *was* a piece that belonged to the museum and I go asking about it. Shit!

'OK, fair point. My instinct says that the gutless prick who hit me from behind, dropped it. If we find out about this coin …we find out about him.'

Skye lifts his head. 'S'pose that's all we've got to go on.'

I snatch up the coin and go look for Gervais, the concierge. I find him attending to someone's luggage.

'Ah, Monsieur Fulton. How is your stay?'

'Good. Good. I wonder if you know of somewhere in Paris that sells old coins.'

Gervais takes a closer look at the coin. His thin eyebrows come together. 'I don't know of anywhere, sorry, monsieur.'

My body deflates. Life begins to cease for me as Ember slips further and further away. I start to walk back to Skye.

'Oh, Monsieur?'

I turn around, weary, my heart craving just one small smile from her, even if that smile isn't for me.

'I don't know where you can buy coins, but my father used to be … how you say, conservateur …'

'Conservateur?' My French kicks in. 'You mean, curator?'

'Yes, curator. He was curator of Le Louvre fifteen years ago. He has a small villa in Chatillon Sur Marne. He might be able to help you if you want information about the coin. I can call him if you wish.'

Hope is re-kindled.

315

Another restless night.

Uncomfortable.

Too hot one moment.

Too cold the next.

I got up several times, adjusting the heater, robbing me of more sleep. And then a musty, almost damp smelling aroma kept waking me, ripping me from crucial moments when I swear I could hear Ember's muffled cries, but couldn't see her. Couldn't reach her.

Skye looks just as rough when we meet up for breakfast. No smile. No sarcasm. No stupid jokes. Broody doesn't suit him at all and for the first time since we met, I wish he would be his smart-arse self just so that something feels normal.

Salvatore arrives on time and with the windows down and his customary Latin Swing music bellowing through the speakers, we travel west to Chatillon Sur Marne. It gives me a good hour and a half to think.

Officially, Ember is now a missing person. Skye had suggested reporting her disappearance to the authorities, but for some reason, I'd advised against it. This isn't something to get *La Police* involved with.

Too many questions.

Not enough answers.

I turn to see Skye curled up on the back seat, asleep, his mouth slightly open. The scenery changes dramatically as we leave the hustle and bustle of Paris behind us. Quaint farms and villages pop up and pass us and I pay them little attention. There is a shake in my muscles I can't seem to stop and all I want to know is how much further we have to go until we're there. I think I might have a temperature too, because it's chilly outside, cold enough for gloves and balaclavas and yet sweat continues to gather on my neck.

Salvatore turns down the music as he pulls onto a dirt track. 'We are here, monsieur.' Three words I'd long to hear.

Gervais's father's villa looks like something out of the 1850's and was probably built around that time, gaging the style of houses in the area. The grey stone-pitched walls have a rustic, prison look about them and the roof, which could have been thatched at one time, but now is a bit of everything, is in need of repair. Random tiles are missing between straw clumps with plastic covering it, and the eaves and guttering jut out at unsymmetrical angles. The windows are more dark than dirty and the paintwork, which looks to have been pale blue at one time, needs some love and attention.

'Nice place,' mutters Skye sarcastically and yawns. His words are straight out of my head. I scowl at him, but he lifts one shoulder in question. 'What?' He hisses out some kind of protest as I shake my head.

I determine Henri du Garcia is an oddball before he invites us in to his comfy but cluttered living room.

Sincere.

Friendly enough.

But odd.

It may have something to do with the specks of red nail varnish on his fingernails labelling him as a cross-dresser or perhaps it's the tonne of women's clothes laying over the backs of sofas and chairs, that does it, especially after he informs us his wife died eight years ago and wouldn't be back to disturb us any time soon. But whatever he is, he seems harmless and eager to talk.

'Excuse my poor English. I 'ave never 'ad much use for it, living down 'ere.'

'Sok, Henri. My French is a little rusty too.'

Skye chokes on a laugh. 'Sh-try speaking Australian. No bugger gets ya.'

Henri nods and narrows his eyes at Skye as though he has no idea what he's said. 'Please. Sit. Gervais tells me you 'ave a coin you wish me to look at.' I sit on the edge of the chair, careful not to crease a flowered printed dress draped over the back. I feel as awkward as Skye looks.

The décor is the same inside as it is out, apart from the addition of clay pots, tapestries, old brass helmets, and a myriad of antiquities doing their best to hide the steely grey of the walls.

Henri removes a saucepan from a black wood-oven. 'Soup? I 'ave made it sis morning.' Skye struts over and looks in the pot. He turns to me and shakes his head very subtly.

'Errr, no, we're good thanks.'

'Yeah, we just had brekkie,' adds Skye.

Henri makes his way over to what looks like his favourite armchair and places the bowl of soup on a flimsy table next to it. Skye is left with the sofa, where every square inch is adorned with skirts and blouses of every colour and design. He looks to me as to what he should do. I give him a smirk and a wink, like I'd expect from him, and watch how he clumsily picks up the women's garments to make space to sit. Henri pays him no mind either.

'So, let me see sis coin of yours while my soup cools.'

I get up, taking the coin out of my pocket as I go. I pass it to the old man, his hands deeply lined and ingrained with a lifetime of dirt.

He looks at me and back at the coin. 'Sacré bleu,' he says, rubbing the coin with his thumb. 'But sis cannot be.' He spits on it and rubs it some more. In my peripheral vision, I see Skye's mouth draw downwards in disgust.

'I found it,' I offer. 'At Le Louvre.'

Henri looks up, disturbed. 'You come to my 'ouse and bring me stolen coin?'

'NO,' I protest. 'I found it, or rather, it found me. You see, this guy was following …'

Skye clears his throat. A slight shake of his head.

'There was this guy and well, to cut a long story short, he dropped something, and we picked it up. We tried to catch up to him, but we lost him, and now we want to return it to him.'

Skye exhales loudly.

For a pathological liar, that was the most pitiful lie I've ever come up with.

And Henri knows it.

They both do.

'Do you know where it comes from?' I ask, eager to pick up the conversation again.

'Sat is not the problem.'

Skye frowns. 'What is then?'

Henri gets up and paces back and forth in front of a small leadlight window, mumbling to himself in French. He is clearly agitated. Skye looks at me in bewilderment. I mouth the words 'I don't know,' and wait for Henri to continue.

'You shouldn't be worried about where it comes from, rather than 'oo it belonged to.' I recall my assailant. 'These coins were part of a lost collection. They haven't be seen for 'undreds of years.' Henri looks up at me first and then at Skye. 'It is has value of ten times more than my petite village.'

'Wh ..?' begins Skye. 'Are you saying this coin is *valuable*?'

'Sat is the biggest understatement of the century. It is, how you say … has no price.'

'*Priceless*?' whispers Skye to me.

'And what do you know of its history?'

Henri returns to his seat. He carefully balances the coin on the arm of the chair and picks up his bowl. He stirs it for two full minutes, flicking his gaze back and forth to the coin.

'So the story goes, five 'undred of these coins were crafted from the blood of the sun god, Sol, and given to 'igh ranking Roman soldiers as a token of their devotion.'

'Devotion to what?' Skye and I ask at the same time.

Henri slurps down some soup, getting most of it on his mushy pee coloured jumper. He picks up a chequered yellow blouse, wipes the soup away and begins to eat again as though we aren't even here.

'Devotion to what?' Skye asks again. His fingers

won't stop drumming against the outside of his leg.

Henri brushes back his hair - hair that was once black, according to the colour of his black eyebrows, but now a dirty grey colour like used dishwater left to stagnate. His face creases slightly, the skin more weathered than wrinkled. I'm guessing his age at around eighty, but who knows. He could be more. His eyes tell another tale of youth and health and adventure.

Henri rests his spoon against the edge of his bowl. He takes turns in looking at us, a curious smile teasing his lips.

He looks up and points to the ceiling. 'To the almighty.'

There is a pause.

Apart from the sound of the pot boiling on the stove, the room is silent.

'*God*?' I hear Skye ask.

'Not *our* god. Sol. Sol or Ra, as he was known in Egyptian times, believed his philosophy would live on through the blood of these coins.' Henri picks up the coin from the arm of the chair and flips it back to me. 'And that his legionnaires would uphold his beliefs and protect the seven initiations, all under the command of his right hand man – Mithras.'

I open my mouth to ask what initiations, and who the hell is Mithras, when Henri continues.

'Mithras was a Persian god. According to philosophers, some say he was born from a rock, which is why he felt the need to hold his secret cult meetings in caves.' Henri's eyebrows rise and he seems to drift off to some faraway place. 'You know, if you go to Le Louvre, you will discover a lot about Mithraism, although, I wasn't into it myself. My area of expertise was Greek mythology and the Celtics. You know the Celts had …'

I'm not interested in the Celts and have to cut the old man off. 'What else can you tell us about Mithraism?' Henri stops in mid-sentence. 'Yes, Mithraism. Sorry, but I know only a small amount. I had to learn a little when I was *curator*.' He looks to me on his pronunciation and I nod and wait. 'It was a strange cult, mysterious, and even today they do not know how or why it was formed, although some believe it was supposed to rival Christianity.'

Skye turns his gaze to me. The slight recognition I see in his eyes is all I need to believe this isn't some random stalker. 'What happened to this "*Mithras*"?' asks Skye.

'Nobody knows. He was looked on as a god, so who knows.'

'And what about these initiations?'

Henri places his bowl back on the table and folds his arms across his chest. 'There were seven of them. I think raven is the first.'

'Raven?' Skye's face has turned from one of nervous excitement to deathly white. 'Are you sure it's a *raven*?' His voice wobbles on the word.

'Oui.' Henri is frowning. 'You know something about sis, don't you?' His elbows dig deeper into his knees as he leans forward.

'It's nothing. I just really hate ravens, that's all.' I recall his fear from before and I'm determined to get to the bottom of his little mystery as soon as we get back.

'Anyway,' says Henri, 'you should go and have a chat with Abigail Martineau at Le Louvre. She can tell you more about Mithraism. She is the world expert on the subject.' I make a mental note of the name, although getting a personal interview tomorrow might be tricky.

As though Henri's has read my mind, he says, 'mention my name and you'll have no problem getting in to see her.'

It is the start of a plan.

'Well, thanks, Henri, but we won't take up any more of your time.' I rise out of the chair at the same time Skye does. 'We should be off.'

Henri nods once and groans his way upright. 'It was nice to have visitors.' Skye goes to shake his hand, but Henri withdraws. 'Sorry, I cannot,' is all he says.

I find Salvatore sitting on the passenger side of the car, door open, legs stretched out. He looks to be finishing the last of a sandwich.

Heading back to Le Louvre, my thoughts wander to the darkest parts of my soul. I don't want to imagine Ember tied up in some dingy basement, held against her will, wondering why the hell I haven't come for her yet, but I can't get the vision out of my head.

A fist squeezes around my heart.

I glance up to see Skye staring at me, his eyes full of sorrow and his mouth agape.

'I'm sorry, man. I truly am.'

TWENTY-FOUR

THE return trip doesn't seem to take as long and I find myself back in the foyer of the hotel. Gervais is stapling a pile of papers together. He looks up and smiles.

'Did you see Henri?'

'Yeah.'

'And he 'elped you with the coin?'

'Yeah,' is all I can say again.

'He is smart. No?' says Gervais, 'and his place is amazing, yes?'

'It would be an awesome place to show visitors if it wasn't for the clothes,' says Skye in a flat tone.

I must have a strange look on my face because Gervais laughs. 'No, he's not like that. He does the laundry for the women's auxiliary club.'

'Right.' I'm not convinced. It still doesn't explain the nail varnish though.

'Do I have any messages for me?'

'No, Monsieur. No message. No phone calls.'

I sigh. 'Thanks.'

The light is beginning to fade as I step outside again. I look out onto the street, hoping against hope she'll come around the corner and tell me this was all a big joke.

Skye is beside me in an instant.

What are we going to do ...? My thoughts are interrupted when Skye answers.

'I don't know, dude.' My teeth find their same old clenched position.

'Can't you track her? Turn on your spidey senses and locate her.' I can't help keeping the animosity out of my voice.

'You think I haven't tried that, stud.' He's pissed off and we're back to the name calling again. 'Normally it's no problem, even if someone is in a building, it still works.'

A flash of something crosses my vision. 'What if she's underground? In a basement or *cave*? Would you be able to pinpoint her?'

Skye's frown lifts. 'It would certainly explain why I'm getting absolutely zero signal. But it still doesn't help us much. She could be anywhere.'

'Suppose the only thing we have to go on is this.' I flip the coin up and catch it. 'I suggest we head back to Le Louvre first thing in the morning and go and chat to Abigail Martineau.'

'And in the meantime ...' Skye looks as helpless as I feel.

'In the meantime ... we wait.'

And I need a shower or a woman.

I end up with neither.

Five thousand laps of the small hotel pool before I go to bed and another at five am subdues the beast. The urge is as strong as always, and yet these last few days, I seem to have developed a better resistance to its taunts.

I did dream last night, but not of Ember, which makes me more anxious when I wake. I can't ever remember a time where I went more than a day without seeing her face.

The dream was about Nereus. *And* the beast. But they weren't separate entities. They were the same. Merged together.

A master of emotions.

A ruler of sexual pleasure.

Nereus was a tall man with a mane of long blonde hair. An image of how I've always pictured him. He didn't speak, but I can't escape the fact that he was trying to tell me something.

Breakfast was even quieter than yesterday and as we enter Le Louvre, somehow, it doesn't have the same flavour as it had yesterday. There is a staleness in the air as though too many people had breathed out and forgot to inhale. Tiny sweat beads have gathered on my upper lip and I wipe them away, acutely aware my mouth tastes like copper.

I feel Skye on my heels.

He's hardly spoken this morning, other than to ask questions I didn't have answers for. I sense his apprehension as easy as he's just read that thought out of my head.

'Bonjour.' The lady behind the counter has a bright, cheery face.

'Bonjour,' I reply. 'We were wondering if we could see Abigail Martineau. We are friends of Henri du Garcia and I have an incredibly unique artefact I think she would be extremely interested in looking at.'

The lady picks up the phone. My broken French manages to ascertain that she is on the phone to Abigail. The conversation is short.

'She will be here very soon. Would you like to take a seat?' Her ring-clad fingers directs us to a couch. Skye takes up her offer.

I can't sit. I can't eat. And I won't rest until I find her.

'I hear ya, brother,' mumbles Skye. He looks down at the floor, refusing to meet my gaze.

A few minutes later, a lady appears from a side door.

She has a confident stride and her grey skirt and jacket remind me of Iris. The thought of Iris and sex stirs in my loins. *Shit! I should have done six thousand laps.*

My first instinct is to lay on the charm and get what I need from this woman, but for some reason, I don't think I'll need to. She is already intrigued.

'Keep it in your pants, lover boy. I've got this.' Skye is up and standing next to me.

'Have I ever told you how pathetically annoying your little stalker brain is …' Any urge I did have is gone. He is the best anti-hard-on I've ever experienced, and it brings a smirk to my lips as I hear him groan in disgust.

Her hand is out, ready to shake, and I push past Skye to get there first. 'My name is River Fulton, and this is my friend, Skye.'

'Very nice to meet you.' She has an American accent. I wasn't expecting that. 'I'm Abigail Martineau.'

Being the total amateur that Skye is, his response is nothing less than I expect. 'I thought with a name like Martineau you would be French.'

She graces me with a smile and Skye with half a grimace of sympathy.

'I am French, but my parents divorced when I was a baby. Afterwards my mother moved to the US.' She glances over at the clock behind the reception desk. 'I am terribly busy.'

I've already retrieved the coin from my pocket. 'What can you tell us about this?'

Her eyes come alight with all kinds of wonder, but she refuses to touch it. 'Come this way.' We follow her through the door she'd previously entered and through several offices until we come to a large glass panelled room, which has all the airs of an ancient library, smell included. Books are heaped everywhere and there are helmets, statues, paintings and other artefacts positioned around the room.

'Sit,' she says, gesturing to a pair of leather chairs. The long, white, plastic table that stretches the length of the room seems out of place. 'Let me take a closer look.' She pulls on a pair of lint free gloves and takes the coin, before sliding it beneath what I can only imagine is some kind of high tech magnifying glass.

The next, silent, half an hour is torture with Abigail raising her hand at us whenever we even contemplate speaking. She is up and down from her seat, thumping large encyclopaedia books onto the table in front of us and muttering to herself as she flicks through page after page. Precious minutes are ticking by.

When the last book slams shut both Skye and I jump. Abigail reclines back in her seat and shakes her head. She has an incredulous look on her face.

'Where did you say you got this from?'

Before I can speak, Skye butts in. 'We didn't.' His tone is sharp and unimpressed.

She slides the coin out from under the magnifying glass and smooths her thumb over the rough metal surface before handing it back to me.

'You have an exceedingly rare and mythical piece of history there.' She frowns as though what she's said has no place in her mouth.

'Tell us about it,' I ask.

'This belonged to a Roman Legionnaire.' I smile. So the old man wasn't telling us stories. 'Or so the story goes.'

'You mean it's not true.'

'There is no evidence to suggest either way. Most stories stem from myths, lost and changed over time to suit the age. A false story about a painting, a map to a Templars treasure, all still myths.'

'Templar? You mean like a knight-of-the-round-table, Knights Templar?'

'Yes. Their history also dates back to this era, again with the same air of mystery surrounding it.'

'So, they were allies.'

'No, they were sworn enemies. Christianity despised the teachings of Mithraism, in their belief of false gods and their frequent human sacrifices.'

'Henri mentioned someone by the name of Mithras and the sun god, Sol. Where do they come into all of this?'

'The Mithraism cult is something I do know a great deal about. The Roman deity, Mithra or Mithras, appears in historical records from the 1AD to 4AD, just after the birth of Christ. Unlike major mythological figures of Greek-Roman times, like Jupiter and Hercules, there are no ancient sources to preserve the mythology of this god. All of our information is derived from depictions on monuments or tablets, some from cave drawings and the limited mentions of the cult in the form of ancient scrolls and parchment. It's all a bit mysterious really.'

Abigail clears her throat and continues.

'The temples of Mithras were located in underground caves. A picture on the outer wall of the cave showing Mithras killing a bull is often seen. Tablets appears in the same format everywhere, but with minor variations.'

She opens a massive book and shows us a picture of it.

'Mythology says that Sol sent his messenger, a raven, to Mithra and told him to sacrifice the bull. It was this ritual that, according to certain theologians, created the beginning of mankind. The blood was first collected in a mixing bowl, and it is said that the holy seed of the bull shaped every creature on earth. When a great light shone down, dark creatures of the earth emerged. A serpent licked the blood spilling from the bulls wound, a scorpion tried to suck the holy seed from the bulls genitals. A lion was also present. With the creation of the world, alongside the bulls death, the struggle for good and evil began – bringing forth the condition of human life.'

Skye seems to have frozen to his chair when I turn to look at him. His eyes transfixed on Abigail. She doesn't notice and carries on.

'Did you say raven,' asks Skye.

He has that same tremble to his voice, and I realise I forgot to question him on it after visiting Henri.

'Yes,' replies Abigail. Skye suddenly appears to be on edge.

'The raven symbolises air, the lion fire, the serpent the earth and the mixing bowl, water. Bringing about the four elements – air, earth, fire and water and from there all things were created.'

Skye and I exchange glances. *We're on the right track.* He nods.

'What happened to Mithra?' I ask.

'Legend says, both he and Sol, banqueted together before mounting the sun gods chariot and venturing across the ocean to the end of the world.'

I take a breath. This is too much to take in.

'The cult was all male and there were seven degrees of initiation.'

Abigail pauses again and glances at the coin rippling across my knuckles.

'Which brings me back to my first question …where did you get this? And don't lie. I have a knack for picking liars.'

I decide to come clean. 'I was attacked by a man in Le Louvre yesterday and when I woke, this coin was on the floor beside me.' I feel no need to divulge the whereabouts of Ember.

'And so you're looking for some payback?' says Abigail.

'He took our friend,' adds Skye. I glare at his big mouth. '*What*?' he says glaring at me, 'you wanna find her, don't ya?'

Abigail is on her feet. I sense that brief, deathly silence before the explosion. 'Do you boys want to tell me what's going on?'

'We can't, and you won't believe us if we do,' replies Skye. There is a smile under his tone that only I can see.

She reaches for an old phone that I took for a relic. 'We need to phone the police.'

I turn to Skye. 'Big mouth. That's why I wasn't going to say anything about Ember.'

'That won't help. Abigail …' I flash her an award-winning smile and turn on my power. 'We just need to find out where we can find more of these coins. Please. We will find her. We just need a little help … from you.'

Abigail softens and drops back into her chair. I have her just where I want her. Out of habit, I look to her hand and notice a wedding ring. This complicates things, even if I did promise to be on my best behaviour. I never go for married women, but she is just my type. Or the beast's type, I should say. Thirty, sophisticated and underneath that prim and proper suit, a wily bobcat waiting to be unleashed. 'Can you please help us?'

Abigail deliberates for a few seconds. 'Okay. I'll give you twenty-four hours and then I'm going to the police.'

'We are forever in your debt. Now … about those coins?'

'There's not much to tell really. Only one museum in the world actually has one on exhibition and like I mentioned before, they're very rare *and* extremely valuable. Whoever has lost it, will be mighty disappointed it's gone.'

Skye leans in closer to me. 'Is there any chance *he* might come looking for *us*? I mean, he knew exactly where to find us yesterday.'

'Then why hasn't he found us already to claim it. No, we need to look for him.'

Abigail rises and plucks a newspaper from a shelf where hundreds of newspapers are stacked up. She spreads it out on the table and reopens one of the books she'd been looking at previously to a page where a Roman Legionnaire is standing with a spear and the picture of our coin beneath it.

'Here's your coin,' she says, pointing to it. In the picture, it shows both sides of the coin. It's a perfect match for the one in my pocket. Abigail then turns to the newspaper. The date at top of the page says *June 3, 1876*.

She lifts the pages very carefully until she comes to a photo of a grand cathedral. 'Here is one of the very first photo's ever to be taken in history, *and* it so happens to be a picture of the last sighting of any Roman coin found.'

'Where is this church?' asks Skye.

Again, I shake my head at his lack of education. 'It's a cathedral, you moron.'

'It's called the Cathedral of Our Lady of Chartres in Chartres, fifty miles southwest of Paris. Three Roman coins were found on the steps of the Cathedral. Two, from later documents, state these coins simply disappeared from existence and the third ended up in a museum in Brussels.'

I stare at the picture, my eyes blurring in and out of focus. Something, or more to the point, someone, has been captured in the foreground, loitering around the top step.

'Will your magnifying glass work for photos?'

'Yes, it was made for photos. Why?'

'Would you mind?' I gesture to Abigail to carefully slide the photo into place. I look through the lens. 'Can you sharpen the image a little more?' She presses a button on the edge of the machine and the image comes into focus.

'Get out of here.'

The breath in I'd taken is worthless when I realise the shadowy figure is none other than my assailant from yesterday. It was his unnatural height that originally caught my attention, but the deep scarring down one side of his face, I can see quite plainly, is a dead giveaway.

I turn to Skye. 'Take a look.' He already knows what to look for after tweezering the information from my brain.

'Are you sure?'

'Never been surer in my life. Looks like we have a place to start.' I pull out my phone. 'Hey, Salvatore, can you come and pick us up from Le Louvre in ten minutes. We want you to drive us south.' I check my watch. It's only 10:30am, leaving us most of the day to explore the Chartres Cathedral.

Skye casually sifts through my thoughts in regard to our one hundred and seventy year old roman coin collector, but the look on his face, as we speed towards the cathedral, tells me he wants to discuss it further … in private.

So, we travel in silence. No Latin music. No polite conversations. There is a tense feeling in the air and it's not just me that notices. Salvatore's driving is more erratic than usual, and Skye looks over at me several times as though he totally agrees. It's a relief to get out when he finally pulls into the car park in front of the Cathedral. 'Do you need me very soon?' he asks.

'We'll be a few hours, Salvatore, so go and get some lunch or something. I'll give you a call when we're ready.'

'As you wish.'

'You want a water?' I ask Skye, spying a small Patisserie.

'Sure. And get something to eat too. I'm starving.'

We end up sitting on the steps of the cathedral to eat after reading their NO FOOD policy inside.

'How about that photo? Do you think it's the same bloke? And if it is, he'd be *well* over a hundred and fifty years old.'

'Pictures rarely lie,' I tell him.

'Unless you photoshop them.'

I roll my eyes. 'Don't think that was around a hundred years ago.'

'What if he's a Roman Legionnaire? You know, like a real, proper one. What do you reckon, Riv? Is it possible?'

'Anything is possible. I mean, look at us. He probably even belongs in the same family tree as Mr Butcher.'

'And what do you think he wants with us, I mean Ember. Or is it all of us, or just her?'

I shrug my shoulders. 'I don't know. But I have a feeling we will find the answers inside.'

TWENTY-FIVE

SKYE and I approach the cathedral.

The enormity of the building is staggering. I shield my eyes from the sun as I look up at the two colossal spires. They stand obediently, like two resolute soldiers, either side of a massive stain-glass rosette window - the colourful pictures and images only truly appreciated from within the cathedral itself.

It's pretty impressive for a pile of white stones but no different really than any other cathedral I'd visited on the multitude of school excursions. The French gothic architecture, featuring hundreds of sculptured figures, adorning the impressive archway we're about to walk through, aren't the only eyes I feel on me.

I collect myself.

Push away the anxiety driving into my heels.

There's no putting this off and I take a quick glance at Skye before we mount the white marble-like steps into the cathedral.

The same familiar long, high ceiling and drafty,

slightly musty aroma is present as always. Not forgetting of course, the big man himself, just hanging around at the back of the cathedral, looking like he's just waiting for a miracle to happen. I look to my left as we walk in to see two sticks of incense burning.

'This is the coolest place I've ever been,' says Skye, taking in his surroundings. 'I betcha any money, whoever took Ember, is holding her in the crypt.' He shows me the picture of it on the pamphlet he'd just picked up off the table.

Initially, the crypt doesn't interest me. 'That's so cliché. It's the first place *anyone* would look.' What does interest me is the way people are walking around in circles looking at the floor.

'Okay, Mr Know-It-All. Where would someone of *your* intellect look first?'

'I don't know. Somewhere a little less obvious.'

'I think you're wrong, dude. Trust me on this.' I cast my eyes in the direction he's pointing. A beautiful blonde woman is standing in front of a group of people.

'The tour to the crypt is this way,' she says in a sexy, French accent. My body automatically pulls in her direction. The urge to rip off her clothes and make her scream out my name is more powerful than anything I've felt in weeks.

'Attaboy,' says Skye, clapping me hard on the back. 'I knew you'd come around.'

'Just so you know. I fucking hate that you can hear my every thought.'

'I know, stud. I know.' He laughs heartily. 'But think where we'd be if I couldn't.'

I acknowledge him with a sniff.

We head over to the group, tacking onto the back. I've no idea why I try to hide behind the other tourists because the blonde notices me straight away.

I feel a nudge in the ribs from Skye. 'Do your thing,' he whispers. He stifles a groan as I grind my heel into his foot.

The blonde weaves her way through the group and holds out her hand to me. 'My name is Rhebbeka. You wish to join the tour?'

'Yes.' I take her hand.

My body tightens and instantly, I want her.

I can tell she wants me too.

'Easy there, pitbull,' mumbles Skye, placing his hand on my shoulder. His words break the hold I have with her. 'My name is Skye, and this is River.' I feel dizzy in my body although my head is still focussed and sharp.

'Nice to meet you, River.'

She disregards Skye.

Her hand skims against mine, sending ripples of desire through me. 'Come up to the front, where I can keep my eye on you.'

Obediently, I follow, taking in her hypnotic aroma of Christian Dior's, Poison.

I hear Skye behind me, cursing under his breath. 'Don't forget, this was your idea,' I say over my shoulder to him. He mumbles again.

Rhebbeka directs our group through a large archway to a set of stairs that have been roped off.

'This crypt was only discovered a hundred years ago, long after the Cathedral was built. You will notice from the paintings on the wall, as we move further into the Crypt, and the raw precision of the stonework, what has drawn experts to believe the Crypt dates back to ancient Greek times. Historians are certain, that over the last three thousand years, many large structures have taken their turn to act as a tombstone for the god, Osiris. In the last few centuries, the Cathedral has become one of these tombstones. Osiris had a particularly strong interest in the concept of immortality. The five tombs below are meant to house the remains of Osiris after he was dismembered by his brother, Set, who wanted his throne. Normally, in drawings, Osiris is pictured with a whip and crook over one shoulder.'

Rhebbeka winks at me and continues. 'Distraught by

the news of his death, Osiris's wife, Isis, collected up the fourteen pieces of her husband and joined the fragmented pieces together. The only missing part was the phallus.'

Rhebbeka pauses and looks directly at me, lifting one eyebrow.

'*Phallus*?' says Skye.

'His dick,' I reply.

'Ewww, gross.'

'So she fashioned a golden phallus, and briefly brought Osiris back to life using a spell she learned from her father. This spell gave her time to become pregnant by Osiris and then, she took off to the desert and gave birth to her son, Horus. So the story goes, the gods were impressed by the devotion of Isis and resurrected Osiris as the god of the underworld.'

'That's a little freaky,' says Skye.

'Depends on your needs, I suppose.'

Skye frowns at my response, and he steps to one side as Rhebbeka unclips the red rope.

'How far down is it?' asks an elderly woman to her husband. 'I won't be able to get back up with my bad knees if it's down too far.' She has broad a Scottish accent.

'Five steps, that is all,' I hear Rhebbeka say to the woman.

I take the lid off my water bottle and sluice back half the contents.

Stop!

Something strange is happening to me.

My body is numb. Neutered. The gentle buzz has disappeared, along with the burning urge to drag Rhebbeka off into one of the tunnels and screw the living daylights out of her. Even the lure of her perfume makes me scrunch up my nose. It smells like paint stripper.

She reaches out to touch me, and instinctively I back away.

'This is wrong. I can't go down there,' I whisper to Skye.

'Scared of the dark,' he says, chuckling. I grab him roughly by the sleeve until we are back in the main hall.

'Will you let go of me.'

I drop his sleeve; not even conscious I'm still holding on to it.

'What's a matter, man. You look like your gonna chunder.'

'What?'

'Chunder … vomit … throw up,' says Skye.

I feel like it. 'I don't know. Call it intuition, if you like, but that woman was weird.'

'You didn't seem to think so to start with,' he says, making delicate thrusting movements with his pelvis.

'Well. I do now. And quit doing that. People are staring at you.'

He doesn't stop, so I walk away, leaving him to explain himself to a man in a brown suit who is walking towards him with a security guard.

I try to act normal, like a standard tourist, gazing up at the stain glass windows and reading small plaques hung on pillars and walls. Skye re-joins me in less than five minutes.

'Thanks for dumping me. That guard wanted to chuck me out. It's a good job I told him I was your *lover*, and that throwing me out could lead to a huge discrimination suit. Oh, and by the way, I also told him you were a lawyer.'

I turn to him. 'Does it ever stop … for you.'

There is a confused expression on Skye's face. 'Does what stop?'

'The childishness. The charade that life is one big joke.'

The light disappears from his face. 'Hey, when you've lived the life I have, and been pummelled from pillar to post, what else is there to do but eat buckets of ice-cream and chocolate, dope myself up on anti-depressants for twenty years and then finally shoot myself in the head. You tell me, Riv? You're the one with all the answers.'

He offers me a grin, but it's fake. 'Or, I could turn out like you – only thinking about yourself, using people for his own purpose and treating everyone with contempt.'

I'm thoroughly ashamed of myself.

'I'm sorry. I really am. I'm just so worried about Ember, I can't think straight, and then that woman ...'

'Don't sweat it, bro. It's forgotten already.'

I realise for all the things that really piss me off about him, he is a much better guy than I am. I look to change the subject.

'What's going on there?' I stare at the way people are following a strange maze on the ground.

'It's the labyrinth,' I hear Skye say, waving the pamphlet in my face. 'It says here that on a Friday, the labyrinth is open for anyone who wishes to walk a pilgrimage of healing and enlightenment. On any other day, there are chairs covering it. Oh, let's be tourists, Riv, and walk the Labyrinth. Can we, Riv? Can we?' There is still a smirk on his face after I stare him down.

At last, he is silent which allows me to think. I don't know why, but this whole situation is like the worst case of déjà vu.

'You have to complete the entire 860 feet of it and follow it to the middle where you will find a copper or brass plate that once depicted Theseus and the Minotaur fighting,' continues Skye. The swirling pattern on the floor makes my eyes ache when I look at it.

'Minotaur?'

'That's what it says.'

Again, more about Greek mythology. How does it make its way into a catholic church? Don't the two contradict each other?

'The Greeks were here first, dude. Catholicism didn't come about till two thousand years ago.'

I half listen as I look around the cathedral for clues to hear Skye still babbling on about how some queen was impregnated by a bull and that her offspring – half man, half bull, the Minotaur, was incarcerated in a labyrinth where human sacrifices were sent to feed the beast.

'This is really interesting stuff, Riv? You should take a look.'

He pushes the pamphlet into my face. 'I haven't got time for fairy tales, Skye. They won't find Ember, will they?'

'For fuck sake, man. Will you just listen to me for a minute? I really think there's something in this. Didn't that chick earlier mention something about a bull ...?'

I swing around to face him. He has a point, and I can't deny, the Labyrinth has a much stronger hold over me than the crypt.

'You're damn right I have a point, dipshit.' I bite down at his rudeness and lack of respect for my privacy.

'It can't all be coincidence, can it?'

I nod in agreeance. 'Yes, there's a connection, but where do we start?'

Skye walks off in the direction of the labyrinth and then looks back at me, gesturing to the maze on the floor. 'If it was me, I'd go for the Crypt, but I'll indulge. Let's follow the Yellow Brick Road, Dorothy.'

I tag on behind him and watch as he takes his first steps. It looks pretty impressive on the floor of this massive and elegant cathedral. The Labyrinth is the size of a small English roundabout and has one hundred small candles surrounding the entire perimeter and seven candles which border the centre copper plate in the middle according to the pamphlet I'm now reading with interest. A sandstone pathway weaves one way, and then back on its self, making up the circular shape.

'C'mon. Enlightenment awaits,' jokes Skye.

I smirk and take the first step. I don't notice anything unusual at first, but as I take quicker steps and catch up to Skye, my feet begin to tingle.

'Do you feel that?' I say to Skye, placing a hand on his shoulder to get him to stop for a minute.

He stops instantly. 'What? The buzzing? Yeah, I feel it, but I'm pretty sure it's not from me. It's coming from you.'

'How do you mean?'

'It doesn't feel like me. It's like it's removed from me, but I get a sense of it. Like how I can hear your thoughts and my own too - the same, but different enough for me to distinguish.'

'What do you think it means?'

'What am I ... a frigging historian? I think it means to shut the fuck up and finish this poxy maze. It's beginning to give me a headache.'

I know what he means. My head is beginning to hurt too. Each step I take feels as though I'm winding up a tightly coiled spring. Each step is getting harder, like I'm walking through heavy snow with the wind pressing against me.

Skye is struggling too, and when he stops to take a breath, I squeeze past him and take the lead. I have no idea how much further we have to go, because it's too difficult to see a clear path ahead.

'Something tells me we shouldn't be doing this,' says Skye between short pants. I don't see anyone else out of breath. Do you, Riv?' I glance around. Everyone else seems to be unaffected.

'Oh, now you tell me. This was your stupid idea, remember?'

Coupled with the metallic taste of copper that has returned to my mouth, the pair of concrete boots that I seem to have stepped into, are also an unwelcome side effect. I now drag each leg in front of the other.

I stop. Stretch my neck. I don't even get this fatigued from 5000 laps. But one thing I can't escape is that dreaded feeling you get when you're being watched. Head aching. Heavy on my shoulders. My neck, like the trunk of an old fig tree, thick and unyielding, struggling against movement or rotation. A familiar figure is staring at me from across the room.

Scarface.

He is dressed in a long black sheepskin coat. Beneath,

340

I see the silver, shimmer of armour. Even if I want to race after him, I know my feet won't let me. I have to finish the Labyrinth.

I also have another problem.

I'm sure Ra-Mon is here.

I don't know where, but I sense his same icy, cold presence and just like the way my muscles freeze to my bones, the life in the room churns to a grinding halt.

Time has stopped. Which means only one thing ... he has come to duel. He's come for Nereus whilst I'm incapacitated and unable to fight back.

'Yeah, that's really fair of you,' I call out to the room, knowing he can hear me. 'Coming at me while I'm helpless, and in no position to defend myself. Yeah, real heroic.' I glance back at Skye, who is in mid-stride, frozen, an anguished look on his face.

'He can't hear you. But I can.' I don't recognise the voice.

My assailant is the only person in the room who isn't affected by Ra-Mon's witchcraft. And he is striding toward me with purpose.

His voice is hollow and mean. 'By entering the Labyrinth, you are summoning passage to the underworld.

'Why should I believe you?' I rub the back of my neck to remind him.

'I never struck that blow. You were deceived by another.' The giant navigates around a family of statues, two parents and three children, his colossal feet striking the ground with steely thuds. 'I have been waiting a long time for you, but I only truly knew it was you when I saw you use your water power on me.' He stops a foot from me and bows his head solemnly. 'My name is Tomas Julius Siricus.'

This sheer size of him throws my body into shadow as he looms over me, erasing the words I need to introduce myself.

'I found you before you lost consciousness and

dropped my only possession into your hand so you would come and seek me out.' He puts out his hand. 'I'll be taking it back from you.'

I place the coin into his hand. 'If you're not my enemy, then why disappear?'

'Because your emotions are weak and override your logic and I had to get to the girl before ...' He cuts off, his eyes downwards, his shoulders slumped. 'I had to wait until you were in the Labyrinth before I could reveal myself to you.'

'And Ember?

'I'm sorry. I was too late. She is being held in the Labyrinth.' I stare down at the pattern on the floor, confused. '*If*, she is still alive.'

I die for a whole second, then jolt back to life. My brain won't allow me to even consider that possibility. 'We have to continue on.'

Tomas stares into the space above my head, a thick scar running from his eyebrow to his jawline. 'You are about to open the doorway to the true Labyrinth that lies thirty feet beneath this cathedral. You will need to be on your guard. A terrifying monster roams free there.'

I disregard the fairy tale. 'You know she's there? How?'

'I followed them.'

'Followed them?' I'm astounded he sounds so casual about it. 'Who took her, and *why* didn't you stop them?'

'I could not. She is with HIM and his witch.' This is all becoming too much. He continues. 'You are the key to my salvation. You, are the only one who can open the True Labyrinth, where I can finally, fulfil my destiny.'

'Destiny? *You've* got a destiny? Then guess what, buddy. Take a ticket and get in line. There's a lot of that going around at the moment.'

Tomas frowns, like he doesn't understand. 'I am here to kill the Son of Osiris. You will not stop me.'

'I don't wanna stop you, but *I'm* here to save the entire human race and save my girlfriend from a weird, religious

342

freak. Suppose we both have our problems today?'

We regard each other.

In hand-to-hand combat he'd finish me on the first strike. I look to the 375ml bottle of water in my hand. There's not much I can do with it, that would aid my chances. Still, I clench the bottle as my only weapon.

'The Son of Osiris is invincible above ground, but in his own domain, I can kill him. He has expelled much energy today and is vulnerable. If you take me with you, I will help find your friend.' Tomas draws his sword. Something until that moment, I hadn't noticed.

I think for a second, but really don't have a choice. 'Okay. What about my friend?' I look at Skye.

'The instance you take your next step, everyone will return to normal, unaware anything had happened. Time stopped, Water Channeller, because you stopped it.'

I return my attention to the maze, and just like Tomas said, the room springs back to life the second I step forward. Except …

'What the hell was that?' groans Skye. 'We're now working alongside Leonidas from 300.'

Tomas steps forward. 'I'm Roman, you feeble-minded fool, not Spartan. Speak the truth or not at all, and I suggest if you want to see your friend again, then hold your tongue.'

'Way to go, big mouth. Piss off a Roman Warrior with a huge sword. He is our only hope of finding Ember.'

'Sorry. I couldn't hear everything that was being said.' He taps his temple. 'Was like listening to a rusty old radio with static.'

'Let's move on,' says Tomas impatiently.

Again, each step is as arduous as the one before. The muscles in my legs and back, driving me forward, feel the onslaught of fatigue. The headache is getting worse too, much worse than any I've had. The constant looking down, backward and forward, is making me dizzy. I feel as though I'm about to lose consciousness at any moment, but then a voice.

'Keep going. You're almost there.'

I turn to Skye and Tomas. Their faces look tired too. 'What?' mutters Skye.

'Did you say something?'

'River, it is I, Nereus. You must complete the path before you, even at the cost of a life.'

'Who's life? Yours? Ember? Skye? Who?'

There is no answer

'Nereus?'

'What dude?' answers Skye.

'Nothing.'

I grind my teeth and push forward through the maze. Just when I think I've travelled as far from the middle as possible, I see a clear path directly back to the centre.

'We're almost there,' I call out behind me.

'Water Channeller, once you reach the copper plate in the middle, the doorway will only remain open for a few seconds. So, don't hesitate.' He looks directly at Skye.

Skye answers with an indignant 'What?'

'You've done this before?' I say to Tomas. There's a glimmer of hope in my voice.

'No. But I have seen it many times.'

I take those last few steps, the passage becoming much easier. A vortex draws me in, pulling at my legs like a magnet.

'You ready,' I call out.

I take that longed for step, except my foot doesn't hit solid copper.

It hits nothing.

Suction drags me under, fast and out of control. It's like I'm underwater again at the lake, except being pulled against my will. Deeper and deeper, blacker and blacker, until I land ... on my back. It winds me and I cough.

I find myself lying on *sand*, looking up at the *moon*? It's not right. It shouldn't be there. Like the world is upside down or something. Currents of cool air sweep across my face when I sit up, confusing me even more. Two marble stone pillars connected to an archway lay a few metres away. I can only guess it's the entrance to the Labyrinth. I don't know why, but I expected a green, hedge-like maze, the kind you might find on the front garden of a nobleman's house. Instead, it looks like it was made by the gods of Olympus.

I hear one more thud and hope it's Skye, then another. Shit. That must be Tomas. Then *another*?

I glance around to see Skye rolling on to his side, clutching his ribs, and Tomas springing to his feet. The fourth person I don't recognise.

'Who's that guy?' Skye beats me to the question and then coughs, rubbing his ribcage as he stands.

'I have no idea.' The man is dressed in a brown suit and tie.

'You alright, fella?' asks Skye.

The man's head swings left and then right. 'Where is sis place?' he says. There is a shaky edge to his voice.

'We don't have time for this,' remarks Tomas. 'I have the instructions on how to get through the Labyrinth.'

'I'm not going with you,' says the man, eyeing Tomas's sword. 'I will find le *guide touristique* and find my own way out.' Without another word, he marches off in the opposite direction, leaving Skye and I watching Tomas marching towards the pillars.

'Wait,' shouts Skye to Tomas. 'We're coming with you.'

TWENTY-SIX

THE light of the moon guides our way through the many
twists and turns. The majestic twenty-foot white walls of
the maze, *and* our prison, hold no clues as to where we've
been or where we're going, but Tomas seems to know
exactly where it is leading us.

Each turn seems calculated.

Taken with confidence.

The loamy sand beneath our feet, closes over our
footprints the moment we step out of them, concealing
them, leaving no trace of us being there.

This is no ordinary maze.

But then again, this is no ordinary world we've found
ourselves in. Even our own world, the one that lies god
knows how many feet above us, is a lie … is hidden
behind a smokescreen of myths and magic.

Skye sniggers at my thought. 'This whole fricking
thing belongs in a movie. All we need is a bit of
bloodshed, and we'll have a winner at the Grammys for
sure.'

Tomas looks over his shoulder at Skye, but doesn't stop walking. 'Bloodshed is something you *don't* want to look forward to.' As slight as it is, I hear the crack in his voice. My innate ability to sense emotions is firing on all cylinders again. I noticed it the second I landed. Stress is beginning to mount from Skye, making me sick to my stomach, and yet I sense nothing from Tomas. He is solid. Unemotional. Focussed.

I glance behind us, checking we are not being followed and although perhaps not the time for a deep and meaningful conversation, I'm intrigued about Tomas and his life.

'What happened?'

Tomas is silent for so long, I wonder if he heard my question. I open my mouth to repeat it, but he gets there before me.

'I joined the Roman army when I was no more than a boy, giving my life willingly to the empire. Naturally, they trained me in the art of war and servitude. I became a Legionnaire as a young man under the command of Horus Cavius. He was brutal and lacked compassion or remorse. This is the reason why I must kill him. He crucified my three children in front of me, and before their lives expired, he set fire to their tiny bodies. And then …' He pauses. 'The entire regiment pleasured my wife before he removed her breasts with a knife and then cut off her head.'

Skye sucks in a breath but says nothing.

'That certainly gives you grounds to kill him. Why would he do that to your family?' I ask.

'It was because I would not drink the blood of his witch. It was in exchange for eternal life and a lifetime of servitude to him, but I'd seen what had happened to those men who had drank the blood. The spark of their life had gone. They had no feeling, no sense of belonging. They had become mindless killers.' He pauses for a second. 'I had no idea that he would …'

Skye frowns. 'So, you *are* human, then?'

347

'Yes. I am made of flesh and blood.'

'Which would make you two thousand years old, give or take a few years?'

'Time has no meaning when avenging those you love. In the end, I was forced into drinking the blood anyway. We were all given a coin once we joined the Mithraic Cult.' He retrieves it from under the shoulder of his armour. 'It was our duty to hand over our coin in order to receive eternal life and in return we drank the blood of his witch. Most men did so without thought. I was told by an old man in a marketplace not to, so I buried my coin and stole another's. They then forced me to drink the blood and relinquished me of the coin. I pretended for a few days that he had my allegiance…'

He pauses again but this time looks away from us.

'I then ran, like the coward I am. I could feel the life slipping from me. So, I dug up the coin. It saved me. I don't know how. But a small part of the man I used to be still remains inside me. Horus never destroyed me, but now is my chance to wreak revenge on him.'

'You mentioned the Mithraic Cult?'

'We prayed to a god by the name of Mithras. All the temples were underground in caves, just like this one. The entrance to these caves were adorned with a stone tablet known as the Tauroctony. It depicts Mithras slaying a bull. I have also come to learn that Horus was not Roman but hails from Egypt and then Greece.'

'Hang on a minute,' says Skye. 'These are *Gods* we're talking about? Right?'

'Yes.'

He turns to me and mutters, 'I did Greek mythology at school.'

'And just so we are crystal clear on this Tom, … this Horus … he is the real Horus, son of Isis and Osiris?'

'Yes.'

Skye sighs. 'Great,' he says to me. 'More frigging immortals to deal with. I thought one nutjob was enough, and now we've got another one to deal with.' He rolls his eyes.

'What I want to know is, if he's been alive this long, how the hell do you think you can kill him.'

Tomas freezes. 'Quiet.'

Air battles to find its way in or out of my lungs.

'He has commanded his pet to do his dirty work.'

'*Pet* ?' mutters Skye softly. 'And what dirty work?'

'We need to hurry.'

I agree.

We do need to hurry.

The further I venture into the Labyrinth, the more my body is aching for a woman. And not just the old familiar ache. A pain more intense, more crippling than anything I've felt before. If I didn't know any different, I feel as if I'm being summoned, or more to the point, Nereus is.

Time is no friend here.

And Ember's time is slipping away.

Moving at a glacial pace and in single file now, which for the record, is turning me more neurotic by the second, we take each corner with caution. The air has lost what little freshness it had and the smell of a hundred rotting rats soaks into my clothes, my hair, tastes like death on my tongue.

Skye grimaces and rubs his nose. 'I can barely breathe,' he says, clutching at his throat.

Tomas stops. 'We are close.'

'How can you tell,' I whisper.

He holsters his sword to pick up a decomposed arm. 'That's how.'

Skye stifles a groan. 'That's probably the grossest thing I've ever seen.' The arm had been roughly severed from the elbow, leaving bone and straggly pieces of flesh hanging out. The long, painted fingernails and cygnet ring identifies its owner was female.

'Who did this?' I whisper.

'Not *who*.'

'*What* then?'

A blood-curdling scream pierces the silence.

Tears through me like a great shard of glass.

The kind of scream you never want to hear. Will never forget. The kind that stops seconds from passing, forces fear in limitless quantities into your head and feet, pausing all movement. Relinquishing your ability to think.

It sounds close.

'Too close for my comfort,' whispers Skye.

Ember's name trembles from my lips.

'It was not a woman,' says Tomas confidently. 'But it soon maybe if we don't get there in time.'

Muffled, throaty, gurgling cries of pain, continue.

'We have to do something,' says Skye.

Tomas shakes his head. 'We cannot.'

'But …'

All is quiet again.

'Hurry.'

The rotten smell intensifies, and I notice Skye dry reaching a few times as we run behind Tomas. The smell doesn't seem to bother Tomas, or maybe it does, although nothing in his face shows it.

We dodge more dismembered limbs strewn on the ground, including several cleanly picked skulls.

'Do you get the feeling we are walking straight into a trap?' says Skye, whipping his head around to talk.

I do. 'Keep going,' I urge.

Our terrain starts to change.

The perfect white walls and pillars appear more battle-scarred and unkempt. Scuff marks from swords and war and splashes of blood, dried and aged, are ingrained into the stonework.

The sand is thinning out too, replaced by a thick, bog-like swampland that doesn't quite reach the top of my trainers. The Labyrinth is also widening enough to allow us to walk three abreast.

Tomas draws his sword. 'Whatever weapons you have, prepare to use them.'

I glance at my bottle of water and then at Skye, who looks down at himself. He shrugs. 'We're screwed, aren't we?'

'Yep.' There's no time for sugar-coating.

Tomas raises his sword. 'Are you ready?' A low mist begins to gather around our ankles.

Skye and I say nothing.

'If we get separated or something should happen to me … take every *third* turn left to every *two* turns right, and that should see you out of the Labyrinth.'

We turn the last corner.

I expect to see Ember gagged and tied to a post, her assailant standing over her, brandishing a weapon.

I couldn't be more wrong.

Underground, in the middle of 'I don't know where', is a forest. Sinister looking trees, some covered in lichen, are clumped together, unnaturally and oddly shaped and unlike any tree I've seen before, and yet my brain tells me that's what they are.

Skye jabs me in the ribs and points at them. I nod, to let him know I've seen them. 'I don't think they're made of wood, somehow,' he whispers into my back.

I focus harder. My heart becomes a stone I've swallowed and now lodges in my throat. 'They're bone.'

'Wha …'

A few steps closer reveal they are, or were, human.

Bodies, torso's and limbs have all been strung together in a perverted, twisted collage. Four people, back-to-back create the trunk, and one poor victim is thrust into the middle, probably standing on a block to make them taller than the rest. Arms and fingers are broken to resemble the natural curvature only a branch can create. It's totally sickening.

Skye nudges me. 'Dude, look.' The expression on his face should warn me *not* to look, but I do anyway. One tree has a newly formed trunk and limb. The victim has a gaping wound in his neck, savaged in haste and still running with blood. All of his teeth have been removed, his nose is missing, and the one arm he has left looks ragged and mauled. It is the man in the brown suit who fell through the Labyrinth with us. His face spells out the horror he has endured.

'Come out and fight me, you coward,' booms Tomas. The volume of his voice makes me jump.

The sound of something in the undergrowth gets closer. Man-made twigs and branches snap, footsteps vibrate through the earth. Whatever is coming … is bigger than us.

I look around to warn Skye to get behind me except I can't see him anywhere. 'Skye? Skye.' My voice a desperate whisper.

'Keep quiet, or you're gonna get us all killed,' he says quietly. He has turned invisible. A handy trick to have. One that I wished I had right about now.

His footprints in the mud alert me to the direction he's going. He is walking or should I say running, in the opposite direction.

Tomas also notices and throws off his sheepskin coat to reveal full tunic and battle armour. All that is missing is the shield and helmet.

Through the human trees, *it* appears. Well over nine feet tall, making Tomas look insignificant in comparison.

Me, I might as well be a rabbit.

It is not a man, well, I don't think it's a man. It stands on two legs, hooves for feet, covered in a shag of thick, light brown fur, has arms like a man with lethal one-strike claws, and the head of a bull. Its chest and arms are muscular and well-defined. The horns, by far, are its most impressive feature. They are long and curve outwards in a flat arc, spanning some one and a half metres across.

That was until it roared.

Row upon row of teeth, still containing the threads of its last meal, are exposed.

'Is that a … a ….'

'Minotaur,' finishes Tomas. 'Yes.'

The Minotaur looks hungrily at Tomas. 'You look

tired, old man. Have you come to die?' There is a twist of humour to his deep and menacing voice.

'Horus, come out and face me. Do not send your pet in your stead.'

A roar of anger rocks the silence. 'PET! I shall teach you who is worthy of who.'

The Minotaur launches itself at Tomas and all I can do is look on in horror. Tomas is quick for a big man. Almost lightning speed and the Minotaur goes gliding past him, stopping short of the entrance back into the Labyrinth.

It's up on its feet so fast and swipes again at Tomas, only missing him by inches this time. Tomas swings for the animal, and skilfully, his sword finds its mark. A red ribbon flutters across the creature's muscular thigh. It lets out a mighty roar.

Tomas grins.

'You will pay for that blood with your own,' growls the Minotaur.

It lunges again, slashing wildly with its claws. Again, Tomas smiles. 'You will have to try harder than that.'

I look around to see how I can help, not that Tomas needs it. He looks to be handling everything quite well on his own. My bottle of Evian is two thirds full, probably enough water to temporarily blind the monster, especially if I could fire it at his eyes with the pace of a bullet behind it. I remove the lid, waiting for an opportune moment.

Tomas retreats behind a huge boulder, which moments ago had been part of the Labyrinth wall. The Minotaur's powering fist had missed its target sending part of the wall to the ground in a shower of rubble.

This brute has strength and stealth on his side, hunting his prey by scent and instinct but he is no match for Tomas as a warrior.

And he knows it.

As though he's read my mind, he comes for me.

I'm glued to the spot, not knowing what to do first.

Run?

Hide?

Stand and fight …

I wrap my fingers tightly around the bottle, conjuring and praying my power is ready and willing to act. I don't sense Nereus anymore. It's only me.

Without too much effort on my part, the water powers out of the bottle hitting the Minotaur directly in the eyes *and* with the right amount of pace behind it. I'm pretty pleased with the result although it doesn't have the effect I'm looking for. It aggravates him rather than throwing him off. I have nowhere to hide and no more tricks up my sleeve.

He comes at me, his arm swinging, fist clenched clumsy and slow. I now see how easy it was for Tomas to dodge the Minotaur's blows. It's not quite slow motion, but certainly slow enough for me to steer clear of it.

Tomas stands between us, the hilt of his sword ready and poised at shoulder height. He lunges twice, the sharpness of the blade having no trouble slicing through the Minotaur's flesh.

The creature screams out. 'MASTER. One chance to make him pay.' I deduce from his statement; we are being watched.

Suddenly, as though a switch had been flicked, the light of the moon is snuffed out. Our arena has fallen into the darkest shadow.

I stand inside the blackness. Not moving. Not daring to blink for fear it might alert him to my presence.

The loud thump of my heart echoes in my ears.

I hear a heavier breath. Probably Tomas.

And I hear IT.

Creeping.

Flanking me.

Sizing me up.

I cry out as he grabs me from behind, restraining me, crushing me in his powerful grip. His claws rake into my skin, stinging, peeling back layers as he jostles me into his grasp.

As though dawn is breaking, the light slowly returns.

Tomas is still in his semi-hunched position, preparing to attack. When he sees me in the Minotaur's vice like grip, he stands tall. The concentrated look on his face drops away.

'This has nothing to do with the boy,' says Tomas. 'Release him, unharmed, and I will meet you in unarmed combat.'

'NO.'

The word "no" was in my mind to say, but never came out of my mouth. I'm sure it was the same answer that the Minotaur thought, but it wasn't from him either. The voice came from someone else.

Skye.

He hadn't left after all.

He was assessing the situation, I tell myself.

'Skye.' I know he won't answer back and give away his position, but at least he knows I know he's there.

I hear clapping from behind me, just what I expected from him. The creature swings around to see where the noise is coming from.

Skye is still invisible, although the perfectly aimed skull that narrowly misses my head, hits the Minotaur straight in the middle of the forehead.

It stuns him.

Angers him.

He tightens his grip on my torso until I hear a break. I scream out, sure that was one of my ribs. I take in a breath and immediately cough. Broken rib and possible pierced lung.

The Minotaur stares down at Tomas. 'If you want him, you will have to prise his lifeless body from my dead hands, Legionnaire.'

Tomas, sword in hand, still poised for battle, makes his move. His eyes are wild, untamed. He runs at us, slicing the air around me. The sensation of searing pain across my forearm doesn't compute until the Minotaur throws me to the ground, roaring with its own agony. Several clawed fingers are missing.

I look to my own wound. It's serious, and I don't have any water nearby to heal me.

I rip off the sleeve of my shirt and turn it into a tourniquet. Pulling it tight. Grimacing at the pain.

The sword, Tomas once had, is now at my feet. True to his word, he's relinquished his weapon.

A snort of laughter comes from the monster's frothing mouth. 'You have a death wish, Roman. But it matters not. Whether I live or die, I will see to it that you become immortalised within my gallery of admirers. You will be my masterpiece.' He gestures to the trees.

'Never,' says Tomas, ready to attack.

In a hunched stature, he steps around the Minotaur with precision. He has a battle strategy in place, moving deftly between the Minotaur's heavy-handed blows. His choreography is poetic, every movement, measured and thought out.

Strike after strike, the Minotaur misses Tomas, giving me more confidence that the Legionnaire has this in-hand. I back up further to where a marble pillar has fallen, clutching at my ribcage. Blood is still seeping from the wound on my arm and I retighten the tourniquet. I need to heal. I need water. I sense it but cannot see any. I feel utterly hopeless.

I lift my eyes.

In that pivotal moment … in the gap between gaps, when you want to cry out to warn someone, the chance is gone before it's begun. I'm too late.

The Minotaur spins around in desperation to miss a boulder to his left flank, gaining the advantage of higher ground.

Tomas is unprepared.

He steps too short.

A thundering blow sends him sailing through the air, his body making a sickening thud as he makes contact with a stone slab.

He lands heavily.

Unconscious.

The Minotaur lumbers towards him with colossal strides and a horse-like gait, ready to deal that final blow.

There's no way I can let that happen.

I summon my power, knowing no water exists, but desperate to try anything.

The earth suddenly begins to shift beneath my feet. The Minotaur also notices and stops dead in his tracks. He turns to look back at me, and then again at Tomas, evaluating his choices. I look to be the best option, with Tomas still out cold.

Between us, a skull hovers in mid-air.

Skye.

'Don't worry,' he calls back to me, 'it's all part of my illustrious plan.'

His visibility returns, the human skull actually poised on the flat of his hand. He raises it to his lips and winks at me. 'You're gonna love this.'

He draws in a mighty breath.

The force on his exhale comes out in hurricane proportions, sending the skull flying towards the creature at great speed. Even I have to brace for the impact, lying down.

The skull cracks him above the eye, opening a gash that only a sword would be proud of. Blood spreads across the creatures' face, matting in his fur.

The animal howls in pain, his partially mutated hand seeking out the damage.

He stares at Skye … through Skye, to me.

Frenzied, his eyes bulge with his hatred for me or any human. Enraged, head down, nostrils flaring, horns deadly … the Minotaur charges.

My protective instinct comes out and all I can think of is getting Skye to safety. 'Turn invisible,' I holler.

'S'ok. I've got this. Bigfoot is history.'

Coming full throttle, the Minotaur suddenly hits an invisible barrier just inches from Skye, the same one I experienced when I tried to right hook him that day outside the pool. It face-plants into the ground, stunned.

'What kind of magic is this?' the monster demands, shaking its colossal head.

'One that can kick your sorry arse,' answers Skye laughing.

I glance over at Tomas, who still hasn't moved. With the Minotaur dazed, I hobble over to him, ribs aching, hardly able to breathe without pain.

'Tomas. Tomas.' I shake him by the shoulders.

Slowly, he comes around.

'We're not out of the woods yet,' I explain. 'Can you still fight?'

Tomas gets to his feet. 'I'll finish this.' He snatches his sword off me and runs at the Minotaur, the blade high over his head.

The Minotaur shakes off its stupor.

Tomas prepares to thrust his sword into the Minotaur's back just as the creature turns its head. There is confusion on Tomas's face - a grimace of something not being quite right, but not fully understanding what has happened. He looks to me, searching my eyes for answers and then down at his abdomen.

One of the Minotaur's horns had found its way beneath the breastplate, impaling him, the tip protruding through his back armour.

The creature throws him to the ground like a ragdoll. Blood trickles out of Tomas's mouth.

I glance over at Skye. 'I've got nothing left,' he mouths to me.

It's up to me now.

I don't know what I can do, but feeling the earth shake before when I summoned my power gave me hope.

Invigorated from his triumph, the Minotaur jumps to his feet. Skye, who is on his hands and knees, doesn't know what's hit him as he's grabbed around the throat and lifted three feet off the ground.

Skye's hands grapple against the gigantic mitt of the Minotaur, desperate for those precious seconds of air as I engage my power.

I settle myself, amidst such chaos. Pain has increased to a whole new level inside me. Rising like a demon. Scattering my strength. Pulling at my core. Something is stirring. Awakening.

I summon my power to arise.

There is a tremble under my feet as the earth is questioned by my power.

'There's water around you,' gasps Skye.

I look around. I see nothing. 'Where?' I reply.

'In the air, in the ground,' says Skye, struggling with every breath.

I then understand.

The mud sticking to my shoes. The low lying fog. They all contain water.

A plan forms.

I jump onto a rocky ledge and concentrate all my effort on sucking up all the water - my body taking on the form of a human sponge.

I syphon as much liquid as my body will allow and before my eyes, the ground goes from a rich chocolate in colour to light beige, the swampland becoming a desert. In parts, the earth has begun to crack open like a dry creek bed waiting for the monsoons.

If I could trap the animal's feet, it might just give me enough time to grab Tomas's sword and finish this.

The Minotaur also notices.

The earth around its huge hooved feet have become solid, acting like quick set concrete, imprisoning him to the ground.

'Unhinge me, or I'll break this weakling's neck.'

I hadn't thought of the repercussions.

'Don't do it,' says Skye. His face is pale.

I'm at a crossroads. I can't hold this water in any longer, and the strength it took to gather it was all I had left.

I need help.

TWENTY-SEVEN

OUT of nowhere, a dark shadow in the form of a bird, flies across my vision. It's as black as the midnight sky and as sinister as my own soul.

Skye also sees it, but he looks more shocked from the raven than he is from the gigantic creature who's throttling the life out of him.

'River. Kill it. Please. It's come for me. It's here to kill me.' There is terror in his voice that I've never heard before. In a pathetic attempt, he tries to shoo it away. But it persists in swooping him.

The Minotaur waves his free hand at the bird too, trying to swat it like an annoying wasp. For a reason I can't explain, the creature doesn't seem surprised to see it. It flies around his head three times, and then directly into the Minotaur's face. With razor sharp precision the raven's pointy beak plucks the monster's eye from its socket.

The Minotaur immediately drops Skye and he scrambles out of the way before the brute has chance to recover. It is also my opportunity to act.

The water I'd taken in has done its job.

All of my wounds are healed.

And I feel strong.

Powerful.

I inhale, relieved there's no more pain.

I locate the sword, point down in the mud. It's only a few metres away. I sprint for it before I have chance to think it through properly and grab the hilt of the sword. I reef it out of the hardened mud and to my surprise it comes out easily. I then drive the sword hard into the chest of the Minotaur.

It's jaw drops, eyes wide with the realisation of its own death. It falls to the ground, allowing the sword to continue its journey into its back.

I sink to my knees.

It's over.

'It's not, dude,' huffs out Skye, exhausted. 'It's only the beginning.'

From the corner of my eye, I see Tomas move.

I kneel by his side. His wound is mortal.

'Chop off the beast's head.' Tomas pauses. 'That way he can never be resurrected.' A gurgling sound comes from the back of Tomas's throat. His life is ending.

'And Ember,' I say. 'She isn't here. Do you know where she could be?'

'Ch-check the altar ... in the middle of the forest.' Tomas takes his last breath. 'Every third right, every second lef ....' His eyes close, and his head rolls to one side.

I can't take my eyes off his broken body.

I refuse to let *anyone* degrade such a brave and righteous man. And a friend.

He will not become part of the human forest. I will not allow him to be condemned to an eternity of humiliation.

Skye and I haul his body to the edge of the Labyrinth and place him gently between two propped up pillars. Then head back to the Minotaur. It takes both of us to roll

361

the monster over to retrieve the sword. The muscle and sinew around the creature's thick neck are harder to get through than I first thought, and it takes a few mighty chops before it's head comes away from its body.

'What now?' asks Skye, wiping a spray of blood from his face.

I look to the forest. 'Wanna take a walk in the woods with me?'

Skye smirks. 'You're even starting to sound like me. But …you need to tweak that Pommie accent… then we'll be real brothers.'

'Fat chance.'

The forest isn't as thick as I thought it would be. Behind the first six rows of *trees*, we come across a dark, grey pillar. It's similar to a gravestone except eight foot in height and comes to a peak at the top. There is an emblem of a sun with rays coming down etched into the stone, and underneath are two rings embedded into the stone where I imagine shackles could be attached.

'Nice,' says Skye. 'Live bait for the Wookie over there.'

I laugh and then abruptly stop.

My heart ventures a million miles away, so far that I can't even feel it beat anymore. A strand of hair, long and red, is stuck to the stone. I pluck it away.

'She *was* here,' says Skye. He swings his head around, looking in every direction.

'EMBER!' he yells out.

Silence.

Some part of me knew she wouldn't answer.

'*Was*, being the operative word. There has to be a back door to this place.'

'You go that way and I'll go this way,' says Skye, pointing in opposite directions, 'and we'll meet up again, in say ten minutes if we haven't found anything.'

'I don't think we should split up. Who knows what else is lurking down here.'

'But we can cover twice as much ground that way.'

I reluctantly agree.

The alternative to finding her too late is beyond any horror we might find here.

Skye heads off in his direction and I turn, taking one last look back at him before moving on. Twenty seconds later, he's already out of sight. The eerie sensation we are still being watched hasn't left me since the Minotaur called out.

I need to think.

Figure out where we are?

Underground ... outside?

Where?

'You are where I want you to be,' answers a low, melodic voice. There is something strangely familiar, almost hypnotic about it. It's soft and enticing like a woman out of breath.

But not Ember.

Definitely not Ember's voice.

'*Where* are you? *Who* are you?' I yell to the forest of skeleton trees.

'Seek me out,' replies the voice.

A web of wispy fog comes in from my right. Swirls at my feet. I decide it's as good a sign as any and follow it. The sweet tones of angels singing fills my head, making me forget about Skye, about Ember, overriding any logic. I know I'm in some kind of trance, although I can't break free from it.

The human trees begin to thin out, and in front of me, at the entrance to what I can only imagine was once a cave, is the most beautiful woman I've ever seen.

Her hair, copper red, hangs down to her waist in a mass of curls. Her eyes, dark and alluring, beg me closer. Her skin, silky white with a glow of sunshine beneath it, screams out for me to touch it.

'Come closer,' she whispers.

Blinded. Unable to stop myself. Not sure I even want to. I walk towards her.

She smiles at me. Seductive.

'You have proven your worth, WaterLover. Now, here is your reward.'

The singing stops.

A blast of electric blue light from her eyes hits me in the chest, winding me, knocking me off my feet.

Pain … the kind that crushes you from within until your insides become some brutal kind of agonising chaos.

Where shock and panic find a safe place.

Where normal becomes malformed, twisted into a wound that has never known peace.

Where every cell in my body screams out, begging for this torture to stop.

And then burning.

My whole body is on fire. Hot, searing pain that should've killed me already, punches through my chest, taunting me, keeping my alive. I lie there in the dirt, my body shuddering.

And then nothing.

I can't move.

I am paralysed.

My eyes close.

'Dude? You okay?'

I open my eyes.

Skye is standing over me. 'What happened to your shirt, stud?'

'Shirt?' I palm my chest and cough and wince, pushing myself into a seated position.

I vomit.

'What the hell happened to you?' He is pointing at my chest. I look down and see a burn the size of my fist.

'I leave you alone for five minutes …' begins Skye.

There is a dizzying thump at the back of my head as though my brain has been pummelled within an inch of death.

'There was a cave, with a woman,' I stammer.

Skye frowns. 'I think you hit your head, man. There's no cave. No woman.'

I stagger to my feet.

'Are you sure you didn't see anyone else around?' I mutter.

'No. I backtracked after ten minutes, just like you said, and found you on the ground at the edge of the Wookie's forest. Did you even bother looking? You must have searched all of a hundred yards.'

I decide not to tell Skye what happened as the image of the woman re-enters my thoughts. I reprimand myself for forgetting his mind-reading ability the second the thought disappears, except nothing registers with him this time. His face is relaxed and there are no pending questions in his eyes. Not even a quick snipe.

'We need to go,' I say, casually scanning the environment for any signs of my shirt.

'Where? This place doesn't exactly have google maps.' He's standing with his hands on his hips. 'I found nothing back there, just a solid stone wall, which is why I figured I'd head back this way.'

I find I am grinding my teeth back and forth. 'Can't you tune into her thoughts or *airwaves* or whatever you call it. She can't be too far away.'

A heavy frown works its way across Skye's forehead. 'You think I haven't tried that already.' His words come out in a rush. 'Whenever I think of her, all I get is this weird smell like lilacs.'

I recall the bath salts I placed in her bathroom that night I rescued her from her molesting foster father. *Could it be that easy?*

Hope ignites. 'Can you track that?'

'I guess so, now that I know what I'm looking for, or more to the point, smelling for.' Skye lifts his head and takes in a deep inhalation. He smiles. 'Air never lies.'

Like an obedient bloodhound, Skye tracks Ember as I subserviently follow behind him. He seems to be enjoying himself, occasionally stopping to sniff the air, before venturing on. The more I think about what happened with the woman, and the burn on my chest, which has now of course, miraculously healed, the more I expect Skye to question me on it, and yet, he says nothing. It's like he can't hear my thoughts anymore, and as thrilled as I am to have some privacy, now may not be the best time for such a miracle.

We haven't walked for long before the stone wall, Skye spoke about, comes into view. It is freckled with lichen and moss and so high I can't see the top of it. It appears to be another dead end.

The labyrinth was simple compared to this. At least it had a guiding path. This is a different kind of maze. Instead of old ruined stone pillars, cracked and fallen, half buried in the earth or swamp-like wastelands, this new scenery is one of scrubby bushland that doesn't seem to change. It feels like we are going around in circles.

'Fuck,' I hear Skye say, looking at the colossal wall. 'It's like this whole place is surrounded by this thing.'

'Wait.' I shift my head slightly to one side and laugh. Ingenious. 'It's an optical illusion. Don't you see it?'

Skye mimics my movements. 'I don't see anything.'

I nudge him in the back to take a few more steps closer to the wall. The image is even clearer. 'See it now?'

He frowns. 'Just tell me what I'm supposed to be looking at.'

Relief overwhelms me. 'The stairs.'

Walking adjacent to the wall reveals nothing more than a stone wall. Walking towards it at the right angle, a stone staircase is visible.

'We fell down God knows how far. Only fair to assume, we have to go *up*, to get out.'

It's not until I'm standing at the foot of the wall do I discover the stairs actually disappear into the stonework. Only the first twenty or so steps are visible. I peer into the dark, cavernous opening. 'God, I hope no-one is home.'

Skye rubs his chin up, a dubious look on his face. 'You've just killed a Minotaur, Hercules. What's a few cyclops' or werewolves to a warrior like you?'

I roll my eyes at him. 'Forever the joker.'

My legs welcome the heavy exercise as we begin our ascent. Skye mumbles more about running into different kinds of monsters as we climb, but he shuts up pretty quickly as I hear him gulp down air from the exertion.

The stairs seem to go on forever.

An hour later, or maybe its two, I couldn't say for sure, but the rise of the steps become less steep.

'How many more to go, do you reckon?' he says between sharp breaths.

I power on. My legs started to shake about ten minutes ago. 'I can't see the top yet,' I say. 'Keep going.'

The air around us has changed too. It's hot and tastes like burnt toast. We might as well be travelling through the earth's crust. My tongue sits in the bottom of my mouth, useless, like a piece of thick rubber and every time I part my lips, they sting. I would kill for a drink of water. I need to rest.

'Stop here for a minute,' I say.

'What's going on? You said keep going.'

'That was ages ago,' I say slowly, struggling to get my mouth to work. If there was *ever* a time where Skye could use his mind reading skills it would be now. Anything, so I don't have to talk.

'Something doesn't feel right,' I say, slurring out the words.

'I think you overdid it, drawing up all that water. You know, these powers aren't to be messed with. There are repercussions.'

I suddenly realise I haven't released the water I sucked up out of the ground and air, and it's having the complete opposite effect on my body, drying me from the inside out.

'How much longer can you hold on to it for?'

I wish I could see his face to determine where he is going with this. 'Why?'

'I think it could come in handy if we find ourselves in a tight spot.'

I have to admit, he's right.

Again, the comeback I'm expecting from him doesn't happen. This new heightened power must somehow be blocking Skye's ability to read my thoughts.

With renewed energy and purpose, I rise. 'C'mon. Let's go.'

We continue to climb the stairs again, and no more than five minutes later, my body jolts as my anticipated step up, finds a level footing.

We made it.

Whether my eyes have adjusted, I'm not sure, but the darkness ahead, doesn't seem so dark anymore. We are in a stone tunnel of some sort, only wide enough for single file. The walls are smooth and the ground feels like wet, grainy sugar.

'You still got your mobile?' asks Skye.

'What? Of course I have.'

'Then put the flashlight on, dipshit.'

I don't know why I hadn't thought of that before.

I stop. 'Can you hear voices?'

Skye rams into the back of me. 'No. All I hear is your heavy breathing. Work out, much?'

My well-aimed elbow finds his sternum. He coughs. 'A joke, bro. Jeez.'

'Listen.' This is no time for his jokes.

There is silence, and then more voices. I freeze and pin Skye to the wall with my arm, sending the flashlight beam up the opposite wall. I draw Tomas's sword that I'd holstered in my belt.

'Do you think its Ember?' he whispers, 'because her scent is weaker and all I can smell is donuts.'

'No.' I would know her voice anywhere.

'How can you be so sure?'

I don't have to answer. A baby cries.

Footsteps, lots of shuffling footsteps are coming our way. 'What shall we do?' I hear Skye ask.

'Sshhh.' I've been wanting to do that to him since that first night in the alley, and I relish the payback as I hear him tut behind me.

The footsteps stop.

I'm about to whisper, 'let's move', when the voice starts again. I flick off the flashlight, plunging us back into darkness.

'The Crypt is the last part of the tour, thank you for coming. For those who wish to walk the Labyrinth, follow me.' The voice is English, laced with a heavy French accent. It's as clear and as loud as though he is standing directly in front of us.

'It sounds like a Tour Guide,' whispers Skye. I hear the relief in his voice. The warm fuzzy feeling that we'd found our way out soon disappears when the loud, clanging sound of an iron door shutting, echoes in my ears.

'We're in the Crypt. Didn't I tell you we needed to look here for Ember?' I can't bear how smug he sounds.

'It doesn't mean anything.'

'Gimme your phone,' demands Skye.

'What?'

'Give me your phone,' repeats Skye.

Reluctantly, I hand it over. He switches on the flashlight and aims it at the wall opposite us. 'I thought I saw something before.' Skye traces his hand over the stonework. 'This doesn't feel right, somehow. Riv, feel it.'

He's right.

This wall isn't cold, like it should be, and not rough in texture either when I touch it.

'It feels like … like a warm mattress.' He snorts.

It's a strange anomaly, even for Skye, but I kind of know what he means.

The battery is fading on my phone and just as Skye flicks it at the top of the wall, something catches my eye.

'Wait. Up there.'

Skye shines the light above my head.

'It's a latch. Most of these service tunnels had escape routes when they were originally built,' I inform him.

Instinctively, I reach up for it.

'Wait!'

'*What now*?'

'You've seen Raiders of the Lost Ark, right? You might end up triggering a booby trap or something.'

I ignore him and pull against the latch.

Nothing happens. 'See, told you.'

'There could be another one.' I drop my hand while Skye scours the wall.

'Hurry up. The light is fading.' We are in almost complete darkness except for a small yellow glow.

'I think this is it.' His voice sounds lower to the ground. He's on his hands and knees. 'Got it.'

I feel the wall tremble as though it knows we've discovered its secret. 'Pull on it when I count to three. One ... two ... thr ....'

I am falling.

Again.

A few seconds later, the ground finds me.

'Well that was the best ride in the park. NOT,' says Skye, landing on top of me. 'And for the record, I'm sick of falling through mystical doorways.'

'At least you got a soft landing. Get off of me.'

We get to our feet.

We're in a stone corridor, not as dark as the tunnel and more updated, better crafted. My eyes adjust easily. 'Looks like a light up ahead.'

We keep our backs to the wall, just in case, as the light in front becomes brighter. I can see my hand in front of my face.

Something hits me in the back of the leg. I look back.

'I kicked something?' says Skye. He bends down and picks it up and then promptly drops it. 'It's another bone.'

I bend down to take a closer look. It appears to be the long bone of a human leg.

'That's a tad concerning,' I mutter.

'A tad? I'd say we're up shit creek without a paddle.'

'Calm down. We've faced worse.'

I straighten up and take my next step. I also kick something. It doesn't feel stick-like this time, more football shaped. My fears are unveiled when I reach down and pick up a human skull.

'This poor chap could've got lost and died down here.'

Skye isn't buying it. 'That doesn't instil much confidence that we're both going to get out of this alive, let alone find Ember. And anyway, you and I know those other people were eaten, not lost.'

'Maybe?' I mutter.

As we move further and further up the passage, more skulls and bones litter the floor. There are also shields and spears and the occasional roman helmet. I think of Tomas's corpse left to rot in the Labyrinth.

'It's so random. Like they've been chewed up and spat out,' says Skye. A chill runs over my spine.

The light we'd been gaining on, turns out to be a flaming torch hooked to a wall. 'You ever get the feeling someone's expecting us,' I say to Skye. He nods and releases the torch from its holding.

Having the light is comforting but not a good move if you're relying on the element of surprise as your only ally. I debate for all of two seconds before giving Skye the nod of approval to move forward.

We seem to be making little ground and yet the ache in my body tells me we are pushing along at an impressive pace. I only wish I could sweat some of it out, but my water power refuses to relinquish one drop.

'What the … Are we going downhill?'

'Yes.' I thought the same about a hundred metres ago. The passageway then begins to widen considerably, and we can walk side by side rather than one behind the other. The bones are fewer too and I'm sensing we are close.

I feel Skye tense up beside me. 'Shit. Now which way?'

We have come to a crossroads.

'Straight, left or right?' I try to hone-in on where Ember might be, hoping she can send out her whereabouts to me. This is nothing like the Labyrinth, but feels as though we're caught up in some kind of cat and mouse game.

'I think we should go right,' says Skye. I agree. Right, was what I was about to say. Finally we agree on something.

Just like all the other corridors, this one is no different.

'Douse that torch,' I say to Skye. The light in front of us is growing in intensity.

'With what?'

I blow in his face.

'Oh yeah. Great idea.' He grins widely and with one huge breath, the fire is extinguished.

TWENTY-EIGHT

WITH the rugged, natural rockface of the tunnels behind us, the chamber is pretty much how I imagined it would be – dark, damp and smelling of wet newspapers and mushrooms. I wish I still had my shirt, if only to wrap over my nose and mouth, just like Skye is doing with his hoodie.

The room we find ourselves in is primitive in design but not in structure. Large, heavy stone blocks, shaped to precision, probably fashioned by a qualified stonemason, make up the walls and floor. The ceiling is too far away, and too dark to determine. Rough-sanded stone pillars break up the expanse, standing tall at regular intervals throughout the room, all perfectly chiselled.

'Gross,' says Skye, pretending to gag. Bodies have been mummified and embedded into the walls in grotesque poses. 'We're definitely in the right place,' he continues, stepping away from them. 'You know what, though … if I had to pick, I think I prefer the forest of skeleton trees.'

He stops, his head tilting slightly. 'Did you hear that?'

I find myself frowning. 'What?'

'I thought I heard ...' His voice trails off.

'As spooky as it is in here, I really need you to keep your head and not get freaked out right now.'

I'd rather not be here either.

The mummified remains would freak anyone out ...mouths stretched open in terror. Arms extending towards us, fingers grasping the air, and to make matters worse, the room has become a haven for menacing shadows that disappear as soon as you see them. 'Someone has gone to a lot of trouble to welcome us.'

'I was thinking the same thing,' says Skye, glancing up at the hundreds of lit candles, perched on a high ledge above us.

Five stone tombs also share the room with us – four in a square pattern in the middle of the room, and one in the centre. Skye runs his hand along the top of the nearest one.

'I wouldn't do that if I was you,' I say, not trusting that the occupants inside are truly dead. 'There's too much that is NOT of this world to assume death lasts forever here.'

Skye ignores me. 'Check these out.'

He is bending down looking at the front of the tomb. In the poor light, I can make out carvings into the stonework. I trace my finger over the intrinsically sculptured warriors, ready for battle, swords drawn and spears held high, frozen in the supreme moment before blood is spilt.

Skye stands up. 'What do you suppose is up there?' he asks, pointing to a flight of stone steps that span the entire width of the room.

I shrug my shoulders. 'Go and have a look, while I check out down here. And ...' He stops in mid step. 'For the love of God, DON'T touch anything. I'd like to get out of here with all my fingers and toes.'

'And your girlfriend,' he says with a hopeful look. He

374

takes off, up the twenty or so steps, stops and cocks his head as though listening to something, before continuing on.

A moment later.

'River, I think you should come and look at this.'

I follow in the direction he went and let out a low whistle as I clear the last step. At the end of the chamber is a monstrous altar, hideous in appearance, fifteen feet tall with a massive bulls-head on top. The stone table in front is bigger than my king size bed back home. And then there are thrones.

'It's like something out of Narnia,' says Skye. Four smaller thrones surround a larger one. 'Are they made from bone too?'

I take a closer look and run my hand along the back of the tallest throne. A cold shiver finds its way down my spine. 'It looks like it.'

'I've got a bad feeling about this,' says Skye, backing away.

I don't like it either. An unknown fear is beginning to grow inside me.

'It smells of death in here,' whispers Skye. 'I think we need to find Ember ASAP.'

I nod and follow him back into the crypt. He is still turning to look around every few feet.

Skye stops again.

'What's up with you *now*?'

Half of his face is in darkness, but I see his other cheek lift into a smile. 'She's here, River. I can hear her thoughts. I wasn't sure at first, but it's definitely her.'

I feel myself frowning. 'You can hear her thoughts, *too*? Why haven't you mentioned this before?' I knew he could read *my* mind, but Ember ... I hadn't even contemplated it.

'Dude, this really isn't the time to get into this. She's frightened. Oh, fuck it. Em ...' I clap my hand over his mouth.

My teeth clench. 'Not a good idea. Let's use our inside

375

voices, shall we. No need to alert any *unwanted* attention.'

He rips my hand away from his face, irritated. 'What's your plan, then?'

'Use your senses.'

Like a sulky kid, he stomps into the middle of the room and starts to walk in circles, each one bigger than the previous. It's an intriguing way of tracking after I realise what he's actually doing. It takes us to the furthest corner of the room, where no light hits the floor and where we find ourselves standing in complete blackness.

'She's close,' says Skye.

'Skye?'

I hear her too. 'Ember?' My head whips around to see where she is.

'Up here,' she replies.

'Where are you, Em?' asks Skye, his voice just above a whisper.

'I can't see anything. Grab a torch,' I say to Skye, pointing at the fire torch slung on the wall. He hovers ten feet and lifts it easily from its cradle and continues upwards.

And then I see her ... trapped in a cage, suspended in mid-air.

I hear a soft whimper. 'Ember?'

'Skye. River. It's a trap,' she says. 'Get out of here and save yourselves.'

Of course, it's a trap, but I'm not going anywhere. I stand underneath, trying to figure out how to get her down.

'Can't you float it down?' I say to Skye.

He hovers at eye level with Ember and pokes his hand through the cage to hold her hand. 'Don't worry. We'll get you down,' he mutters to her.

'I've already tried that. Whatever is keeping her up there is way more powerful than me,' he calls down to me. By firelight, I witness the knowing smile on his face. 'But I could try ...' He pulls up short on what he was

376

going to say. 'Guess what? This cage is made out of bone too.'

I'm not surprised.

I see Ember's arms protrude through the cage. She lunges for Skye and he brings her into him, hugging her tightly. 'It's okay. It's okay.' I hear him say. 'We're going to get you out of here.'

She starts to cry. 'I never wanted this to happen,' she says, 'and I don't know who to trust anymore.' She looks down at me for one short but powerful moment and then looks away. 'You're the only one who hasn't lied to me. If you say you can get me out of here, I will believe you.'

That dreaded shift in my body, more fearful than any nightmare, sharper than any blade, tells me I have lost her forever. There will be no way back from this.

Without her, I have nothing.

Without her, I am nothing.

What is the point in living half a life? What is the point in living …

I gaze up to see Skye struggling to free Ember. I suddenly see things so much clearer. I know what I have to do.

'Come down. I have a plan,' I call up to Skye.

He floats back to earth, leaving Ember imprisoned and alone in the dark.

'The only way to do this, is together,' I add.

'Okay, I'm listening.'

I'm referring back to our day at the fire brigade. 'Ever used a high-pressured hose before?'

'Yeah. Course.'

'I have a tonne of water in me that needs to come out, and you have the means to fire it up to that cage.' I point upwards.

Skye raises his eyebrows. 'Have you gone completely mad? That will kill her, and if not, then definitely strip the flesh from her bones.'

'What's happening, Skye?' calls Ember.

'Sok, love. We'll get you down in a jiffy,' he says to

her.

I bite at his familiarity with her. 'NOT if you are careful.'

'Riv, Christ, man. Are you *serious*?'

'Yes. No. I don't know. I don't have a fucking idea. Do you have another suggestion?'

His face goes blank. I know Ember will listen to him.

'Get her to hang upside down at the top of the cage and we'll blast it from underneath on a side angle.'

Skye has an incredulous look on his face. 'Are you sure about this?'

'No, I'm not sure, but what other choice do we have.'

'Skye?' Ember whimpers.

'Okay,' he says through gritted teeth. 'Okay. Em, can you cling to the top of the cage. We're going to make a hole in the bottom to get you out.'

Immediately, Ember links her arms and legs through the roof of the cage, gripping with her elbows and knees.

'We'll have to be quick,' I whisper to Skye. 'I'm not sure how long she can hold on.'

He nods and takes a deep breath.

I also breathe deeply, summoning my power, sitting just on the edge of my resolve, just like my emotions, waiting for a chance to redeem itself.

'You ready?'

'Go,' says Skye.

I glance at my hands, feeling the force of my water power rushing to my fingertips.

My skin resembles dry, brown paper …cracked … that might tear apart at any moment. It is no longer pink flesh, just something that once was, and is now desiccated beyond repair.

I roll my sleeves up. My arms are just the same.

'What are you waiting for?' shouts Skye. 'No water. No rescue.'

I come back into myself when I hear Ember scream.

'Too late, fine sir. Your time is up.'

It's Ra-Mon.

And he has company.

He stands on the top step with two people at his sides. One is the woman who lured me in the labyrinth, now wearing a long red flowing dress. The other, is a man of ethnic descent. His profile is familiar in the waning light, and as he moves out of the shadow, I realise I know him.

'*Salvatore*?'

Skye clicks his tongue. 'I knew there was something dodgy about him.'

Salvatore rubs his hands together. 'You can't tell me you knew nothing of who I am. You cannot be that stupid.'

'I ... I ...' Stupid, no. Shocked, yes.

'Be kind, Horus. Remember who you are,' says the woman. 'Excuse, my son. He knows little of the new world.'

'Enough talking,' bellows Ra-Mon. 'You know why you are here, WaterLover. And you also know what I need from you.'

Ramon is clothed in a white hooded cloak that drops to the floor. His face is the only part of him visible, electric blue eyes shining out as a warning. He looks less threatening than the last time I saw him, but to believe that would be naive on my part.

'Never. I told you before. Nereus isn't up for negotiation' The words are out before I have chance to decide whether it's the right thing to say or not.

There is no hesitation on Ra-mon's part. A spear of blue lightning flies straight toward me.

'River.' I hear Ember scream.

I hold up my arms in defence and the bolt bounces off me without causing any damage.

Ra-Mon sends another and another, and each time, they rebound off my body as though they are matchsticks. I remember Tomas saying how killing the son of Osiris would be easier in his own lair and I wonder if that might apply to Ra-Mon.

'Dude, how are you doing that?' asks Skye.

A smug smile creeps over my lips. 'I've got no idea. I thought you had a hand in this.'

'Not me, bro. But whatever you're doing, don't stop.'

Ra-Mon stops firing thunderbolts at me. Instead, ten-foot flames shoot out of his hands, just like I'd seen Ember do.

I brace myself.

'He must have broken Nuria and stolen her power,' yells down Ember. I expect to feel pain and yet there is none. His power still isn't hurting me.

'Nereus is protecting the boy,' says the woman to Ra-Mon. 'He needs to unleash the power. Only then will Nereus be vulnerable. If he will not yield for you, perhaps my son can change his mind.' In the time it takes to blink, Salvatore had disappeared from his position next to Ra-Mon and is now behind Skye, restraining him.

I think about the gallons of water I have stored up, unconsciously protecting Nereus and about to be released to save Ember. I have a choice to make – hold on to it to protect Nereus or release it to save Ember and Skye. Is this what Nereus meant about at the cost of a life?

It's a no-brainer.

'I'm sorry,' I whisper. 'I really am. But I have to do this.'

I hear Ember crying again as Skye looks sideways at me. I nod at him, hoping he knows what I'm about to do.

'If you give up Nereus, I will let you all leave *together*,' says Ra-Mon. Something in the way he says *together* isn't reassuring. There's together *alive* and then there's together *dead*. I'm not sure Ra-Mon knows the difference.

'Now,' says Skye.

I let go … with everything I have.

All my energy.

All my passion.

All my emotions.

Water gushes out of my hands at such a rate I almost lose myself. It's such a rush, so exhilarating, the most scariest, amazing experience of my life. It's like nothing else in the world matters but water. No agendas. No having to act a certain way or be someone else. Total freedom. No desire. No exploding, consuming lust. Just me. Me to be who I was born to be.

And nothing else.

I feel peace.

At last.

I tell myself there is still a job to be done, but it is done thinking of others and not myself – a new concept, and one I think I will like getting used to. The concentrated look on Skye's brow as he blasts air at the torrent of water I'm producing, is enough to propel Salvatore backwards.

He is mad, but Ra-Mon warns him off with one wave of his hand.

Ember, obviously is in full telepathic contact with Skye because she has now swung herself into the top half of the cage, out of the way of where Skye is aiming the jet blast.

'It's working, says Skye. 'I can see it cracking …'

And then Ember is falling … falling fast, but Skye is there, slowing her descent so that she lands on the ground without a sound. She gets up and rushes behind him, holding on to the back of his hoodie with everything she's got.

The force of Skye's air power slows. 'Ease down, Riv,' he says, closing the gap between us.

I try to turn off my faucet, but nothing happens. 'I can't.' Panic sets in. 'I can't turn it off.

'Try harder,' says Skye.

Water continues to cascade out of me and I can already feel the water levels rising to my ankles. I dig deeper, searching for an on/off switch. There is nothing.

'Nothing is working,' I cry back to Skye.

Ra-Mon laughs loudly.

'Oh, Nereus, come forth, my old friend. This is just like old times.'

My torso jerks erratically.

'Give in. You have always found self-control so difficult and I will show you how to overcome that. I will teach you to become a master of control. No longer will your emotions rule you. No more will you be dictated by them. Come, Nereus, do not hide within this bag of flesh and bones. Release yourself, and join me.' Ra-Mon gestures to the throne on his right. 'This is where you belong. You *and* Nuria.'

Ember peers out from around Skye's body. 'Nuria,' she whispers.

An orangey apparition is seated on one of the thrones. My whole body lurches forward, sending my muscles into spasms. 'No, Nereus,' I say softly. 'It is a trap.'

A shift is happening between my body and soul.

A voice trembles inside me. 'I need to be with her. The same way you need to be with the earth girl.'

'But ...'

'This is a place of great sacrifice, and I am offering myself so that you may be free.'

'But ...' I haven't even put up a fight to save him. I look to Ember who fought with everything she had to save Nuria.

'Release everything you have. Release your love for the earth girl too and it will be enough to save you.' I gasp, reach out, die a little as I feel a tearing inside me. 'Remember, learn from each other. Find the fourth Elementar and then, and only then, will you have the strength to defeat Ra-Mon.'

A final rip, tearing me from navel to nape, releases Nereus from my body.

My immediate reaction is relief.

The overwhelming urges of screwing the nearest female have reduced to almost nothing. I feel strangely *normal*. Whatever *that*'s supposed to feel like.

The cold water swirling around my thighs brings me back to the moment. My eyes cut across to Ember, still clinging onto Skye.

She looks back at me. 'Can't you stop this?' she asks.

'If you don't, we're all going to drown.' The speed in which the water is gushing out of me has tripled, making the water level rise so much faster now.

'Now that I have what I came for,' says Ra-Mon jovially, 'you may leave.' He disappears, leaving behind a haunting laugh.

The woman and Salvatore vanish too.

'Any ideas?' asks Skye.

'Up there.' I point to the steps. 'We need to get to higher ground.'

'What good will that do,' says Skye. 'You're flooding this entire chamber. We need a way out.'

'It will give us more time to come up with a plan.'

We half swim, half wade through the water and by the time we reach the stairs, the second to top step is already underwater.

'Hurry.'

The water is rising quickly now, and although we're back on solid ground for now, it doesn't take long for the water to start swishing around our calves as we run for the far end of the chamber.

'Look around. There has to be a way out of this place,' I say to Skye.

'I could blast through the wall, just like with the cage,' Skye suggests, looking about hopelessly.

Some unnatural impulse makes me reach for Ember's hand. She looks down at it, but doesn't let go. I hold no hope for us, but my need to protect her is still the most important element in my life.

'It'll take too long,' I tell him, turning to Ember, our clasped hands now underwater.

'River, there must be something you can do,' she says, 'can't you at least slow it down. I don't want to drown.' She grips my hand tighter.

Panic invites its way into my body.

'I wish I could, but I have no control over it. Nereus told me to release everything.' I pause. 'To be honest, I didn't think I was holding on to this much. All the swimming I've done in my life must have soaked in, contributing to this.' I shake my head, finally understanding the realisation. It has nothing to do with swimming. It's my emotions or lack thereof. Every emotion I should've had, should've felt, is finally being released.

Ember closes her eyes. Squeezes them tight. 'I'm scared.'

TWENTY-NINE

I search inwards, begging for the water to stop.

Nothing is working.

I can't find an off switch.

I feel strangely limp. Energy at an all-time low. And yet everything I'm feeling is uniform and catalogued just as it should be. Fear for my own self-preservation. Anguish for the plight of two friends. Useless that I'm unable to do anything to get us out of here and yet a surge of belief is growing inside me. Belief that all is going to be ok.

I've no idea where it's coming from.

The water is now past my shoulders.

Ember has been treading water for awhile, when she isn't holding on to me for dear life. In five more minutes, that will be me too, and I can't help wondering, now that Nereus is gone, whether my ability to hold my breath has gone with it.

And then the revelation comes.

The massive bulls-head altar.

I remember reading in Skye's brochure about the secret passageway that religious leaders would use to come and go from the Crypt. *God, what are the chances it could be that easy.*

I wrap my arms around Ember. She clings to me, shivering, as the water swirls up to her chest. 'I need you to hold on to this for a moment.' I guide her towards a pillar. 'I need to check something.

Skye looks to be scanning the walls for a lever or something. 'Skye, quick, get over here.' He swims over. 'Look after her.'

'You're *going*?' she asks, her teeth chattering.

'I'll be back in a few minutes. Trust me.' Her eyes give her away – they say they're not sure.

Inhaling a deep breath, I slip below the surface.

First thing I notice, I can't see quite as clearly as I could in the lake, but it's manageable. I can make out Ember's legs, the sunken pillars around us and the tombs on the bottom level, considering there is very little light.

Less than two minutes later, my lungs are searching for air. I'm not desperate, not gagging for breath, but again, my ability is lessened. I reckon I'll have five to ten minutes, tops.

I think …

I hope …

I break the surface and swim over to Ember. I have a plan.

She is still clinging to the post, her knuckles white from cold. I attempt to stand and realise in those few short minutes, I can no longer touch the bottom.

'We're going to die, aren't we?' she sobs.

I shoot a glance over at Skye. 'Of course not. I won't let that happen.' There is more water in the chamber now than air, the ceiling getting closer and closer.

'The chamber behind the altar looks to be our only way out,' I say to Skye. 'I have to check. I'll be quick.'

'You'd better be, or we'll both be dead.'

Without thinking, I duck dive under the water and

swim to the Altar. The passageway behind it, is dark, and I propel myself along, using the torch holders on the wall to increase momentum. Every stroke seems to be getting me nowhere. My muscles are a mess of stabbing pains and aches ...my emotions a complete train-wreck. But I can't think about that. The thought that Ember and Skye could be taking their last breaths only pushes me harder.

I see a wall approaching. *I hope to god it's not a dead end.* A sliver of light cuts through the gloomy dark water, rekindling hope.

I take the corner; aware the water is becoming more and more shallow with every stroke. I no longer see the cracked stone ceiling of the tunnel anymore, but the surface of water.

I burst through.

Take a huge breath.

And then power on again.

Another corner and my feet finally touch on ground.

The water level continues to drop as I venture on, but what's to say that by the time I swim back, this area won't be underwater.

I half-run through the water, until it's ankle deep. To my left, is an impressive flight of stairs that I'm sure would take us back into the main hall of the cathedral. It's all the evidence I need.

I rush back down the way I came, through the shallow water, and back into the dark tunnel, praying with everything I have, they are still alive.

The second I see the back of the Altar, I kick harder, grimacing at the stiffness in my legs. I slip through the secret passageway and back into the Crypt. Finding the surface, however, sends a thump through my heart. And my head.

I break through to see a few inches of air left. Ember has come apart, sobbing uncontrollably.

'Is there a way out?'

'Yes. But it's a bit of a hike,' I say, swimming over to them. I sweep a thick strand of hair from Ember's eyes.

'Oh, River,' she mumbles. 'I'm so sorry.'

There's no time for apologies. We need to leave … now.

'I just want to try something,' says Skye to Ember. 'Do you trust me?'

'With my life,' she says.

All that *remains* is one inch of life left.

They are already face to face, but then Skye cradles her head in his hands. *Don't you dare do what I think you're going to do.*

He kisses her.

It's a long, slow, hard kiss that rips out my heart and replaces it with stone. I want the water to take me, fill me completely, dull the pain and then put me to sleep, but we don't have that kind of relationship anymore. He then wraps his arms tightly around her neck. She doesn't even seem to mind. Seconds dissolve and drown, hates me even more, bashes against my head so I can hardly see, they slip beneath the surface.

Take me.

I'm ready to die.

I blow all the air out of my lungs and let my body sink.

Lower and lower.

Skye and Ember remain locked in an embrace that I can't bear to look at anymore. The only word that comes to mind is … traitor.

There is no more air to breathe.

There is no more life to live.

The chamber is completely immersed.

I turn to swim away from them when I feel a tug on my leg. It's Skye and he's pointing frantically at the altar.

He doesn't want me to see them perish.

Fight and flight take over and my survival instincts kick in. Reluctantly, I slip through the entrance and find myself swimming back along the passageway.

Alone.

The water is lifeless to me now. Is black and

foreboding. Means nothing. Indifferent. No longer comforting, no longer appetising. No longer a friend or companion.

I feel betrayed by *everything* and *everyone* I've ever known.

If for nothing else, muscle memory takes over, weaving a path to my exit. I soon discover I can touch the ground.

I wade through, dragging my legs until the treacherous liquid subsides, leaving my jeans heavy and cold against my skin. I haul myself up a few steps and drop my head into my hands.

This wasn't the way I had envisaged this to go. Tears press against the back of my eyes, ready to fall, finally being given permission to fall.

Nothing happens.

I am dry.

Squeezed out.

I sense the change. Feel the ripple in my body as though everything is resetting … adjusting.

Recalibrating for River Fulton – two point zero.

I look to the water - once my only ally, now dark and expecting. The first chance I get to experience real feelings, and they come at me at a hundred miles an hour.

There are too many to choose from and yet something says it won't be forever. They all want to have a turn and for the first time in my life, I recognise them all individually and by name, even amidst the emptiness that bores away at my heart.

Love is replaced with hatred and sadness and more grief than one single person can bear alone.

Hope battles against anger, that I failed them. Failed myself.

Belief with betrayal.

That I am alive. And they are dead.

I push myself upright and turn to climb the stairs, pausing for one moment in the hope I am wrong.

I am not.

The sunlight provides no peace or relief as I step outside the cathedral. It doesn't warm my skin. It doesn't heal the ache in my heart either. It must be around midday of the next day. God, I hope it was only one day - time meant nothing there.

A flurry of actions and voices erupt behind me as tour guides cautiously usher people out of the cathedral, informing worried visitors a water pipe has burst, flooding the crypt. They pass me, standing in my wet clothes, eyeing me with suspicion.

I look past them, across the street and rooftops. A church bell peels in the distance.

'Just in the nick of time, I'd say,' says a voice behind me. Skye slaps me on the shoulder, spraying water from my sodden shirt. I grab him by the scruff of his hoodie.

I can't believe my eyes …that he's real.

Alive.

I pull him into me and hug him.

'Dude, we're in public. What will people think?'

For the first time in my life, I don't care. I'm just glad to see him.

'They'd think you were lovers.' Ember appears on my other side.

There's a smile on her face. A smile for just me.

My arms peel away from Skye as I drop to my knees. My breath won't start because my heart still hasn't fully grasped the reality that she is actually standing in front of me, pink and breathing and not entombed beneath me, lifeless and grey. I want to say so many things. To say, I'm sorry. To say, forgive me. To say that my life means nothing without her in it. But I don't know where to begin. What is my biggest confession? *Iris?* And she still doesn't know about her. What good will it do to pour my heart out and beg her forgiveness right now when there is so much more I have done to hurt her of which she doesn't know about. What is the point of getting her to trust me all over again and believe in me, when there are still lies to come and so much more pain to endure.

She looks down at me, her eyes full of unanswered questions. I'm even apprehensive about hugging her.

'Awkward,' sings out Skye.

I stand. Shaking. My life a wobbly tightrope.

Luckily, she takes that fear away by stepping in close and throwing her arms around my neck.

'I don't care what's happened between us. I don't care if there are more dramas to come. All I know is, my life won't work without you in it.'

My heart swells.

Emotions come flooding in.

Real emotions.

Something I can call my own - that belong to me now. No sinister voice inside me. No ulterior motive. No beast tormenting me.

It's just me.

Just me.

I hug her tightly. Find the small crease in her neck and whisper into her ear, 'I'm so sorry. Forgive me.'

We arrive back at the hotel, alive and soaked to the skin, and after rescheduling our flights for the following morning, we disappear to our rooms. I'm barely out of the shower when there is a knock at my door.

Wet hair, towel around my waist, I look into the empty hallway. Skye materialises out of thin air, leaves the door wide open and struts inside.

'Fancy room,' he says and sniffs.

'What's up?'

'Riv, man. I just wanted to explain …' He stumbles for words. 'I hope you understand what happened back there in the Crypt … with Ember, I mean. It wasn't like you …'

'You were saving her life, where I could not,' I cut in.

'Remember that time at the lake …'

I nod.

'Something weird happened. I knew I had the power

of air but I didn't realise I could use that to breathe underwater. So I figured, if my body converted the oxygen in the water to help me breathe, why couldn't I use that to help Ember.'

'Quick thinking.'

Skye smirks. 'It happens occasionally.'

'You should give yourself more credit. I … we, wouldn't be here if it wasn't for you.'

Skye shrugs it off. 'All jokes aside.' His face is now profoundly serious. 'I want things to be good between us. I really do. I've spent most of my *recent* life, alone. And it's not a nice place to be. The comedy routine is a cover for how screwed up I really am. I don't want pity and I don't need a father. What I need is …'

'A brother,' I add.

'Is a brother,' he repeats. 'And I think you do too.'

I smile.

'I'll always have your back, bro, always. Never forget that.'

I can feel an awkward man-hug thing coming.

Skye raises his eyebrows at me. 'Come on then, if it'll soothe those watery emotions.'

I could say something smart. I could brush it off with sarcasm. But I don't. I walk straight up to him and hug him like I always wanted to be hugged by my father. Strangely enough, he hugs me back and it doesn't feel weird, even though I am naked from the waist up.

'Am I interrupting anything here?' asks Ember, standing in the doorway of my room.

'Actually, Riv and I were just about to get it on. Do you mind?' Skye laughs but gives me a look to say, "now's your chance. Go sort everything out with her."

'Feeling better?' I ask her. Her hair is also wet and her cheeks have that cherry blossom glow about them that I love and have missed seeing.

'Yes,' she says shyly.

Skye vanishes.

I wait a few seconds.

'Dude, are you still here?'

He flashes back to visibility with a sheepish look on his face before walking out and closing the door behind him.

Ember and I exchange smiles.

She looks at me. At my chest and then quickly averts her eyes when she realises she's been sprung. I'm being a distraction, and I don't need to be. I go to my suitcase and pull out a t-shirt.

She walks over to the window, looks out at Paris, then turns to the table and chairs in the corner of the room.

She sits.

She looks at me ...waiting ... her eyes searching my face for reasons.

'Would you indulge me for one moment?' I ask her.

She frowns as I kneel on the floor in front of her and pick up her hand.

I close my eyes and focus on how she might be feeling. In truth, I want to see whether I still have the ability to read emotions. Obviously it'll be more intense when we kiss, but I want an idea of where she's at now. And it would be so presumptuous of me to think she would ever want to kiss me again.

I am curious to see whether the same residual power that Ember was left with after Nuria was torn from her, is the same for me. Sure, the water from this morning's shower soothed me, but I can't be certain that it wasn't from spending two days underground than any residual power.

Exhaustion is the first to come up – which I expect. I don't need to be an emotion reader to know that.

Confusion is there too.

Then lust - which surprises me. A lot.

And the rest are a jumble of emotions that won't sit still long enough for me to read them. These aren't the intense readings I *used* to get from her. But I can still feel them. Fainter, somehow rewired to a slightly different frequency.

'*River*?'

'Sorry, love. I needed to see if anything has changed.'

'*Changed*?' she asks.

'Yes,' I mutter. Her hand is so smooth, so warm, the burning urge to place it against my lips and relish the silkiness against my face is a desire I *am* in control of now. 'I need to know for sure if *he's* still in here ... inside me.'

I listen in more intently, delving deeper until I reach those dark chasms that have housed him and haunted me. I seek out one word from the beast.

'And?'

I smile. 'All I hear is a hundred million moments of glorious silence,' I say with confidence, patting my other hand against my heart. 'It's just me in here.'

She takes a deep breath and lets it out very slowly.

I continue on. 'I've always known how I feel about you.' There's a tremble to my voice when I say, 'but I need to know one thing ...'

'Yes, it was you I fell in love with ... not some strange, hypnotic power.'

Relief drops in.

Becomes my saviour.

I want to lift her up and swing her around in my arms and scream until my voice ceases to exist that no moment in my life has ever been this good.

'Although ... in the beginning, you were pretty hard to resist.'

I smirk. 'I thought so.'

'My feelings for you haven't changed, River. Just like I told you they wouldn't.'

'You can understand why I had to be certain.' I place my other hand against her cheek, and she leans into my palm, closing her eyes.

'Yes, I understand.'

The urge to lean in and kiss her is overpowering my thoughts, but not because of any insane compulsion anymore. I want to kiss her now because it's real. I know she truly sees me.

I hold back.

I have a confession to make

'I can't remember a time when I didn't know you. You visited me in my dreams for years, so silent, so distant from me, but you were always there. When my parents ignored me, you were there. When I was singled out for being different at school, you were there. And then when you told me your name, I knew I had to start looking for you.'

Her eyes open and she smiles that beautiful smile at me, crumbling me into a thousand tiny pieces.

I continue. 'So, I hired a private investigator to track you down.' I look deeper into her eyes, surprised she isn't upset about this. 'I knew there would come a time when we'd meet and that first day, seeing you outside the school gates, it didn't feel real. I kept telling myself to breathe, to believe, to pinch myself because I thought I had slipped into another dream.' I take a moment. 'Standing there, looking at me, really looking at me, with so many questions in your eyes, I knew, that *somehow*, you knew me.'

Ember lowers her lashes and there's a hint of redness on her cheeks. 'It was a strange day,' she admits, 'I thought I was about to spontaneously combust. But it was Nuria. All along it was Nuria alerting me to who you were.'

I smile for one second and then it's gone. She sees it. '*What*? Whatever it is, I can handle it.'

I collect myself again and press on. 'Em ... finding you came at a price. The woman I hired was unscrupulous in her dealings with me ...'

Ember's head angles slightly to one side. 'You mean you slept with her?'

'Yes.'

Ember exhales a shaky breath. 'I suppose you were a free agent back then. You could choose to have sex with whoever you wanted.'

'The real me was never attracted to her, never wanted to have sex with her. The beast did. She used me, the same way I used her. That's the kind of person I was back then. I would've done anything ... *anything* ... sold my soul to the highest bidder to find you.' She squeezes my hands and brings them to her own lips and kisses my knuckles.

'She wanted me for sex, and I wanted her for information. She meant nothing to me then and means nothing to me now.'

Her eyes glass over. One single tear slips down her cheek and she casually wipes it away.

'Wally isn't my butler either. He's my legal guardian. Terry and Annabeth did take custody of me, but it didn't work out. Wally was my father's ex-business partner and I persuaded him to go along with the story to ... appear normal.'

'There's nothing normal about a butler.' She lets out a little laugh.

'I know that ... now, but in my defence a butler was not that unusual for the life I lived before my parents drowned ... ' I feel a frown settle on my forehead. 'Back then, I wasn't thinking straight.'

Ember smooths the skin on the back of my hands with the softness of her fingertips. 'How old are you, River?'

'I'm twenty.'

Some kind of recognition dances across her vision. 'I thought so. You sounded too old to be seventeen. How on earth did you register for school?'

'I had a fake birth certificate made up.'

She nods.

'I've lied a lot in my life to get me where I need to be, Em.' Blackness tries to cloak me, tries to find its old address again. 'And I've had sex with so many women I've lost count.' I think back to her question about how many.

She raises her eyebrows and waits.

'Over five hundred,' I offer.

She sits back in her chair. Withdraws her hand from me and twists and turns them in her lap. 'And how many people have you had sex since we've been together?'

Confidently, I look her boldly in the eye. 'None.'

She sighs. 'Have you *been* with any girls since you moved?'

My posture breaks rank and sags a little. 'Yes. Three times. Once before we met, a girl I met after Cole's party, and the private investigator, of course.'

She presses her lips together. 'What I don't understand is, if you say you've been in love with me all this time, how can you have sex with other women?'

'Sex isn't love, Em. They're two very different expressions of affection. I never once invested my heart into any of the girls I had sex with. They were a way to keep the pain at bay. I used it to subdue the insatiable lust that drove me almost insane …almost to my death. I called it the beast because I thought the voice was a darker part of myself. I thought, being my father's son, that I was just like him – selfish, self-centred, unable to love or care about anyone other than myself. I thought it was all me – how I was made. I persecuted myself time and time again, made myself believe that I wasn't worthy of anyone's time, anyone's love. But it wasn't me …

It was Nereus.

All along …it was Nereus, and his bottled-up emotions. He was a massive influence, that up until recently, I didn't know he existed inside me. And now that he's gone, I am the man I should've been. You spoke of a voice inside you when you discovered Nuria. I had something remarkably similar except it's been with me since puberty. It was vicious. It was …'

I find I'm clenching my teeth.

'Nereus had an impact on my emotions and sex drive that I had little control of. Having no sex was a punishment of headaches, stomach cramps, and pain. I did what I had to, to survive. I'm sure you understand the concept. You must remember the power you felt with

Nuria, as though sometimes you weren't even in the driving seat anymore.'

She looks away and nods. 'I understand. I'm sorry I was quick to judge you.'

'You have nothing to apologise for.'

Ember drops her head before returning her eyes to me. Shyly she says, 'you once said to me, that you would never be intimate with me, whilst Nereus was inside you?'

'Yes.'

'I want to know what that means for us now?'

'It means, I hope, that we are free to love each other the way we were meant to.'

'I hoped you'd say that.'

Ember stands and removes her jumper. She throws it on the floor.

'Wait! I have more to tell you.'

'It can wait,' she says huskily. 'I can't.'

My breath leaves my body as I take in her perfectness. The light from the window leaves a stream of sunshine across her body, making it shimmer like gold dust.

'You are so beautiful,' I murmur. Words, feelings, and everything that makes up the meaning of love crashes into me in a big hurry.

I'm not sure I can move.

Can think.

Breathe.

The rush is so intense.

I stumble to my feet.

I can't take my eyes off the way she pushes her hair to one side, laying it over one shoulder, partially covering one breast ...leaving her neck and the other shoulder exposed in a way that cries out to be touched. Kissed.

Life is on pause.

The world has frozen.

And I can take all the time I want.

I step closer. Her breath quickens. I sense the warmth from her body as her arms circle my waist.

'Take this off,' she says, tugging at my t-shirt. 'I want to feel you.'

It's off in a blink, thrown in the same spot as her jumper.

Her hands slide over my skin, past my waist, fingers and hands gently painting circles of passion into the small of my back.

My own fingers ache to touch her.

'Kiss me, River.'

My lips find hers. Soft and sweet as always. And I'm falling and laughing and collapsing and my body is singing a tune it's never known the words to before. Coming alive in a way that is as virgin as I feel. Her hands disappear for one second and then are back.

Something is different.

Her bra is gone and she presses herself against my chest - igniting my skin with such pleasure I might die at any second. Sparks race across my skin. Igniting inside me. Becoming fire and water – so uniquely different, so opposite in every way and yet one needing the other to survive. My skin becoming a frenzy of something I don't know how to explain and will never know and it doesn't bother me if I never find out. It's just her and me in a dream – the most wonderful dream.

Inside the seconds I've been lost in my head, she has squirmed out of her jeans. 'Don't go so fast, love,' I hum into her ear. 'I've waited ten years for this moment. I want to savour every part of you.'

She giggles so quietly, before finding a sweet spot behind my ear. I almost come undone. 'It should be me saying that, but don't worry, I'll be gentle with you,' she says in a velvety, sexy voice that I've never heard before.

My hands can no longer be contained. The tips of my fingers trace a line either side of her neck and across to her shoulders, enjoying the shiver it creates over her entire body. Down her arms, my thumbs finding the slight curve of her breasts as they glide past. She moans breathlessly when my hands brush over her hips and onto her buttocks.

'Jump,' I say. Her legs circle me, squeezing against me when I lift her up and carry her over to the bed.

'This is more than I deserve,' I whisper over her face as I lay her down.

She frowns a little, and I kiss it away. I kiss her eyelids, her forehead, her nose … tiny kisses each filled with more emotion than I can turn into words. My thumbs smooth over the apple of her flushed cheeks, so delicate, so incredibly perfect.

There are a hundred places I haven't kissed her yet. A thousand, even, and I want to spend the rest of my life discovering them. I sit back to look at her, my knees resting between her thighs.

'What's wrong?' she asks.

My eyes follow a trail from her eyes, over her lips and down her chin. Then down her neck, across her breasts to her stomach.

'Nothing, love. It couldn't be more right.'

She sighs.

Rewards me with a smile I feel deep inside me.

I drop a kiss just above her belly button and continue dropping them in a straight line until I run out of skin. A tiny pink bow on her knickers receives the last one. Her fingers tangle in my hair and her hips twist as I take my time to kiss one hip and then the other. Her skin is warm and tastes like peaches and coconut against my tongue as I let it roam where it wants to. I have become a swirl of colours and rainbows, dreams colliding with dreams, wishes and desires all happening in one glorious and blissful moment.

Nothing could be any better than this, until she reaches up to me, guiding me to lie down next to her, before rolling me onto my back. She straddles my hips.

'My turn,' she says. Her auburn curls, more dry now than wet, fall over her breasts, hiding them. Teasing me even more.

I close my eyes, turn inward as her hands learn what it

feels like to touch me. And it is the most amazing sensation. No restrictions. No consequences. Just her stroking my chest, my abdomen, my shoulders in a way that can't be real. I think I may have fallen into another world, where pain has no name, where love resides, and where pleasure was created.

When her lips begin to kiss my torso, I come back to myself. Feel my breath quicken. My heart finds a new rhythm.

'Em,' I mumble.

'It's okay,' she says.

She slides under the sheets, removes her underwear and welcomes me in next to her.

I discard my towel on the floor and join her.

'I want you so bad it hurts,' I say tenderly into her ear.

She wraps herself around me, arms around my neck, massaging my neck, her legs around my waist. She presses herself against me, her breath coming in short bursts. 'I'm yours. I will always be yours.'

My heart explodes.

Love like I've never known flows out. Everything I ever dreamed of has been fulfilled. Every kiss, every touch, every waking second of knowing we are going to be together forever is now real – no longer a dream, no longer a wish.

Real.

A tear finds its way to my cheek.

'I'm home,' I say.

Copper curls lay spread across the white linen of the pillow, a beautiful contrast to the most incredible night of my life. It's still early, before six, but I've been awake for an hour, watching her sleep ... the way her back could be sculptured from the finest porcelain as she lays on her side, hugging the sheets at her neck but totally unaware she is uncovered everywhere else. I dust a finger across her shoulder and right down past the curve of her waist to her hips and down her legs. A flurry of goosebumps erupt over her skin.

She stirs and mumbles something, bringing a smile to my lips. I move in closer, shaping my body to hers, tucking her into my hold. Kiss a tiny orange freckle on her shoulder.

She stirs again, 'morning,' she says sleepily. She snuggles in closer to me. 'How did you sleep?'

'Better than I have in years,' I say. 'No dreams.' And for the first time in forever, no stomach cramps, no nausea, no pain, and no compelling urge to swim a thousand laps to beat down the beast. My whole world is shining that much brighter this morning.

And she knows it.

She rolls over to face me and kisses me lightly on the lips. 'I'm happy to see that anguished look that you used to greet me with, is now gone.'

Her hands find my face.

The stubble on my chin.

The dip behind my earlobe.

My Adam's apple.

She pauses here a while, drawn to the movement it makes. Then onto my chest and waist. The curve of my arse. Across my lower abdomen, close to my pubic line. Her fingers concentrate on the skin right there, teasing. I close my eyes, languishing in some kind of wonderful heaven.

'Could you indulge me a moment,' she says so quietly I almost miss what she says. I hear her giggle my words back at me.

She disappears under the covers.

'Em … please…' I try to pull her upwards.

'I want to see what *it* again.'

It's impossible to hide my excitement. Her hair tickles my stomach and I hold my breath. My body tightens in anticipation, so intense and amazing and so utterly alive.

'I didn't understand what it meant last night, but I think I do now.'

The word *what* barely makes it out of my mouth. Her

fingers trace over the same spot on my skin, over and over, and only when she places three kisses over the three words I have tattooed there, do I comprehend what she means. I didn't realise she saw it, but I suppose she knows me intimately now.

'*Conquer From Within*' she says to me like it's a question.

'It fit, at the time,' I tell her. 'I was sixteen and in a pretty dark place. It was just before my parents died.'

She kisses it again before making her way back into my arms. 'You've been through pain. Just like I have. But you'll never have to do it alone … ever again.'

She kisses me, hard, stirring up a wild frenzy of feelings. Then pulls back. Looks at me mischievously and says, 'now, where was I …'

THIRTY

IT'S close to nine thirty by the time we head downstairs for breakfast.

'Hey, there you both are. I was beginning to think you were going to stay up there all day.' Skye has a plate of chocolate croissants in front of him, six in fact, and a bowl of mixed fruit. 'We have about half an hour before the car gets here, and …to be on the safe side, I requested a change in driver.' He smiles his usual boyish grin. 'Soooo, how are we *all* feeling this morning?'

Ember blushes and giggles, and I offer him a very casual wink.

'Good for you guys. It's about time. I'm happy it all worked out.' He leans in like he's about to say something he doesn't want anyone else to hear. 'But we still have a helluva lot of shit to sort out when we get home.'

'Yes, we do,' I say.

'And most of it isn't of the supernatural kind.'

'How do you mean?' asks Ember, digging her spoon into a bowl of muesli and yogurt.

'Your parents, for one.'

'My *parents*?'

I quickly jump in. 'Em, when you told me everything else could wait, your parents were one of them.' I drop the bombshell. 'We believe your parents' might have been murdered.'

Her spoon drops into her bowl. Her eyes widen and her usual rosy glow dissolves in seconds, leaving nothing but white.

There's an apologetic look on Skye's face. 'Riv, man, I didn't know. I thought you'd told her …I'm sorry …'

'It's okay.' I place a hand on his shoulder.

I reach over and weave my fingers into Ember's. She's shaking uncontrollably.

'I'm so sorry.' She doesn't seem to hear me. 'Remember me telling you about that private investigator chick I used, well, she had an entry in her diary and …'

She looks up quickly, her eyes questioning. 'What did it say?'

'I'll show you as soon as we're home, but it looks like it was planned.'

The shake in her hands stop. 'The Creeper said that he knew I was his, the day of the accident and that I wasn't randomly placed into foster care.' Ember squares her shoulders and looks at us both. Her jaw, wired tight. 'Promise me one thing right now. Both of you.' We nod. 'I don't care what it takes, I want the rest of that diary.'

The sky looks moody. Not black, thunderous moody or even bruise purple or grey moody as we land back on home soil, but heading in that direction – in a big hurry.

Life is about to get *very* real!

Wally is there to meet us, just like he said he would be and the relief on his face touches me … surprises me. He pulls me into a hug but not before tilting his head to one side, staring at me, questioningly.

'You look … *different*,' he says loud enough over my shoulder for me to hear but not so anyone else can. He pulls back and holds me by the shoulders, studying me. 'How did everything go?' On cue, Ember returns from putting her bag in the boot and slips under my arm to snuggle into my chest. 'I'd say fairly good,' Wally mutters around a smile.

The drive home is pretty sombre.

Ember ends up falling asleep in my arms before we hit the M40 and Skye isn't fooling anyone with the unease that has settled over his face.

Me ... I feel kind of empty.

At peace ... to some degree but the eerie silence from within is unsettling, like war is brewing. Like things are about to shift gear dramatically in a way none of us are prepared for or even qualified for.

But for now ... I couldn't ask for anything more.

'Can I see it,' says Ember, the second we walk through the front door. She wipes the tiredness from her eyes. I want to say it can wait until after she's had a shower and something to eat, but the determination on her face prompts me not to fight this.

'I'll just go get it,' I tell her, dropping my bag in the main entranceway and heading up the stairs. I expect her to wait for me in the kitchen or lounge room, but instead she tags on behind me.

I pull out a box from the back of my wardrobe and pass her the pages Skye had printed out. It's then I realise she's never been in my bedroom before.

She makes her way over to my bed, and sits down, her hands back to their familiar trembling state.

I stand back.

Give her space.

Halfway through she starts to cry, folds the pages into her lap, before gathering herself and continuing on. When she's finished, she looks up at me, tears staining her cheeks. Her face is tight, pinched, angry.

'My parents were killed because *I* was living a comfortable *life*?' she says between sobs. 'What kind of fucked-up reason is that?'

'I know,' I say in a soothing voice. 'At first, I didn't get it either. But I've had time to think about it. My guess is … Ra-Mon somehow paid off Iris to make this happen.'

Ember sucks in a breath. The longer I stare at her, the more shadows of disbelief seem to leach out of her skin.

'And don't take this the wrong way, but if it was up to me, the best way to provoke Nuria into surfacing would be to eliminate your family and put your life in jeopardy, using her very own element against her.' I pause. Clench my teeth. 'Planting you with that sick, twisted family, I can only guess, was part two of the plan, pushing you to your limits, heightening your emotions, making you aware of your power.'

Ember sniffs. 'And it worked like a charm, didn't it, because she did come to me when I was in the car. When it was on fire, I mean,' she whimpers.

I nod soberly. 'Look, Skye and I lost our parents too, and I'm pretty certain Ra-Mon had a hand in that as well.' Ember reaches for my hand and tucks her fingers into my palm. 'He has to pay for this. He has to …' Tears start to fall more freely.

There's a knock at the door and she abruptly wipes them away.

Skye doesn't enter but calls out. 'Wal said dinner's ready.'

'It can be a temporary arrangement then, just until you find your own place,' I say to Skye, looking around at Ember and Wally. This heated debate at the dining table about him moving in, has been going on for almost an hour.

He shakes his head. 'Wally doesn't need someone else to cook and clean up after.'

'I've told you, you're more than welcome to stay,' says Wally, 'besides, who said anything about cleaning up after you.' There's a smirk on his face and he looks over at Ember and winks. Her blush is adorable, and she tries to hide it with her hands. Wally gets up and takes his plate to the kitchen.

I lean over the table, waiting until Wally is out of earshot. 'To be completely honest with you, I don't want you going back to live with your brother.'

'Awww, I didn't think you cared so much,' coos Skye.

'No seriously, man. I'm done with him using you as his personal punching bag, and besides you're next on Ra-Mon's list. Plus, safety in numbers is just common sense.'

'I agree,' says Ember. 'We need to stick together. We need to be ready for him.'

'Do I get a key?' There is a cheeky grin on Skye's face. I was waiting for this and slide the spare I got cut weeks ago along the table to him. 'And what about a curfew?' He looks to Wally as he re-enters the room.

'How old are you?'

'Nineteen, the last time I checked.'

'Then 2am,' says Wally, picking up Ember's plate.

'What if I'd said twenty-one.'

I laugh. 'Makes no difference to Wally. It's still 2am.'

Wally chuckles. 'I don't mind if you're staying out all night, but if you're going to be home, then it's 2am.'

'Does that include me, Wal?' asks Ember.

'No. You're in by midnight and no overnighters.' Skye makes a face at her.

'What if I'm with River?'

'It's still twelve. You're not eighteen for another few months.'

Ember just smiles and nods. 'I'm happy with that, and while we're on the subject, I'd like to give you some money for my keep. I have some saved up.'

I jump in immediately. 'Em, please ... I don't need any money from you or Skye. Hold onto it. You'll need it for other things.'

My attention is diverted as my mobile goes off. I reach into my pocket.

I stare at the screen.

The room spins.

'Well. Aren't you going to answer it?'

It's Iris.

I still have one debt to repay. But I will never give myself to her again. I will need to renegotiate my terms with her, plus I must find a way to steal that diary. I'm positive there's more in there that will help us.

Skye lifts his chin as I glance over at him. He nods very slightly, letting me know he's up for it too.

I slip down from the table and text her back, asking if she's up for some company tomorrow. I slide the phone back into my pocket.

Crossing Iris isn't a smart move especially if my suspicions about Ra-Mon are correct, but then again, nor is stealing her diary. But if left with facing the end of the world … and killing all I love in it, I'll take Iris's diary any day of the week.

That night as I lay curled around Ember, my lips resting lightly in the crook of her neck, her hair tickling my cheek, her back pressing against my chest and my thoughts at safe distance from Skye, I know in my heart that tomorrow needs to be a solo mission.

I won't risk him being harmed.

I can't knowingly allow him to accompany me, well aware, I could be walking him straight into the lion's den.

I stand outside Iris's door the following afternoon, nervous. I wonder whether she'll be able to tell that Nereus isn't calling the shots anymore.

Skye had bugged the shit out of me, asking where I was going, but I'd held fast, keeping my thoughts on anything other than heading back to Sheffield.

The door swings open.

It isn't Iris who welcomes me in. I don't recognise this new woman.

'Come in. We've been expecting you.'

We?

I find Iris sitting at her dining table, her fingertips

drumming against her diary. This isn't the kind of meeting I was after, although, maybe, she has invited the olive-skinned woman who hasn't taken her eyes off me since I got here, here for some fun. About two weeks too late, mind you.

The woman brings over two tall glasses with what looks like tomato juice.

'Bloody Marys,' says Iris. 'You look like you need a little down time.' This swish of her stockings barely rates at all in my body. She grins, like she knows this is the case, somehow. 'This is a celebration.' She takes a sip of her drink and then pulls the diary out and opens to a page. She takes out a piece of paper and unfolds it. She then shows me the contents.

It's my contract with her.

She smiles sweetly and tears it into four perfect pieces. 'Our agreement is complete, River. You are free.' The other woman giggles from the kitchen. I turn to stare at her until Iris speaks again. 'Come on. Let's celebrate.' She raises her glass to me, waiting for me to do the same.

What the hell. Just when I thought I'd have to adjust my terms with her, my prayers have finally been answered. The irony of it all makes me smile as I take a mouthful of the disgusting, grainy drink.

'This is my sister,' says Iris, getting up to stand beside the woman. There is no resemblance. There is an ethnic Egyptian like feel to the woman and some part of me wonders if we've met before. 'I told you he was quick. And handsome. I think he'll do well.'

I frown. I feel as though I've turned up too late and to the wrong party. Nothing is making sense.

'Do well at *what*?'

'And questions authority. Yes, I agree, Isis. Strong, wilful and deliciously mouldable.'

My head feels foggy and somewhere else.

'What do you mean?' The word slurs out of my mouth. I look to the glass. 'What … are … you … doing?'

Unconsciousness tries to drag me under. My eyes are

dry and heavy, my bones aching right through to the marrow.

A sharp slap brings me back for a few seconds. It's just enough time to see Iris and the woman from the crypt merge together to become one person.

'Hello, honey, my name is Isis.'

I can't believe what I'm seeing.

Her voice is like syrup. 'Toast me, and drink,' she says, 'or I'll kill your little girlfriend.' She waves a photo of Ember in my face.

I lift my head to the glass, just in time to see Skye Buchannan, hovering, staring at me through the window, well … actually screaming at me, though no sound comes out of his mouth. I can tell he is saying the word no over and over again, but it's too late.

The blood of Isis has already begun to poison me.

Consume me.

'Welcome to the family,' says Isis.

About the Author

Lorraine Eljuga was born in Suffolk, England and emigrated to Australia when she was twenty. The Snowy Mountains, in New South Wales, is where she now calls home. Lorraine is a Nutritionist & an Aromatherapist and was also a Writer in the Royal Australian Navy.

FlameMaker, Book 1 of the Elementar series

You can visit her at https://www.lorraineeljuga.com

Coming soon ...

Book 3
AirWhisperer